THE BOOK OF
SONGS

Books and Translations by Arthur Waley

CHINESE POEMS

THE NŌ PLAYS OF JAPAN

TRANSLATIONS FROM THE CHINESE

THE WAY AND ITS POWER:
*A Study of the Tao Tê Ching and Its Place in
Chinese Thought*

THE BOOK OF SONGS

THE LIFE AND TIMES OF PO CHU-I

THE POETRY AND CAREER OF LI PO

THE REAL TRIPITAKA AND OTHER PIECES

NINE SONGS:
A Study of Shamanism in Ancient China

YUAN MEI:
An Eighteenth Century Chinese Poet

THE TALE OF THE GENJI

THE PILLOW-BOOK OF SEI-SHŌNAGON

MONKEY

THE ANALECTS OF CONFUCIUS

THE OPIUM WAR THROUGH CHINESE EYES

INTRODUCTION TO THE STUDY OF
CHINESE PAINTING

JAPANESE POETRY

THE BOOK OF
SONGS

THE ANCIENT CHINESE
CLASSIC OF POETRY

Translated from the Chinese by

ARTHUR WALEY

GROVE WEIDENFELD
New York

Published by Grove Weidenfeld
A division of Grove Press, Inc.
841 Broadway
New York, NY 10003-4793

For this edition, the publisher gratefully acknowledges the support and assistance of the Asian Literature Program of The Asia Society.

Library of Congress Cataloging-in-Publication Data

Shih ching. English.
   The book of songs.

    Bibliography: p.
    Includes index.
    I. Waley, Arthur.   II. Title.
PL2478.F7 1987 895.1'11'08   87-7440
ISBN 0-8021-3021-6

Manufactured in the United States of America
Printed on acid-free paper
First published in 1937
First Evergreen Edition 1960

10 9 8 7 6 5 4 3 2

TO
GUSTAV HALOUN

Contents

Foreword to the 1987 Edition

O ur age is one of complexities, in which the causes of events and
their meanings are never entirely clear. Perhaps for this reason, in
the poetry of our age we respect an answering complexity, which
interprets the world and offers no clear answers. Difficulty is our
common measure of depth. However, as we read more poetry,
particularly early poetry, we often make a surprising discovery: that
there is in some poetry a magic of simplicity, which can be even more
forceful and alluring than modern complexity. We find it, for example,
in some of the medieval English lyrics:

> Ich am of Irlaunde,
> And of the holy londe
> Of Irlaunde.

> Good sire, pray ich thee,
> For of sainte charite,
> Come and daunce with me
> In Irlaunde.

At least on one level we still feel we are included by such poems,
included in the archaic invitation to go off with the singer and dance
with her in that mysterious land, Irlaunde. The poem can still address
us; however, we also recognize we can no longer accept such an
invitation with simple delight, nor could we ourselves be able to offer
such an unself-conscious invitation. A poetry as simple and open as this
is somehow beyond our capacities. And at the moment we recognize

this, we may have an intuition that the complexity and "depth" of our own modern poetry is not entirely a progress, but also a falling away and loss. In reading a poem like "Ich am of Irlaunde," we may have a moment of something like shame, recognizing a basic humanity that can address us, even though we no longer speak back to it. If we are given such a moment of revelation, we can grasp something of the role of *The Book of Songs* in Chinese civilization.

There are many poems in *The Book of Songs* which are, like "Ich am of Irlaunde," invitations. They can speak desire without the wink of embarrassment or the self-conscious crudeness that reacts against embarrassment—the qualities that touch almost all statements of desire in modern popular songs.

> That the mere glimpse of a plain coat
> Could stab my heart with grief!
> Enough! Take me with you to your home. (10)

> A very handsome gentleman
> Waited for me in the lane;
> I am sorry I did not go with him. (20)

> Cold blows the northern wind,
> Thick falls the snow.
> Be kind to me, love me,
> Take my hand and go with me. (28)

Even more wondrous, it is a world in which people can speak not only desire but also the contentment of desire, a happy life between man and woman. The husband can want to sleep just a little longer, and the wife can sing him out of bed with a vision of shared joys:

The lady says: "The cock has crowed";
The knight says: :"Day has not dawned."
"Rise, then, and look at the night;
The morning star is shining.
You must be out and abroad,
Must shoot the wild-duck and wild-geese.

When you have shot them, you must bring them home
And I will dress them for you,
And when I have dressed them we will drink wine
And I will be yours till we are old." (25)

As joy can be spoken, pain can be spoken as well and with an equal
honesty. A woman, driven to a marriage she doesn't want, can respond
with a voice that has no gender, that speaks simply as a human being:

> My heart is not a mirror,
> To reflect what others will.
> (75)

And as she continues her complaint, she finds her metaphors not in a
literary tradition, but in the griminess of everyday life:

> O sun, ah, moon,
> Why are you changed and dim?
> Sorrow clings to me
> Like an unwashed dress. (75)

Such a direct and honest world could probably never have existed in a
real human society, but somehow it did exist in poetry.

The Book of Songs is both poetry and scripture, a work of literature and one of the Confucian Classics. Over the past two and a half millenia, *The Book of Songs* has been interpreted and understood in very different ways; but while the significance of the *Songs* changed from age to age and from reader to reader, the texts always retained their allure, promising access to something basic in the human spirit.

For the tradition of Chinese poetry *The Book of Songs* was a beginning that was never forgotten; echoes of the *Songs* appear throughout classical Chinese poetry, even in this century. For many the *Songs* were the ideal for all poetry, an archaic honesty and simplicity that seemed forever just out of reach to more sophisticated and self-conscious ages. In addition, the *Songs* seemed to their readers to be a permanent embodiment of the inner lives of people in the remote past: in the *Songs* one could discover "what it was like then" more perfectly than in any history. Finally, for the Confucian thinker the *Songs* played a central role in the great Confucian project of educating the human heart back to its natural goodness; it was assumed that if a person heard the *Songs* performed, especially as they had once been performed with their lost ancient music, the emotions of the listener would be shaped to decent, balanced, and at the same time, natural responses to the events of life.

Behind all these different approaches to the *Songs* was a simple definition of what a poem was (the term "song," *shih,* in the title *The Book of Songs* being the same generic word used later for all classical poetry). This definition first appeared in another of the Confucian Classics, *The Book of Documents,* and its authority was immense (as if God had decided to offer a brief pronouncement on the nature of poetry in Genesis). The definition is: "Poetry gives words to what the mind is intent upon." This seemingly innocuous statement had immense consequences: readers found in the *Songs* not an "art" of words, produced by a special class of human beings called "poets," but rather a window into another person's heart, a person like themselves. Behind every *Song* one might find some powerful concern—desire, anger, reverence, pain—set in its living context. Other Confucian Classics treated outward things: deeds, moral precepts, the way the world worked. But *The Book of Songs* was the Classic of the human heart and the human mind.

Each reader of *The Book of Songs* has sought to understand the poems as they "originally" were, and each reader has found in them his or her own vision of the remote past, a vision of basic humanity. Confucian scholars discovered their own idea of a genuinely moral society; Arthur Waley, the twentieth-century Western reader, discovered a folk poetry that confirmed modern Western notions of archaic society; contemporary Chinese Marxist interpreters find their own version of social history. However, in one sense each different interpretation of the *Songs* has discovered the same thing: that original core of humanity that we all still have within us.

The Book of Songs is an anthology of three hundred and five poems of varying length, drawn from various levels of Chou society. It contains folksongs, songs of the nobility, ritual hymns, and ballads on significant events in the history of the Chou people. The oldest poems, the temple hymns of the royal house of Chou, may date as early as 1000 B.C.; but most of the songs seem to have reached their present versions shortly before the anthology was put together, probably around 600 B.C. Although it is likely that versions of many of the individual poems continued to be sung in peasant society, the anthology itself clearly belonged to the Chou court and courts of the feudal states into which the Chou kingdom had disintegrated.

Western and modern Chinese scholars have often expressed puzzlement that early China, unlike so many other cultures, has no epic, in which some central myth of the people is shaped into a narrative whole. In Chinese literature *The Book of Songs* occupies the place where Western notions of literary history assume an epic ought to be. However, when we reflect on the nature of *The Book of Songs,* we find in it a different vision of wholeness, and one perhaps more persuasive than the narrative unity of an epic. *The Book of Songs* is a work that attempts to embrace every aspect of its world: the dead ancestors and the living, past history and present, men and women, the ruling house and the common people. And between each of these divisions in their world, the *Songs* create relations that bind them together: the living do homage to the ancestors and the ancestors watch over the living; the present acts with past examples in mind; men and women speak to one another in love or anger; the common people praise or blame their rulers, and the best rulers act in the interest of the common people. The anthology constitutes a whole without possessing any simple unity. Moreover, its wholeness has an ideological basis which would preclude the possibility of epic. Epic unity demands a focus that speaks for one group and excludes other voices: the voices of the common people, the voices of women, voices from all aspects of life outside the heroic ethos. When Andromache begs Hektor not to go out to fight in the *Iliad*, her voice is only a foil against which Hektor can declare his fatal commitment to heroic values. Odysseus' commoners exist poetically only to serve the hero in his hour of need. But the legacy of Chou culture prohibited deafness to those other voices: it was essential that they have their say, that attention be paid to them.

One of the most remarkable tenets of the Chou monarchy was the notion of "Heaven's charge," that the right to rule was given to the house of Chou by Heaven only so long as the Chou watched over the interests of the people it ruled. The real Mycenean warrior who fought below the walls of Troy might well have worried about the peasants at home, who were tilling the fields and keeping the sheep; but to the literary warrior in Homer these are invisible or allowed to appear to aid the hero's progress: each warrior seeks his own private glory. The rulers of Chou were less confident: archaic Chinese writings, including many of the *Songs,* are filled with notes of anxiety lest the ruler stray and Heaven, in its wrath, withdraw its charge from Chou:

Mighty is God on high,
Ruler of His people below;
Swift and terrible is God on high,
His charge has many statutes.
Heaven gives birth to the multitudes of the people,
But its charge cannot be counted upon.
To begin well is common;
To end well is rare indeed. (242)

This anxiety is reminiscent of the caution that the house of Israel
needed to show, always under the watchful eye of God; but the
situation of the Chou was even more precarious: they were not, like the
people of Israel, chosen forever, but merely given an office which they
could keep only so long as they carried out its duties and remained
successful. And the clearest evidence of Heaven's support was to be
found in the voices of the common people. The Chou were constantly
reminded of the fate of the dynasty they had conquered, the Yin or
Shang Dynasty, which had in its day enjoyed Heaven's favor and then
lost it:

Bright they shone on earth below,
Majestic they blaze on high.
Heaven cannot be trusted;
Kingship is easily lost.
Heaven set up a foe to match the Yin;
Did not let them keep their frontier lands. (246)

That "foe" was the Chou itself. Kingship is indeed easily lost.
Although the power of the Chou monarchy had disintegrated and
largely passed to the Chou's feudal lords by the time *The Book of Songs*
was compiled, a concern for the attitude of the common people
remained part of the Chou legacy. The warrior class of early Greece
and the later citizens of the city states, who looked back fondly on that

warrior past, were content to listen to the deeds of heroes alone. And, with very few exceptions, the folk poetry of Greece is lost to us. The same is true of archaic India. But over half of *The Book of Songs* is either folk poetry, modified folk poetry, or inspired by folk poetry.

There is a noticeable lack of violence in *The Book of Songs*.[1] There is some glorification of Chou military power—fast chariots, blazing valor, rank upon rank of warriors—but blood is hardly ever shed. Among the songs of the dynasty are those that bear the memories of the great folk migrations that brought the Chou people into the Chinese heartland. Here we might expect the stuff of epic, monumental struggles in which the Chou people show their power and fitness to rule. But this is how "stalwart Duke Liu" begins the migration into the land of Pin:

> He stacked, he stored,
> He tied up dried meat and grain
> In knapsacks, in bags;
> Far and wide he gathered his stores.
> The bows and arrows he tested,
> Shield and dagger, halberd and battle-axe;
> And then began his march. (239)

The value of wholeness, which governs the compilation of the anthology, can also be seen in these individual poems: the ordinary work of provisioning the people must be celebrated along with the conquest, for in this activity Duke Liu also shows his fitness to rule. Indeed, the only point where the principle of wholeness is violated is in the presentation of violence. Having made ready "Shield and dagger, halberd and battle-axe," Duke Liu must anticipate some resistance from the people into whose lands he is leading the migration, but:

---

[1] For a longer discussion of this question and the avoidance of violence, the reader might consult C.H. Wang, "Toward Defining a Chinese Heroism," *Journal of the American Oriental Society* (95), January–March 1975, pp.25–35.

He made his royal progress, proclaimed his rule;
There were no complaints, no murmurings
Either high up in the hills
Or down in the plains. (239)

Duke Liu's fitness to rule is demonstrated by the willing acceptance of his overlordship on the part of the people whose land he has invaded. It is as sure a mark of Heaven's favor as David's strong sling-arm or Diomedes' prowess.

There is military heroism in *The Book of Songs,* but it is directed more often to public rather than private glory. The Chou's heroes are praised for their valor, but also for their sagacious execution of state policy. The army is essentially a collective force, "the king's claws and fangs":

The king's hosts swept along
As though flying, as though winged,
Like the river, like the Han,
Steady as a mountain,
Flowing onward like a stream,
Rank on rank, in serried order,
Immeasurable, unassailable;
Mightily they marched through the land of Hsü. (139)

However, such exultation in Chou military might represents a threat of violence, which must be balanced by some statement justifying the use of force, as in the stanza that immediately follows the one above:

The king's plans have been faithfully effected,
All the regions of Hsü have submitted,
All the regions of Hsü are at one;
It was the Son of Heaven's deed.
In the four quarters all is peace;

The peoples of Hsü come in homage.
The regions of Hsü no longer disobey;
The king goes back to his home. (139)

Moral power and peace here are a transparent disguise for the brute conquest of Hsü. The peoples of Hsü had probably thought of themselves as independent rather than "disobedient." We must never forget that here we are reading the values of Chou rather than social fact. We must not suppose that Chou was any less bloody than any other branch of the human family. But they felt uneasy enough about their acts of violence to try to conceal them in royal propaganda.

The principle of wholeness in the anthology does not allow such praises of Chou military might to go unquestioned. Poems by soldiers complaining of military service are even more numerous than ballads glorifying Chou campaigns:

Minister of War,
Truly you are not wise.
Why should you roll us from misery to misery?
We have mothers who lack food. (127)

What plant is not faded?
What day do we not march?
What man is not taken
To defend the four bounds?

What plant is not wilting?
What man is not taken from his wife?
Alas for us soldiers,
Treated as though we were not fellow-men! (130)

What Homeric warrior would have declared that he was prevented from desertion only by fear of punishment?

> Oh, bright Heaven high above,
> Shining down upon the earth below,
> Our march to the west
> Has led us to the desert wilds!
> . . . .
> Of course I long to come home,
> But I fear the meshes of crime. (143)

The "meshes of crime" are what we would call "the arm of the law," which will catch him if he deserts the campaign.

The songs of courtship and marriage are generally the least marked by cultural differences and perhaps the easiest of the *Songs* for a modern Western reader to appreciate immediately. Many of these poems might have come from any tradition of folk lyric in the world. There is an *alba* or dawn song (26), in which the anxious girl urges her unwilling lover to get away before he is discovered, that might just as easily be a translation from the Provençal or Old French or medieval German. There is a voice for each step in the delicate dance of courtship: invitation; celebration of the dashing good looks or beauty of the beloved; exchanges of love-gifts and love-words; love-tests; the laments of women seduced and abandoned; and the man who waits for the girl who never comes.

> By the willows of the Eastern Gate,
> Whose leaves are so thick,
> At dusk we were to meet;
> And now the morning star is bright. (57)

The native speaker of English has difficulty avoiding reading the second line "Whose leaves *they* are so thick," thus assimilating the stanza entirely to our own folk lyric. And here, as so often, what at first seems only incidental finally proves essential to the scene: the willows are not simply the place chosen for meeting, their thick leaves, now observed wistfully, would have served to hide the lovers.

The Chou was an agrarian dynasty, and their sense of beauty and order is closely related to the cycles and abundance of the agricultural year. In a society of warriors life is directed to a single intense and uncertain moment of decision, crisis; this plays a powerful role in understanding the structure of time and events, hence of narrative. Agrarian time is cyclical, a complete and repeating series of acts and events, all of which are equally necessary and all of which contribute to the whole. In *The Book of Songs* we often sense a sheer delight in naming all the parts of things: all the different kinds of millet, every activity to be performed in its season. Poems of *The Book of Songs* never begin "in the middle of the matter," *in medias res,* as Horace advised the writer of epic; the *Songs* begin at the beginning and follow through to the end. The need for wholeness in this poetry of the Chou goes far deeper than the dynasty's need for assurance of universal support: it embodies a larger sense of how the world and events in it are structured. Each actor and act must be placed on the stage. The farming hymns are filled with that pleasure in abundance and order in the following celebration of the planting:

> They clear away the grass, the trees;
> Their ploughs open up the ground.
> In a thousand pairs they tug at weeds and roots,
> Along the low grounds, along the ridges.
> There is the master and his eldest son,
> There the headman and the overseer.
> They mark out, they plough.
> Deep the food-baskets that are brought;
> Dainty are the wives,
> The men press close to them.
> And now with shares so sharp
> They set to work upon the southern acre.
> They sow the many sorts of grain,
> The seeds that hold moist life. (157)

It is not enough to say that the lowlands were weeded; we must remember the ridges too. The absence of suspense, the delight in things in their expected order, is one of the most difficult qualities for the Western reader to appreciate in these earliest poems of *The Book of Songs*. It is a world with anxiety but without terror: there is no incomprehensible divinity, god the hunter, who tracks men down, good men like Job and men who follow the proper customs like Pentheos, whom Dionysios destroyed. There are, however, a few poems that recall a darker and even more archaic past, times when retainers were killed and buried with their lords, to keep them company in the afterlife. One of the few datable poems in *The Book of Songs* comes from 621 B.C., the date of the death of Duke Mu of the state of Ch'in, a border duchy where the old customs still survived:

> "Kio" sings the oriole
> As it lights on the thorn-bush.
> Who went with Duke Mu to the grave?
> Yen-hsi of the clan Tzŭ-chü
> Now this Yen-hsi
> Was the pick of all our men;
> But as he drew near the tomb-hole
> His limbs shook with dread.
> That blue one, Heaven,
> Takes all our good men.
> Could we but ransom him
> There are a hundred would give their lives. (278)

The stanzas of the song continue with the oriole alighting on a series of different plants; and each time it alights, a new member of the Tzŭ-chü clan is sent to join Duke Mu in the grave. Many of the *Songs* begin with some natural image whose relation to the topic of the *Song* is oblique (as the English "Green grow the rushes, o"), but in this case there seems to be some magic correspondence between the plant on which the bird stops and the man named in the following lines, as if an augur were present who could read Heaven's choice of victim in the movements of the bird.

The sense of arbitrary and inescapable doom in the poem above stands out from all other poems in *The Book of Songs*. The anthology presents the full human share of unhappiness and pain, but usually the reasons behind suffering are quite clear: desertion by a lover, misgovernment, the hardships of forced military service. In the increasingly turbulent and violent centuries that followed the seventh century B.C., much in *The Book of Songs* seemed indeed to come from a lost era in which the world was comprehensible; and the anthology contributed much to the Chinese myth of the Chou as the ideal polity.

Out of this diverse body of hymns, ballads, and folksongs current in the seventh century *The Book of Songs* took shape. We know that the *Songs* were performed in the feudal courts of the period, and that they became an authoritative body of texts with which everyone in the courts was familiar. They served as one of the few unifying cultural legacies of the Chou in an age of political fragmentation and interstate warfare. Like the Homeric epics in Greece, an aura gathered around the *Songs,* and, known to all, they were frequently quoted in court discussions to lend force to arguments. This practice of quotation would usually involve taking lines or stanzas out of context and applying them, with varying degrees of appropriateness, to contemporary situations. From this custom (and from the reaction against its egregious abuses) individual *Songs* gradually acquired general interpretations.

Confucius (551–479 B.C.) placed great emphasis on the study of *The Book of Songs,* both as an essential part of a moral education and as training for political life in the courts. In his *Analects,* we can see the *Songs* well on their way to becoming a Classic; they are recommended as paradigms of the moral heart: "There are three hundred *Songs* and one phrase covers them all: 'No straying from the path'" (*Analects II.2*). However, since many of the *Songs,* as honest they may seem to our eyes, did not conform to certain aspects of Confucian morality, they were reinterpreted to make them accord with their presumed moral perfection. The Traditionalists, whom we now call "Confucians," made *The Book of Songs* a central text in their schools; they based ethical discourses on them and, as earlier in the courts, cited the *Songs* to prove their points. This practice is amusingly illustrated in a cruel parody by the greatest foe of the Traditionalists, the Taoist Chuang-tzu (ca. 369–286 B.C.). Note that the verse quoted isn't really from the *Songs,* but does sound like one:

Some Confucians were robbing graves according to *The Book of Songs* and Rites. The senior Confucian gave a dictum to his subordinates, "Sun riseth in the east; how goeth the matter at hand?" A junior Confucian answered, "We haven't stripped off his robes yet, but there's a pearl in his mouth." The senior Confucian: "Ah, indeed it is as the *The Book of Songs* says:

'The millet is green, so green,
It groweth on the slopes.
If ungenerous in life,
What good a pearl in the lips when dead?
I'll grab his whiskers in one hand and yank down on his beard with the other. You prop his jaws open with a metal spike, then gently, gently spread his cheeks so as not to damage the pearl in his mouth.'"

If the Traditionalists believed that the *Songs* could make a person good, Chuang-tzu saw them as a potential disguise of evil. There is a venerable Taoist principle in this: when interpretation and practical application appear, possibilities of misinterpretation and misapplication appear with them.

When Confucianism finally was fully institutionalized in the Han Dynasty, *The Book of Songs* became a standard part of the scholastic curriculum, each poem carrying with it an orthodox interpretation, which explained how that poem responded to the moral and social conditions of the age in which it was produced. By this point the an-

thology had come to lead the double life mentioned earlier, both as
literature and as a Confucian Classic. There was always some tension
between the clear and natural surface of the text and the weight of
moral interpretation attached to it. Perhaps the best analogy in the
Western tradition would be the "Song of Solomon" in the Bible,
where a surface of erotic love poetry played counterpoint to orthodox
interpretation as the soul's love for God (or Christ's love for the
Church). And as with the "Song of Solomon," that tension in *The
Book of Songs* worked both ways, lending the natural responses of the
Songs a quality of moral value, and casting on moral positions given in
the exegeses the glow of natural response.

The interpretation of *The Book of Songs* is filled with difficulties,
both the philological interpretation of individual words and lines and
of whole poems. Arthur Waley was a scholar in his own right, as well
as being a remarkably gifted translator; and he has done his best in
these translations (which are at the same time interpretations) to
restore to the *Songs* some of the freshness of their Chou origins. Many
aspects of these poems will always seem strange to us: unfamiliar place
names and vanished folkways. Very few readers indeed have ever ridden
in a chariot, nor do we wear belts with carved stones dangling from
them (Waley's "girdles"). But in many of the *Songs* something basic is
still transmitted, even across the barriers of translation, a different
culture, and over two and a half millenia of history. And when we
catch that basic human note, we may recognize that it is we who have
become strange and alien, not the *Songs*. We find in them words we can
feel but no longer say, such as the following words of a woman to a
lover who has abandoned her:

> If along the highroad
> I caught hold of your sleeve,
> Do not hate me;
> Old ways take time to overcome. (56)
>   —Stephen Owen, Harvard University

Preface to the Second Edition

THIS book was first published in 1937. In 1941, owing to a fire caused by incendiary bombs, it went out of print. Some years later when my other books were reprinted, I held back *The Book of Songs*, feeling that it needed a leisurely revision. In making this revision I have had the advantage of constantly referring to Professor Karlgren's word-for-word translation and notes, which appeared between 1942 and 1946.[1] Anyone using my book for documentary purposes, that is to say, for the study of comparative literature, folklore or the like, would do well to see what Professor Karlgren has to say. There are many cases in which, after again weighing the evidence, I do not find myself in agreement with him; but few where I feel quite certain that he is wrong.

About a dozen corrections, chiefly of small misprints, have been made in the text, and I have separately listed a similar number of corrections and additions which it would have been technically difficult to incorporate in the text.

A point which I did not make clear in the first edition is that in the transcription of proper names I have ignored the abnormal pronunciations sometimes indicated by phonetic glosses and have, for the convenience of the reader, used the commonly accepted pronunciations that figure, for example, in the Harvard-Yenching index to the songs. The separately bound little volume of Textual Notes is still in print.

In the preface to the first edition I spoke of my deep debt of gratitude to Gustav Haloun, who shortly afterwards became

[1] *The Book of Odes.* Stockholm, 1950. *Glosses on the Book of Odes,* Bulletin of the Museum of Far Eastern Antiquities, 1942, 1944, 1946.

Professor of Chinese in Cambridge and died there in 1951. The book was (and still is) dedicated to him. In a sense it is his book as well as mine, and I think it would have pleased him to see it in print again after an interval of thirteen years.

Preface to the First Edition

THE collection[1] here translated consists in the original of three hundred and five pieces. I have omitted fifteen of these, all of them political laments, partly because they are much less interesting than the others and partly because in many passages the text is so corrupt that one would be obliged either to write nonsense or to leave many blanks. With these omitted pieces I have dealt elsewhere.[2] Such of the songs as are datable range between 800 and 600 B.C.

I am deeply indebted to Professor Gustav Haloun, Director of the Sinological Seminary at Göttingen, who not only put at my disposal the resources of the splendid Chinese library which has been formed at Göttingen under his care, but also directed my studies and borrowed for me from other German libraries books which would not otherwise have been easy to procure. I wish also to express here my gratitude to the editors of the Harvard–Yenching Index Series for their *Concordance to the Shih Ching*, published in 1934. This work has furthered our understanding of the songs more than all the thousands of volumes which have dealt with the book since the second century B.C. Indeed, before its appearance no serious, independent study of the text was possible. I have also to thank Mr. Alan Clutton-Brock for valuable literary criticism, Mr. R. C. Trevelyan for help both before and after printing, and Mr. John Layard for advice about kinship terms. Miss Alyse Gregory and Mrs. Ætheldreda Penderel also kindly helped me with the proofs.

[1] For its customary English titles, see p. 18.
[2] In the periodical *T'ien Hsia*, October 1936.

Introduction

Imagery

EARLY Chinese songs do not as a rule introduce a comparison with an 'as if' or 'like,' but state it on the same footing as the facts that they narrate. European traditional poetry sometimes uses the same method. Our English folksong does not say, 'My feelings after being forsaken are like those of a person who has leaned against an apparently trusty tree and then found that it was insecure.' It says:

> I lean'd my back against an oak;
> I thought it was a trusty tree.
> But first it bent and then it broke;
> My true love has forsaken me.

Compare a Polish song:

> They have cut the little oak, they have hewn it;
> It is no longer green.
> They have taken away my lover,
> Have taken him to the wars.

That is exactly the way that images are used in the early Chinese songs. For example:

> The cloth-plant grew till it covered the thorn-bush;
> The bindweed spread far over the wilds.
> My lovely one is here no more.
> With whom?—No, I sit alone.

If we want to understand that poem, we cannot do better than compare it with this *uta* from the old Japanese anthology *Manyōshū*:[1]

---

[1] Book XII, No. 4352.

> From you with whom I am entwined
> Like the bean-plant that has crept
> Over the face of the thorn-bush
> That grows by the road
> Must I now be parted, go away?

The Japanese poem, besides helping to explain the image in the Chinese one, handles this image in a way that is a stepping-stone between the early Chinese method and that of modern poetry; for the comparison is linked to the question with which the poem ends only by a frail particle, *no*, which probably means no more than 'so' or 'thus.' To put in a 'like' or 'as if' where there is none in the original, is to alter the whole character of a song, and I have, out of a hundred instances, not done so more than once or twice, in special cases where it did not seem to matter. The flight of birds, their cries, the movements of animals, the condition of flowers, dewy or rain-dabbled, the restlessness of insects, the sound of their wings, the fading of the stars—all these play their part in early Chinese imagery; as symbols, illustrations, or omens according to the context. Many of these images are such as we should ourselves use. That the soughing or sighing of the wind should be interpreted as a sound of sorrow, that showers of fertilizing rain should symbolize princely bounties, that wet leaves should recall tearful cheeks, seems to us natural enough. That the cries of birds should be interpreted as words with real meaning strikes us at first as odd. But we must remember that such cries as caw-caw, coo-coo, cluck-cluck, quack-quack, are typical of the sounds that actually existed in early Chinese vocabulary. It was difficult to believe that birds and beasts did not use them with the same intention as human beings. Such interpretations are not confined to poetry. For example, in 543 B.C. a bird flew out of the national shrine of the Sung people crying 'hieg, hieg!' Hieg[1] means 'to moan in agony,' and no one was surprised when shortly afterwards a great fire broke out at the capital and the duke's wife perished in the flames.

[1] I give an approximate Chou pronunciation.

Some images are common to Chinese and Japanese poetry, but do not so far as I know occur in the West. For example, the river that divides and joins again, as a symbol of reunion after a bitter parting; and the rocking of boats as an image of the turmoil in a lover's heart, as in the Japanese poem[1] 'Tossing, tossing even as some great ship that rides at anchor in the bay I am worn out with longing for her that is another's girl,' or in No. 75 below:

> Tossed is that cypress boat,
> Wave-tossed it floats;
> My heart is in turmoil, I cannot sleep.

Other images recall those of folk-tales; for example, bundled firewood as a symbol of mutual aid and cohesion. It was by a similar image that the mother of Chingiz Khan warned her sons against dissension.

Often nature seems to work with man and share in his moods. But in certain moments of horror and anguish it is the indifference of nature that adds a last touch to the poignancy of human suffering. The lament (No. 278) for the warriors who followed Duke Mu to the grave has the refrain: " 'Kio' sings the oriole, as it lights on the brambles."

> "And bonny sang the mavis
> Out on the thorny brake"

says the Scotch ballad *Lamkin*, in describing the execution of the 'false nourice.'

Again and again it is as contrasts and not as comparisons that the things of nature figure in early Chinese songs. The lotus is in the pool and the pine-tree on the hill. Nature goes its accustomed way, only man changes; such is the burden of many songs. The birds and beast come back to the farm at dusk; but the warrior knows no rest (No. 100). The kite soars into the clouds, the fish hides in the depths of its pool; but for man there is no escape.

[1] *Manyōshū*, No. 122 (Book II).

> How can ye chant, ye little birds,
> And I so full of care?

writes Burns, and it is this feeling of unendurable contrast that is expressed in many of the Chinese songs. This was misunderstood by later commentators. For example, the same phrase that in No. 187 admittedly means 'gorgeous its yellow' (speaking of flowers), is taken in No. 289 quite arbitrarily as meaning 'they wilt and turn yellow,' despite the fact that the next verse describes the flourishing condition of the same tree. In reality the singer is contrasting the miseries of man with the glowing profusion of nature.

In the courtship and marriage poems the beloved, much as in Japanese poetry, is compared to plum-blossom, to peach-blossom, to beautiful creepers, to slender bamboos, to the pepper-plant, to lotuses, to the Chinese gooseberry, and once or twice to the sun and moon; the comparison almost always being made in the form:

> On the hill grows the cherry-tree
> And lovely are its flowers;
> I have seen my lord,
> And splendid is his dress.

Hardly ever, as I have already pointed out, are words such as 'like,' 'as,' or 'even so' employed. Anyone reading the poems must be struck by the frequency with which clothes and articles of personal adornment are mentioned. Interest in clothes may be of many different kinds. It may, for example, be purely aesthetic, as it often is in the *Tale of Genji*,[1] and may be concerned with the sense of beauty and harmony shown by the wearer in his choice of textures and colours. Or again, clothes may be regarded simply as an indication of personal status. If a girl in a garrison town turns down one lover in preference for another who has more stripes on his sleeve, she does not do this because her sense of beauty is better satisfied by the additional stripes. She does so because more

[1] A Japanese novel of the eleventh century A.D., which I have translated.

prestige attaches to walking out with a sergeant than to walking out with a corporal. In which way were the lovers in the *Book of Songs* interested in dress? According to my view, wholly in the second way. 'The lover I am with has blazoned coat and broidered robe' (No. 29) is not a eulogy on the young man's taste in dress or an expression of aesthetic delight in the beauty of his clothes, but a cry of triumph at having hooked (the words are preceded by an angling metaphor) a lover of high social standing.

These Chinese songs play on words exactly as Japanese poetry does, though much less frequently. *Pien*, for example, means 'change,' *p'ien* means fluttering of wings or leaves. So that the *p'ien-p'ien* of leaves or wings becomes an evil omen for the lover. Sometimes the existence in the commentaries of two quite different explanations of a word or phrase is due to the fact that in reality both senses were intended. Fortunately for the translator, the meaning of a song seldom depends exclusively on a pun; play on words is merely an additional decoration. I have called attention to the most obvious and certain of these puns in the course of my translation. There are other cases where I suspect a double meaning, but am not sure enough to feel justified in pointing it out.

I do not think that in these songs the nature-references have ever become mere meaningless refrains, as they sometimes appear to have done in our own ballads—'*the bird and the broom grows bonnie*' being put in merely to fill out the tune. But there are probably cases in which the clue to their full meaning has been lost. It is not likely that we can recreate all the mental associations of people in China three thousand years ago. We must be content to miss a great many small points, expecting the songs, handed down from so long ago, to be at times somewhat baffling, seeing that even our own ballads (some two thousand years less ancient) are so often mysterious.

This volume consists of translation and such notes as can be understood by those who are not students of Chinese. My supplement (Textual Notes) deals with technical questions and is meant only for specialists. There remains a host of points philological, geographical, historical, which I have altogether evaded. A list of them will be found in Appendix V.

A word about the form of the songs. This is to some extent apparent from the translations, which (with very rare exceptions) are line for line. Head-rhyme, internal rhyme, and alliteration, all occur as occasional ornaments. But the only sort of rhyme used systematically as a metrical basis comes, like that of our own poetry, at the end of the line.[1] In a quatrain the second and fourth lines must rhyme. Sometimes all four lines rhyme together; sometimes lines one and three have a rhyme of their own. Arrangement in rhyming couplets occurs, but is not frequent. The normal form of the courtship and marriage songs is three verses of four lines each. There is (apart from the very fragmentary dynastic hymns) only one song that consists of a single quatrain—the form so popular in later Chinese poetry. Like our own ballads, the longer songs are irregular in the formation of their stanzas, using four lines and six lines promiscuously.

The collection was in early days known to the Chinese simply as the *Shih* (song-words); later, as the *Shih Ching* (song-word scripture). It has been known to Europeans as *The Odes, The Confucian Odes, The Book of Poetry*. The songs are indeed 'Confucian' in the sense that Confucius (who lived *c.* 500 B.C.) and his followers used them as texts for moral instruction, much as Greek pedagogues used Homer. There is no reason to suppose that Confucius had a hand in forming the collection.

I would much rather have kept to the traditional order, which does not arrange the poems according to subject. But after experimenting in this direction I came to the conclusion that the advantages of an arrangement according to subject far outweighed, for the purposes of the present book, the disadvantages of tampering with the accepted order. I hope

[1] For the rhymes, see B. Karlgren, *Shi King Researches* and *The Rimes in the Sung section of the Shi King*.

that the tables at the end of the book will enable the specialist to identify the pieces without difficulty. If any reader possesses a copy of the *Songs* in which the pieces are not numbered 1–305, as they are, for example, in the Harvard–Yenching Index text, he will find that it is a very easy matter to insert the numbers. The *Songs* ought to be referred to by means of a consecutive numbering, and not by their transliterated headings. Such a reference as 'Mien Shui' is of no practical use.

Finally, a word about plant names. Structural classification of plants is a modern European invention. It did not exist in ancient China any more than it existed in ancient Europe. I have tried wherever possible to use general, non-technical equivalents. In the two or three instances where I give a Linnaean name I do so merely in order to indicate the sort of plant that was meant. I do not mean that the ancient name and the modern scientific name exactly coincide.

Readers wanting to know more about the *Songs* in general and their relation to early Chinese culture may prefer to read appendices I and III before reading the translations.

Courtship

1   OUT in the bushlands a creeper grows,
     The falling dew lies thick upon it.
There was a man so lovely,
Clear brow well rounded.
By chance I came across him,
And he let me have my will.

Out in the bushlands a creeper grows,
The falling dew lies heavy on it.
There was a man so lovely,
Well rounded his clear brow.
By chance I came upon him:
'Oh, Sir, to be with you is good.'

2   IN the lowlands is the goat's-peach;[1]
Very delicate are its boughs.
Oh, soft and tender,
Glad I am that you have no friend.

In the lowlands is the goat's-peach;
Very delicate are its flowers.
Oh, soft and tender,
Glad I am that you have no home.

In the lowlands is the goat's-peach;
Very delicate is its fruit.
Oh, soft and tender,
Glad I am that you have no house.

[1] The goat's-peach was later identified with the Chinese goose-berry, which now only grows a long way south of the Yangtze. The same names were applied to the *Actinidia Chinensis*, which grows in the north and is probably what is meant here.

3   HEY-HO, he is splendid!
Magnificent in stature,
Noble his brow,
His lovely eyes so bright,
Nimble in running,
A bowman unsurpassed.

Hey-ho, he is glorious!
Lovely eyes so clear,
Perfect in courtesy,
Can shoot all day at a target
And never miss the mark.
Truly a man of my clan.

Hey-ho, he is lovely!
His clear brow well-rounded,
When he dances, never losing his place,
When he shoots, always piercing.
Swift his arrows fly
To quell mischief on every side.

4   SUN in the east!
This lovely man
Is in my house,
Is in my home,
His foot is upon my doorstep.

Moon in the east!
This lovely man
Is in my bower,[1]
Is in my bower,
His foot is upon my threshold.

[1] The word that I have translated "bower" means the back part of the house, where the women lived. The sun and moon are symbols of his beauty, and do not mark (as one might at first sight suppose) the time of his visit. Compare No. 32.

5   'How can you say you have no bedclothes?
                Why, you have seven!'
    'But not like your bedclothes, so comfortable
                and fine.'
    'How can you say you have no bedclothes?
                Why, you have six!'
    'Yes, but not like your bedclothes, so com-
                fortable and warm.'

6   In skins of the young lamb
        Sewn with white silk of five and twenty
            strands,
        Going home to supper from the palace
        With step grave and slow!

    In hides of the young lamb
        Sewn with white silk of a hundred strands,
        With step grave and slow
        From the palace going to his supper!

    In skins of the young lamb sewn
        With white silk of four hundred strands,
        With step grave and slow
        Going home to supper from the palace!

The more numerous the strands the more potent the
personal magic (tê) of the wearer. Thread of a fixed
number of strands is often used in attaching amulets,
charms, etc.

7 THERE in the oozy ground by the Fên[1]
I was plucking the sorrel;
There came a gentleman
Lovely beyond compare,
Lovely beyond compare,
More beautiful than any that ride
With the duke in his coach.

There on a stretch by the Fên
I was plucking mulberry-leaves;
There came a gentleman
Lovely as the glint of jade,
Lovely as the glint of jade,
More splendid than any that attend
The duke in his coach.

There in the bend of the Fên
I was plucking water-plantain;
There came a gentleman
Lovely as jade,
Lovely as jade,
More splendid than any that escort
The duke in his coach.

[1] Tributary of the Yellow River, south-western corner of Shansi.

8   THE seeds of the pepper-plant[1]
Overflowed my pint-measure.
That man of mine,
None so broad and tall!
Oh, the pepper-plant,
How wide its branches spread!

The seeds of the pepper-plant
Overflowed my hands as well.
That man of mine
Big, tall and strong!
Oh, the pepper-plant,
How wide its branches spread!

9   ELMS of the Eastern Gate,
Oaks of the Hollow Mound—
The sons of the Tzŭ-chung
Trip and sway beneath them.

It is a lucky morning, hurrah!
The Yüan girls from the southern side
Instead of twisting their hemp
In the market trip and sway.

It is a fine morning at last!
'Let us go off to join the throng.'
'You are lovely as the mallow.'
'Then give me a handful of pepper-seed!'

---

[1] The fine stature of the lover is compared to the luxuriance of the pepper-plant, which at the same time symbolizes the heat of his passion.

10   THAT the mere glimpse of a plain cap
Could harry me with such longing,
Cause pain so dire!

That the mere glimpse of a plain coat
Could stab my heart with grief!
Enough! Take me with you to your home.

That a mere glimpse of plain leggings
Could tie my heart in tangles!
Enough! Let us two be one.

11   How well your black coat fits!
Where it is torn I will turn it for you.
Let us go to where you lodge,
And there I will hand your food to you.

How nice your black coat looks!
Where it is worn I will mend it for you.
Let us go to where you lodge,
And there I will hand your food to you.

How broad your black coat is!
Where it is worn I will alter it for you.
Let us go to where you lodge,
And there I will hand your food to you.

12   IN the ten-acre field
A mulberry-picker stands idle,
Says: 'If you're going, I will come back with you.'

Beyond the ten-acre field
A mulberry-picker has strayed,
Says: 'If you're going, I will stroll with you.'

13 DOWN below the town-gate
It is easy to idle time away.
Where the spring flows by
It is easy to satisfy one's desires.[1]

Must the fish one sups off
Needs be bream from the river?
Must the girl one weds
Needs be a Chiang[2] from Ch'i?

Must the fish one sups on
Needs be carp from the river?
Must the girl one weds
Needs be a Tzu from Sung?

[1] Not by drinking the water, as has usually been supposed, but by
picking up one of the girls who haunted the fringes of the town.
[2] Name of the clan to which the rulers of Ch'i belonged.

14   WHEN the Chên and Wei[1]
    Are running in full flood
    Is the time for knights and ladies
    To fill their arms with scented herbs.
    The lady says, 'Have you looked?'
    The knight says, 'Yes, I have finished looking;
    Shall we go and look a little more?
    Beyond the Wei
    It is very open and pleasant.'
    That knight and lady,
    Merrily they sport.
    Then she gives him a peony.

    The Chên and Wei
    Run deep and clear;
    That knight and lady,
    Their flower-basket is full.
    The lady says, 'Have you looked?'
    The knight says, 'Yes, I have finished looking;
    Shall we go and look a little more?
    Beyond the Wei
    It is very open and pleasant.'
    That knight and lady,
    Merrily they sport.
    Then she gives him a peony.

The commentators, no doubt rightly, connect this poem with a spring festival at which there was a custom of general courtship and mating. So we must take our knight and lady not as an individual romance, but as typical of the general courtship that went on in the land of Chêng in the third month. The peony has, of course, a great reputation for medicinal and magical powers, both in the West and in China. It shares some of the mythology of the mandrake. It was probably the root rather than the flower that first interested the Chinese; for the second

[1] Two streams in northern Honan.

element in the name (*Shao-yao*) means 'medicinal herb,' and it is the root of the peony that has always been used in medicine. It probably figured in courtship first as a love-philtre, and later (as in this poem) merely as a symbol of lasting affection, like our rosemary. A popular etymology makes it mean the 'binding herb.'

15   DRUMMING and dancing[1] in the gulley
     How light-hearted was that tall man!
     Subtler than any of them at capping stories.
     And he swore he would never forget me.

     Drumming and dancing along the bank,
     How high-spirited was that tall man!
     Subtler than any at capping songs.
     And he swore he would never fail me.

     Dancing and drumming on the high ground,
     How gay was that tall man!
     Subtler than any at capping whistled tunes.
     And he swore his love would never end.

I think that too many of the songs have been explained by M. Granet as being connected with a festival of courtship in which the girls and boys lined up on opposite sides of a stream—a type of festival well known in Indo-China. This song, however, is clearly connected with such a meeting. An interesting book on courtship by exchange of songs has been published by N. van Huyen (*Chants Alternés des Garçons et des Filles en Annam*, 1934).

----

[1] Literally 'bending the legs.' That particular kind of dancing (with bent knee), so common in the Far East, must be meant.

16 THE pond by the eastern gate
    Is good for steeping hemp.
    That beautiful Shu Chi[1]
    Is good at capping songs.

    The pond by the eastern gate
    Is good for steeping cloth-grass.
    That beautiful Shu Chi
    Is good at capping proverbs.

    The pond by the eastern gate
    Is good for steeping rushes.
    That beautiful Shu Chi
    Is good at capping stories.

17 PLOP fall the plums; but there are still seven.[2]
    Let those gentlemen that would court me
    Come while it is lucky!

    Plop fall the plums; there are still three.
    Let any gentleman that would court me
    Come before it is too late!

    Plop fall the plums; in shallow baskets we lay them.
    Any gentleman who would court me
    Had better speak while there is time.

[1] Literally, 'third daughter of the clan Chi.'
[2] This poem is akin to love-divinations of the type 'Loves me,
loves me not' and 'This year, next year, some time, never.' Seven,
as with us, is a lucky number.

18 SHE threw a quince to me;
      In requital I gave a bright girdle-gem.
      No, not just as requital;
      But meaning I would love her for ever.

      She threw a tree-peach to me;
      As requital I gave her a bright greenstone.
      No, not just as requital;
      But meaning I would love her for ever.

      She threw a tree-plum to me;
      In requital I gave her a bright jet-stone.
      No, not just as requital,
      But meaning I would love her for ever.

   I have here used the term 'requital' because it is
technical in our own pastoral poetry. For example, in
Michael Drayton's *Pastorals*:

      His lass him lavender hath sent
      Showing her love, and doth requital crave;
      Him rosemary his sweetheart . . ., etc.

   Modern botanists identify the fruit of verse 1 as
Cydonia Sinensis (Chinese quince), that of verse 2 as
Cydonia Japonica, and that of verse 3 as the common
quince. The names of the stones very likely indicate
their shape and their position in the girdle-pendant
rather than their quality.

19   AMONG the hillocks grows the hemp;
There works Tzu-chüeh of Liu,
There works Tzu-chüeh of Liu.
If only he would come in and rest!

Among the hillocks grows the wheat;
There works Tzu-kuo of Liu,
There works Tzu-kuo of Liu.
If only he would come in to supper!

Among the hillocks grow the plum-trees;
There work those good men of Liu,
There work those good men of Liu
That gave me jet-stones for my girdle.

20   A VERY handsome gentleman
Waited for me in the lane;
I am sorry I did not go with him.

A very splendid gentleman
Waited for me in the hall;
I am sorry I did not keep company with him.

I am wearing my unlined coat, my coat all of brocade.[1]
I am wearing my unlined skirt, my skirt all of brocade!
Oh uncles, young and old,
Let me go with him to his home!

I am wearing my unlined skirt, my skirt all of brocade.
And my unlined coat, my coat all of brocade.
Oh uncles, young and old,
Let me go with him to his home!

---

[1] I do not here or elsewhere use these textile terms in a technical sense. Words for needlework and weaving are hopelessly confused in ancient Chinese; as they were also in medieval English.

21 HE waited for me at the gate-screen, heigh-ho!
    His ear-plugs[1] were white, heigh-ho!
    And over them, a bright flower, heigh-ho!

    He waited for me in the courtyard, heigh-ho!
    His ear-plugs were green, heigh-ho!
    And over them, a bright blossom, heigh-ho!

    He waited for me in the hall, heigh-ho!
    His ear-plugs were yellow, heigh-ho!
    And over them, a blossom bright, heigh-ho!

22 OF fair girls the loveliest
    Was to meet me at the corner of the Wall.
    But she hides and will not show herself;
    I scratch my head, pace up and down.

    Of fair girls the prettiest
    Gave me a red flute.
    The flush of that red flute
    Is pleasure at the girl's beauty.

    She has been in the pastures and brought
            for me rush-wool,
    Very beautiful and rare.
    It is not you that are beautiful;
    But you were given by a lovely girl.

[1] I take it that ear-rings were only worn on state occasions and
that the 'plugs' took their place at other times.

23   I AM going to gather the dodder
In the village of Mei.[1]
Of whom do I think?
Of lovely Mêng Chiang.
She was to wait for me at Sang-chung,
But she went all the way to Shang-kung
And came with me to the banks of the Ch'i.

I am going to gather goosefoot
To the north of Mei.
Of whom do I think?
Of lovely Mêng I.
She was to wait for me at Sang-chung,
But she went all the way to Shang-kung
And came with me to the banks of the Ch'i.

I am going to gather charlock
To the east of Mei.
Of whom do I think?
Of lovely Mêng Yung.
She was to wait for me at Sang-chung,
But she went all the way to Shang-kung
And came with me to the banks of the Ch'i.

Secret Courtship

THE rural lover, in China as in Europe, paid secret
visits to his lady at night. She expected him to show his
courage and resourcefulness by climbing walls and
forcing doors so silently that the dog did not bark nor
the parents wake. Difficult though it was to tear himself
away, he must leave the house by daybreak. This is a
situation that is familiar to us in hundreds of European
folk-songs and ballads. It is especially typical of German
country-courtship, save that the German lover had an

[1] The places mentioned in the song were all in northern Honan.

easier time of it, being generally let in at a window; hence
the name 'Fensterln' commonly given to such courtship.

The custom belongs to that curiously marginal type of
sexual institution, half illicit and half condoned. It is the
sort of thing about which we say, 'I don't mind what
they do, so long as they keep it to themselves.'

The right, which exists in some countries, of younger
brothers to have access to an elder brother's wife so long
as the connection is a secret one, is another example of
this ambiguous type of institution.

24   I BEG of you, Chung Tzu,
      Do not climb into our homestead,
      Do not break the willows we have planted.
      Not that I mind about the willows,
      But I am afraid of my father and mother.
      Chung Tzu I dearly love;
      But of what my father and mother say
      Indeed I am afraid.

      I beg of you, Chung Tzu,
      Do not climb over our wall,
      Do not break the mulberry-trees we have
         planted.
      Not that I mind about the mulberry-trees,
      But I am afraid of my brothers.
      Chung Tzu I dearly love;
      But of what my brothers say
      Indeed I am afraid.

      I beg of you, Chung Tzu,
      Do not climb into our garden,
      Do not break the hard-wood we have planted.
      Not that I mind about the hard-wood,
      But I am afraid of what people will say.
      Chung Tzu I dearly love;
      But of all that people will say
      Indeed I am afraid.

25 THE lady says: 'The cock has crowed';
    The knight says: 'Day has not dawned.'
    'Rise, then, and look at the night;
    The morning star is shining.
    You must be out and abroad,
    Must shoot the wild-duck and wild-geese.

When you have shot them, you must bring
        them home
And I will dress them for you,
And when I have dressed them we will drink
        wine
And I will be yours till we are old.
I will set your zitherns before you;
All shall be peaceful and good.

Did I but know those who come to you,
I have girdle-stones of many sorts to give them;
Did I but know those that have followed you,
I have girdle-stones of many sorts as presents
        for them.
Did I know those that love you,
I have girdle-stones of many sorts to requite
        them.'

This song and the next could be paralleled by many
'albas,' dawn-songs, in European traditional poetry. The
word used for 'shooting' does not mean shooting with an
ordinary bow and arrow, but fowling with a short dart
attached to a string. Hsü Chung-shu has written an
interesting article on the subject.[1]

[1] See *Academia Sinica*, Vol. IV, No. 4.

26 THE LADY: The cock has crowed;
                It is full daylight.

   THE LOVER: It was not the cock that crowed,
                It was the buzzing of those green flies.

   THE LADY: The eastern sky glows;
                It is broad daylight.

   THE LOVER: That is not the glow of dawn,
                But the rising moon's light.
                The gnats fly drowsily;
                It would be sweet to share a dream
                    with you.

   THE LADY: Quick! Go home!
                Lest I have cause to hate you!

27   TOWARDS the east it is still dark,
     But he bustles into jacket and skirt.
     He bustles into them and hustles into them;
     From the palace they have sent for him.

     The dew of night is not yet dry,[1]
     But he bustles into skirt and coat,
     Hustles into them and bustles into them;
     To the palace they have summoned him.

     'He is breaking the willows of the fenced
         garden,
     The mad fellow in his flurry—
     Never can he judge the time of night;
     If he's not too early, then he's too late.'

[1] The original says, 'Towards the east it is not yet dry.' The first
two characters have been erroneously repeated from verse 1.
   For a different rendering of this song, see *Chinese Poems* (1946), p. 21.
I am still not sure which is right. Here, and elsewhere in this book, the
allocation of lines to different speakers is my own, and is not indicated
in the original.

28 COLD blows the northern wind,
Thick falls the snow.
Be kind to me, love me,
Take my hand and go with me.
Yet she lingers, yet she havers!
There is no time to lose.

The north wind whistles,
Whirls the falling snow.
Be kind to me, love me,
Take my hand and go home with me.
Yet she lingers, yet she havers!
There is no time to lose.

Nothing is redder than the fox,
Nothing blacker than the crow.[1]
Be kind to me, love me,
Take my hand and ride with me.
Yet she lingers, yet she havers!
There is no time to lose.

29 'THE fish in the minnow-net
Were rudd and bream.
The lover I am with
Has blazoned coat and broidered robe.'

'The wild-geese take wing; they make for the
island.
The prince has gone off and we cannot find him.
He must be staying with you.

The wild-geese take wing; they make for the land.
The prince went off and does not come back.
He must be spending the night with you.'

  [1] And no one truer than I.

'All because he has a broidered robe
Don't take my prince away from me,
Don't make my heart sad.'

Separation · Hopeless Passion

30 SHU is away in the hunting-fields,
There is no one living in our lane.
Of course there *are* people living in
        our lane;
But they are not like Shu,
So beautiful, so good.

Shu has gone after game.
No one drinks wine in our lane.
Of course people *do* drink wine in
        our lane
But they are not like Shu,
So beautiful, so loved.

Shu has gone to the wilds,
No one drives horses in our lane.
Of course people *do* drive horses in
        our lane.
But they are not like Shu,
So beautiful, so brave.

31 SHU in the hunting-fields
Driving his team of four,
The reins like ribbons in his hand,
His helpers[1] leaping as in the dance!
Shu in the prairie.[2]
The flames rise crackling on every side;
Bare-armed he braves a tiger
To lay at the Duke's feet.
Please, Shu, no rashness!
Take care, or it will hurt you.

Shu in the hunting-fields
Driving his team of bays.
The yoke-horses, how high they prance!
Yet the helpers keep line
Like wild-geese winging in the sky.
Shu in the prairie.
Flames leap crackling on every side.
How well he shoots, how cleverly he drives!
Now giving rein, now pulling to a halt,
Now letting fly,
Now following up his prey.

Shu in the hunting-fields,
Driving a team of greys.
The two yoke-horses with heads in line,
The two helpers obedient to his hand.
Shu in the prairie,
Huge fires crackling on every side.
His horses slow down,
Shu shoots less often.
Now he lays aside his quiver,
Now he puts his bow in its case.

[1] The two outside horses.
[2] That has been fired to drive the game into the open.

32 A MOON rising white
   Is the beauty of my lovely one.
   Ah, the tenderness, the grace!
   Heart's pain consumes me.

   A moon rising bright
   Is the fairness of my lovely one.
   Ah, the gentle softness!
   Heart's pain wounds me.

   A moon rising in splendour
   Is the beauty of my lovely one.
   Ah, the delicate yielding!
   Heart's pain torments me.

33 THE two of you[1] went off in a boat,
   Floating, floating far away.
   Longingly I think of you;
   My heart within is sore.

   The two of you went off in a boat,
   Floating, floating you sped away.
   Longingly I think of you.
   Oh may you come to no harm!

---

[1] We can only construe *êrh tzu* as 'two sirs'; but I suspect that it
is a corruption of a single name.

34   THICK grow the rush leaves;
Their white dew turns to frost.
He whom I love
Must be somewhere along this stream.
I went up the river to look for him,
But the way was difficult and long.
I went down the stream to look for him,
And there in mid-water
Sure enough, it's he!

Close grow the rush leaves,
Their white dew not yet dry.
He whom I love
Is at the water's side.
Up stream I sought him;
But the way was difficult and steep.
Down stream I sought him,
And away in mid-water
There on a ledge, that's he!

Very fresh are the rush leaves;
The white dew still falls.
He whom I love
Is at the water's edge.
Up stream I followed him;
But the way was hard and long.
Down stream I followed him,
And away in mid-water
There on the shoals is he!

35　THAT mad boy[1]
　　Will not speak with me.
　　Yes, all because of you
　　I leave my rice untouched.

　　That mad boy
　　Will not eat with me.
　　Yes, it is all because of you
　　That I cannot take my rest.

36　OUTSIDE the Eastern Gate
　　Are girls many as the clouds;
　　But though they are many as clouds
　　There is none on whom my heart dwells.
　　White jacket and grey scarf[2]
　　Alone could cure my woe.

　　Beyond the Gate Tower
　　Are girls lovely as rush-wool;
　　But though they are lovely as rush-wool
　　There is none with whom my heart bides.
　　White jacket and madder skirt
　　Alone could bring me joy.

[1] For 'mad boys,' see No. 209.　　[2] Denoting a humble lover.

37   By that swamp's shore
      Grow reeds and lotus.
      There is a man so fair—
      Oh, how can I cure my wound?
      Day and night I can do nothing;
      As a flood my tears flow.

      By that swamp's shore
      Grow reeds and scented herbs.
      There is a man so fair—
      Well-made, big and strong.
      Day and night I can do nothing;
      For my heart is full of woe.

      By that swamp's shore
      Grow reeds and lotus-flowers.
      There is a man so fair—
      Well-made, big and stern.
      Day and night I can do nothing;
      Face on pillow I toss and turn.

38   In your lamb's wool sauntering,
      In your fox-fur at Court—
      Oh, how can I help thinking of you?
      My heart throbs with pain.

      In your lamb's wool roaming,
      In your fox-fur there in the Hall—
      Oh, how can I but think of you?
      My heart is sad and sore.

      In your lamb's wool glossy
      As the first rays of dawn—
      How can I help thinking of you?
      My heart is sick within.

39 IF you tenderly love me,
   Gird your loins and wade across the Chên;[1]
   But if you do not love me—
   There are plenty of other men,
   Of madcaps maddest, oh!

   If you tenderly love me,
   Gird your loins and wade across the Wei;
   But if you do not love me—
   There are plenty of other knights,
   Of madcaps maddest, oh!

40 THICK grows the cocklebur;
   But even a shallow basket I did not fill.
   Sighing for the man I love
   I laid it there on the road.

   'I am climbing that rocky hill,
   My horses stagger,
   And I stop for a little to drink from that
       bronze ewer
   To still my heart's yearning.

   I am climbing that high ridge,
   My horses are sick and spent,
   And I stop for a little while to drink
       from that horn cup
   To still my heart's pain.

   I am climbing that shale;
   My horses founder,
   My groom is stricken,
   Oh, woe, oh, misery!'

In the first verse it is the lady left at home who speaks;
in the remaining verses it is the man away on a perilous
journey.

   [1] The Chen and Wei were two rivers in north-central Honan.

41 THERE is a fox dragging along
    By that dam on the Ch'i.[1]
    Oh, my heart is sad;
    That man of mine has no robe.

    There is a fox dragging along
    By that ford on the Ch'i.
    Oh, my heart is sad;
    That man of mine has no belt.

    There is a fox dragging along
    By that side of the Ch'i.
    Oh, my heart is sad;
    That man of mine has no coat.

42 LOOK at that little bay of the Ch'i,
    Its kitesfoot[2] so delicately waving.
    Delicately fashioned is my lord,
    As thing cut, as thing filed,
    As thing chiselled, as thing polished.
    Oh, the grace, the elegance!
    Oh, the lustre, oh, the light!
    Delicately fashioned is my lord;
    Never for a moment can I forget him.

    Look at that little bay of the Ch'i,
    Its kitesfoot so fresh.
    Delicately fashioned is my lord,
    His ear-plugs are of precious stones,
    His cap-gems stand out like stars.
    Oh, the grace, the elegance!
    Oh, the lustre, the light!
    Delicately fashioned is my lord;
    Never for a moment can I forget him.

[1] River in northern Honan.   [2] A kind of reed-like grass.

Look at that little bay of the Ch'i,
Its kitesfoot in their crowds.
Delicately fashioned is my lord,
As a thing of bronze, a thing of white metal,
As a sceptre of jade, a disc of jade.
How free, how easy
He leant over his chariot-rail!
How cleverly he chaffed and joked,
And yet was never rude!

43   How it tapered, the bamboo rod
With which you fished in the Ch'i!
It is not that I do not love you,
But it is so far that I cannot come.

The Well Spring is on the left;
The Ch'i River on the right.
When a girl is married
She is far from brothers, from father and mother.

The Ch'i River is on the right,
The Well Spring is on the left;
But, oh, the grace of his loving smile!
Oh, the quiver of his girdle stones!

The Ch'i spreads its waves;
Oars of juniper, boat of pine-wood.
Come, yoke the horses, let us drive away,
That I may be rid at last of my pain.

44   WHO says that the River is broad?
      On a single reed you could cross it.
      Who says that Sung[1] is far away?
      By standing on tip-toe I can see it.

      Who says that the River is broad?
      There is not room in it even for a skiff.
      Who says that Sung is far away?
      It could not take you so much as a morning.

45   OH, he is plucking cloth-creeper,[2]
      For a single day I have not seen him;
      It seems like three months!

      Oh, he is plucking southernwood,
      For a single day I have not seen him;
      It seems like three autumns!

      Oh, he is plucking mugwort,
      For a single day I have not seen him;
      It seems like three years!

---

[1] Sung lay to the south of the Yellow River, and Wei (where this song comes from) to the north.

[2] *Ko* is the name applied to various sorts of creeper from the fibres of which cloth was made—*Pachyrhyzus*, yambean, hyacinth-bean.

46 OH, you with the blue collar,
On and on I think of you.
Even though I do not go to you,
You might surely send me news?

Oh, you with the blue collar,
Always and ever I long for you.
Even though I do not go to you,
You might surely sometimes come?

Here by the wall-gate
I pace to and fro.
One day when I do not see you
Is like three months.

47 Do not till too big a field,
Or weeds will ramp it.
Do not love a distant man,
Or heart's pain will chafe you.

Do not till too big a field,
Or weeds will top it.
Do not love a distant man,
Or heart's pain will fret you.

So pretty, so lovable,
With his side-locks looped!
A little while, and I saw him
In the tall cap of a man.

48   HE. BY the clearing at the Eastern Gate
           Where madder grows on the bank—
           Strange that the house should be so near
           Yet the person distant indeed!

     SHE. By the chestnut-trees at the Eastern Gate
           Where there is a row of houses.
           It is not that I do not love you,
           But that you are slow to court me.

49   HEIGH, Po is brave;
     Greatest hero in the land!
     Po, grasping his lance,
     Is outrider of the king.

     Since Po went to the east
     My head has been touzled as the tumbleweed.
     It is not that I lack grease to dress it with;
     But for whom should I want to look nice?

     Oh, for rain, oh, for rain!
     And instead the sun shines dazzling.
     All this longing for Po
     Brings weariness to the heart, aching to the
        head.

     Where can I get a day-lily[1]
     To plant behind the house?
     All this longing for Po
     Can but bring me heart's pain.

     [1] Herb of forgetfulness; the *wasuregusa* of Japanese love poetry,
which was worn at the belt.

50   I WAS plucking liquorice, liquorice,
On the top of Shou-yang.[1]
The stories that people tell—
Do not believe them at all.
Let be, let be!
It is not so at all.
The stories that people tell—
What is to be got from them?

I was plucking sow-thistle, sow-thistle
At the bottom of Shou-yang.
The stories that people tell—
Do not heed them at all.
Let be, let be!
It is not so at all.
The stories that people tell—
What is to be got from them?

I was plucking cabbage, wild cabbage
To the east of Shou-yang.
The stories that people tell—
Do not be led by them at all.
Let be, let be!
It is not so at all.
The stories that people tell—
What is to be got from them?

The magpie's nest, so cleverly contrived, and the other
many-coloured things in the following poem, are symbols
of specious invention.

[1] Near P'ing-yang, in southern central Shansi. The first two
lines in each verse may be comparisons; but I think they imply an
alibi.

51   On the dyke there is a magpie's nest,
     On the bank grows the sweet vetch.
     Who has lied to my lovely one,
     And made my heart so sore?

     The middle-path has patterned tiles,
     On the bank grows the rainbow plant.
     Who has lied to my lovely one,
     And made my heart so sad?

52   That knight of the city,
     His fox-furs so brown,
     His pose unchanging,
     His speech well-cadenced.
     He was coming back to Chou,
     And all the people stood gazing.

     That knight of the city
     In travelling hat and black headcloth;
     That lady his daughter,
     Thick and lovely her hair![1]
     Me, alas, she did not see!
     Sad is my heart within.

     That knight of the city
     With his ear-stops of precious stone;
     That lady his daughter
     They called her Yin Chi.
     Me, alas, she did not see!
     Sorrow is pent up within.

[1] This line is corrupt in the original and the sense can only be
guessed at.

That knight of the city
Dangled a sash cut so as to hang.
That lady his daughter
Curled her hair like a scorpion.
Me, alas, she did not see!
Where can I go to seek her out?

No, it was not made to dangle;
The sash had length to spare.
No, it was not that she made it curl;
Her hair curled of itself.
Me, alas, she did not see!
But what use to pine and sigh?

Broken Faith

53 UNSTEADY is that cypress boat[1]
In the middle of the river.
His two locks looped over his brow[2]
He swore that truly he was my comrade,
And till death would love no other.
Oh, mother, ah, Heaven,
That a man could be so false!

Unsteady is that boat of cypress-wood
By that river's side.
His two locks looped over his brow
He swore that truly he was my mate,
And till death would not fail me.
Oh, mother, ah, Heaven,
That a man could be so false!

[1] Symbol of fluctuating intention.
[2] Before his coming of age. Compare No. 47.

54 HE: The gourd has bitter leaves;
        The ford is deep to wade.
    SHE: If a ford is deep, there are stepping-stones;
        If it is shallow, you can tuck up your skirts.

    HE: The ford is in full flood,
        And baleful is the pheasant's cry.
    SHE: The ford is not deep enough to wet your axles;
        The pheasant cried to find her mate.

        On one note the wild-geese cry,
        A cloudless dawn begins to break.
        A knight that brings home his bride
        Must do so before the ice melts.

        The boatman beckons and beckons.
        Others cross, not I;
        Others cross, not I.
        'I am waiting for my friend.'[1]

        ---

        [1] She says this to the boatman.

55 THE branches of the vine-bean;[1]
A boy with knot-horn at his belt!
Even though he carries knot-horn[2] at his belt,
Why should he not recognize me?
Oh, so free and easy
He dangles the gems at his waist!

The branches of the vine-bean;
A boy with archer's thimble at his belt!
Even though he has thimble at belt,
Why should he not be friends with me?
Oh, so free and easy
He dangles the gems at his waist!

56 IF along the highroad
I caught hold of your sleeve,
Do not hate me;
Old ways take time to overcome.

If along the highroad
I caught hold of your hand,
Do not be angry with me;
Friendship takes time to overcome.

[1] Generally identified as *Metaplexis Stauntoni*, which would fit quite well.

[2] The knot-horn, a pointed instrument for undoing knots, was worn by adult men, presumably symbolizing their right to undo the knot of a bride's girdle; while the wearing of the bowman's thimble signified that a man was of age to go to war.

57   By the willows of the Eastern Gate,
      Whose leaves are so thick,
      At dusk we were to meet;
      And now the morning star is bright.

      By the willows of the Eastern Gate,
      Whose leaves are so close,
      At dusk we were to meet;
      And now the morning star is pale.

   The next song belongs to a category which is, so far as
I know, peculiar to early China.[1] It is what one might
call an elliptical ballad. The theme is one common in
ballads in the West and in later China: a double suicide
following upon a misunderstanding between two lovers.
The man comes, as arranged, to elope with the lady. She
is prevented from turning up punctually and he, thinking
she has repented of her decision, goes away in despair and
kills himself. Whereupon the lady also commits suicide.
The people of the place, moved to pity by their tragic
story, bury them in the same grave.

   [1] Some of our own ballads go fairly far in this direction. Compare
'The Trees so High,' and 'Leesome Brand,' Nos. 156 and 56 in the
Oxford Book of Ballads. Narrative motives can become stylized in
poetry just as decorative motives become stylized in art.

58 'I BROUGHT my great carriage that thunders
And a coat downy as rush-wool.
It was not that I did not love you,
But I feared that you had lost heart.

I brought my great carriage that rumbles
And a coat downy as the pink sprouts.[1]
It was not that I did not love you,
But I feared that you would not elope.'

Alive, they never shared a house,
But in death they had the same grave.
'You thought I had broken faith;
I was true as the bright sun above.'

59 THE whole morning I gathered green;
And in the end had not a handful.
My hair is all wispy;
I must go home and wash it.

All the morning I gathered blue;
But did not get a skirtful.
On the fifth day he was to come;
It is the sixth; and he is not here.

When he went hunting
I put his bow in its case;
When he went fishing
I reeled his line.

And what did he catch?
Bream and tench,
Aye, bream and tench;
On a line I strung them.

[1] Of red millet.

   In the above song a girl, about to be married, goes to
gather plants (perhaps arthraxon and some form of
indigo) with which to make green and blue dyes for her
trousseau-dresses. She fails to fill her basket, which is a
bad omen. Sure enough, the man does not turn up on the
wedding-day. She recalls the happy days of their courtship
and the time when the omens were still good. When he
was fishing he caught a great haul of bream and tench,
which meant that they would be married and have many
children.

60   THE LADY: Heigh, the green coat,
                The green coat, yellow lined!
                The sorrow of my heart,
                Will it ever cease?

                Heigh, the green coat,
                Green coat and yellow skirt!
                The sorrow of my heart,
                Will it ever end?

     THE MAN: Heigh, the green threads!
                It was you who sewed them.
                I'll be true to my old love,
                If only she'll forgive me.

                Broad-stitch and openwork[1]
                Are cold when the wind comes.
                I'll be true to my old love
                Who truly holds my heart.

     [1] Symbol of the new mistress.

Desertion . Love-suits

61 IN the midst of the valley is motherwort
All withered and dry.
A girl on her own,
Bitterly she sobs,
Bitterly she sobs,
Faced with man's unkindness.

In the midst of the valley is motherwort
All withered and seared.
A girl on her own,
Long she sighs,
Long she sighs,
Faced with man's wickedness.

In the midst of the valley is motherwort
All withered and parched.
A girl on her own,
In anguish she weeps,
In anguish she weeps;
But what does grief avail?

T'ui, Siberian motherwort, is also called 'The herb
good for mothers.'

62 WINGS of the mayfly—
    Dress so bright and new.
    My heart is grieving;
    Come back to me and stay.

    Wing-sheaths of the mayfly—
    Clothes so bright and gay.
    My heart is grieving;
    Come back to me and bide.

    A mayfly that breaks out from its hole—
    Hemp clothes, spotless as snow.
    My heart is grieving;
    Come back to me and rest.

If people find a dead deer in the woods, they cover it
piously with rushes. But there are men who 'kill' a girl,
in the sense that they seduce her and then fail to 'cover
up' the damage by marrying her. Such is the burden of
the next poem, its last three lines calling up 'elliptically'
the scene of the seduction.

63 IN the wilds there is a dead doe;
    With white rushes we cover her.
    There was a lady longing for the spring;
    A fair knight seduced her.

    In the wood there is a clump of oaks,
    And in the wilds a dead deer
    With white rushes well bound;
    There was a lady fair as jade.

    'Heigh, not so hasty, not so rough;
    Heigh, do not touch my handkerchief.[1]
    Take care, or the dog will bark.'

    [1] Which was worn at the girdle.

64 THERE is a girdle in the east;
   No one dares point at it.
   A girl has run away,
   Far from father and mother, far from
      brothers young and old.

   There is dawnlight mounting in the west;
   The rain will last till noon.
   A girl has run away,
   Far from brothers young and old, far
      from mother and from father.

   Such a one as he
   Is bent on high connections;
   Never will he do what he has promised,
   Never will he accept his lot.

The girdle is the rainbow. Its appearance announces
that someone who ought not to is about to have a baby;
for the arc of the rainbow typifies the swelling girdle of
a pregnant woman. No one dares point at it, because
pointing is disrespectful, and one must respect a warning
sent by Heaven. The second verse opens with a weather-
proverb. The 'mounting,' here as in the next song,
typifies the swelling girdle; the rain means, I think, the
tears she will shed, when she finds that she has been deceived.
For the lover is bent on forming powerful marriage
connections that will improve his lot in life, and what-
ever promises he may make now, he will certainly not
fulfil them.

65   THAT man at arms
      Bears halberd and spear;
      That fine gentleman,
      Ribboned head cloth and red greaves![1]

      The pelican stays on the bridge;
      It has not wetted its wings.
      That fine gentleman
      Has no right to his dress.

      The pelican stays on the bridge;
      It has not wetted its beak.
      That fine gentleman
      Has not followed up his love-meeting.

      Oh, pent, oh, packed as they mount,
      Those dawn-mists on the southern hill!
      Oh, gentle, oh, fair,
      Those young girls[2] left to pine.

[1] More accurately, demi-jambs.
[2] Whom he has seduced; or we may take it in the singular.

66   O SUN, ah, moon
     That shine upon the earth below,
     A man like this
     Will not stand firm to the end.
     How can such a one be true?
     Better if he had never noticed me.

     O sun, ah, moon
     That cover the earth below,
     A man like this
     Will not deal kindly to the end.
     How can such a one be true?
     Better if he had not requited me.

     O sun, ah, moon
     That rise out of the east,
     A man like this,
     Of whom no good word is said,
     How can he be true?
     I wish I could forget him.

     O sun, ah, moon
     That from the east do rise,
     Heigh, father! Ho, mother,
     You have nurtured me to no good end.
     How should he be true?
     He requited me, but did not follow-up.[1]

Love-suits

Sung 'a recitation,' is probably the same word as *sung*
'a lawsuit'; the plaintiff recites his woes. To-day the two
words are written with different characters; but in old
texts these characters constantly interchange. 'I make this
Sung to accuse you,' says the lady in No. 69. The accused

[1] our love-meeting.

man in No. 67 appeals to 'all you gentlemen,' who are evidently the jury in this love-suit.

The man in No. 68 has picked up with someone who represented herself as being a stray 'girl, without family,' like the girl of No. 2; 'a girl on her own,' like the speaker in No. 61. Now she is trying to force him to marry her, by bringing a lawsuit, which shows that her account of herself was untrue; for unless backed by a large throng of relatives[1] she would never dare to appeal to the law.

'Too much dew in the path' means too many relatives-in-law.

If my view of No. 266 is right, it too belongs to this group. But I have placed it with 'moral' poems in order to be on the safe side; for, however we interpret it, it can clearly be classified as dealing with morals.

67 SHE: That cock-pheasant in its flight
Flaps feebly with its wings;
By this passion of mine
What have I brought myself but misery?
That cock-pheasant in its flight
Cries low, cries high;
Ah, my lord, truly
You have broken my heart.

HE: Look up at the sun, the moon.
Not less enduring is my love.
But the way is long;
How could I possibly come?

Oh, all you gentlemen,[2]
You give me no credit for my good deeds.
I harmed none, was foe to none,
I did nothing that was not right.

[1] Cf. the story of Susanna in the *Apocrypha*, verse 30, 'And she came with her father and mother, her children and all her kindred.'
[2] Who are judging this case.

68   THE paths are drenched with dew.
     True, I said 'Early in the night';
     But I fear to walk in so much dew.
     Who can say that the sparrow has no beak?
     How else could it have pierced my roof?
     Who can say that you have no family?
     How else could you bring this suit?
     But though you bring a suit,
     Not all your friends and family will suffice.

     Who can say that the rat has no teeth?
     How else could it have pierced my wall?
     Who can say that you have no family?
     How else could you bring this plaint?
     But though you bring this plaint,
     All the same I will not marry you.[1]

69   BY the Tomb Gate are thorn-trees;
     With an axe they are felled.
     Man, you are not good,
     And the people of this country know it,
     Know it, but do nothing to check you;
     For very long it has been so.

     By the Tomb Gate are plum-trees;
     Owls roost upon them.
     Man, you are not good;
     I make this song to accuse you.
     Accused you do not heed me;
     After your fall[2] you will think of me.

---

[1] Literally, 'I will not follow up' the love-meeting. Compare
No. 65, verse 3.
[2] When punished by 'all the gentlemen.' The metaphor is perhaps
one of wrestling. Compare No. 109, verse 5. The owl is an evil bird.
Owls roosting means evil deeds being 'brought home' to the doer.

Marriage

THE most important things that happen in Chinese marriage as portrayed in the *Songs* are as follows: The man talks to the father and mother; sends a matchmaker to arrange details. The girl is purified with waterherbs. She is fetched by her future husband or his representatives in a chariot. Her mother ties the strings of her girdle. The bride brings her chattels and also a symbolic gift of things in pairs (shoes, etc.). She brings with her 'understudies' drawn from her own clan. She is accompanied part of the way by carriages sent from her home. She fishes as part of the wedding-ceremony, or at any rate the songs show a recollection of such a rite.

At the bridegroom's house there is a feast. Before the bride sees her husband, she is agitated and weeps profusely; but no sooner does she see him than she is calm and happy. He sits opposite her, making music.

The new bride uses plantain in order to ensure pregnancy. She is presented to her husband's ancestors. She pays a formal first visit to her father's house, bringing luck 'to house and home.'[1]

70 HERE they gallop pak, pak,
Bamboo awning, red leatherwork.
The Lu road is easy and wide;
A lady of Ch'i sets out at dusk.

Four black horses well-groomed,
Dangling reins all glossy.
The Lu road is easy and wide;
All happiness to this lady of Ch'i!

[1] For other forms of marriage, see additional notes.

The waters of the Wên stretch broad;
The escort has splendid steeds.
The Lu road is easy and wide;
A pleasant journey to the lady of Ch'i!

The waters of the Wên rush headlong;
The escort has swift steeds.
The Lu road is easy and wide;
Good love-sport to the lady of Ch'i!

Ch'i corresponds to the northern, Lu to the southern part of Shantung. The River Wên runs east to west through the middle of central Shantung and divides the states of Ch'i and Lu.

71   OVER the southern hill so deep
The male fox drags along,
But the way to Lu is easy and broad
For this Ch'i lady on her wedding-way.
Yet once she has made the journey,
Never again must her fancy roam.

Fibre shoes, five pairs;
Cap ribbons, a couple.[1]
The way to Lu is easy and broad
For this lady of Ch'i to use.
But once she has used it,
No way else must she ever go.

When we plant hemp, how do we do it?
Across and along we put the rows.
When one takes a wife, how is it done?
The man must talk with her father and mother.
And once he has talked with them,
No one else must he court.

     [1] Marriage gifts.

When we cut firewood, how do we do it?
Without an axe it would not be possible.
When one takes a wife, how is it done?
Without a match-maker he cannot get her.
But once he has got her,
No one else must he ever approach.[1]

72   How does one cut an axe-handle?
      Without an axe it is impossible.[2]
      How does one take a wife?
      Without a matchmaker she cannot be got.

      Cut an axe-handle? Cut an axe-handle?
      The pattern is not far to seek.
      Here is a lady with whom I have had a
            love-meeting;
      Here are my dishes[3] all in a row.

This song represents, I think, the popular view that
marriage was a very simple matter, and a match-maker
by no means necessary.

[1] With a view to marriage. It does not, of course, mean that he
may not have concubines.
[2] i.e. someone who has already been married himself.
[3] Of ritual offerings.

73   FIBRE shoes tightly woven
      Are good for walking upon the dew.
      A girl's fingers, long and slender,
      Are good for sewing clothes.
      Hem them, seam them;
      The loved one shall wear them.

      The loved one is very dutiful;
      Humbly she steps aside.
      Jade plugs at her ears,[1]
      Ivory pendant at her belt.
      Only—she is mean,
      That is why I make this stab.

   I take this to be the 'stab,' the wounding, spiteful song
of a girl who considered she had not been properly
rewarded for her toil in making the bride's trousseau.

   [1] The metre shows that a line is missing. I supply one on the
analogy of other poems.

74 SHE: Spray rises from those waters;
The white rocks are rinsed.
White coat with red lappet,
I followed you to Wo;
And now that I have seen my lord,
Happy am I indeed.

Spray rises from those waters;
The white rocks are washed clean.
White coat with red stitching,
I followed you to Hu;
And now that I have seen my lord,
How can I be sad?

HE: Spray rises from those waters;
The white rocks are dabbled.
I hear that you are pledged;
I dare not talk to your people.

The places mentioned are all in Central-Southern Shansi. In the first two verses the white rocks are symbols of the man's fresh, clean ('sauber,' as the Germans say) appearance. In the third verse they symbolize his tears shed because he knows that the lady has been 'ming,' bidden by her parents to marry someone else and that it is hopeless for him to 'kao,' talk to her parents, ask for her hand. For 'I followed you to Wo' compare a similar courtship situation in G. Bateson's *Naven*, p. 145.

This is the song of a lady whose friends tried to marry
her against her inclinations:

75   TOSSED is that cypress boat,
Wave-tossed it floats.
My heart is in turmoil, I cannot sleep.
But secret is my grief.
Wine I have, all things needful
For play, for sport.

My heart is not a mirror,
To reflect what others will.
Brothers too I have;
I cannot be snatched away.
But lo, when I told them of my plight
I found that they were angry with me.

My heart is not a stone;
It cannot be rolled.
My heart is not a mat;
It cannot be folded away.
I have borne myself correctly
In rites more than can be numbered.

My sad heart is consumed, I am harassed
By a host of small men.
I have borne vexations very many,
Received insults not few.
In the still of night I brood upon it;
In the waking hours I rend my breast.

O sun, ah, moon,
Why are you changed and dim?
Sorrow clings to me
Like an unwashed dress.
In the still of night I brood upon it,
Long to take wing and fly away.

76   HERE we are gathering duckweed
        By the banks of the southern dale.
        Here we are gathering water-grass
        In those channelled pools.

        Here we are packing them
        Into round basket, into square.
        Here we are boiling them
        In kettles and pans.

        Here we lay them beneath the window
        Of the ancestral hall.
        Who is the mistress of them?[1]
        A young girl purified.

77   BRIGHT shines the new terrace;
        But the waters of the river are miry.
        A lovely mate she sought;
        Clasped in her hand a toad most vile.[2]

        Clean glitters the new terrace;
        But the waters of the river are muddy.
        A lovely mate she sought;
        Clasped in her hand a toad most foul.

        Fish nets we spread;
        A wild goose got tangled in them.
        A lovely mate she sought;
        But got this paddock.

This song may refer to a story about a bridegroom
who was changed into a toad, which is, of course, a very
widely spread type of folk-story, common in Asia as well
as in Europe. The scene of the song is Northern Honan.
'River' does not necessarily mean the Yellow River.

[1] i.e. for whose benefit is the ceremony performed?
[2] My textual note appears to have been misunderstood. I meant that
ch'ü = clasped, and *ch'u* = toad.

78 WHEN a gentle wind from the south
   Blows to the heart of those thorn-bushes
   The heart of the thorn-bushes is freshened;
   But our mother had only grief and care.

   A gentle wind from the south
   Blows on that brushwood of the thorn-tree.
   Our mother was wise and kind;
   But among us is no good man.

   Yonder is a cold spring
   Under the burgh of Hsün.
   There were sons, seven men;
   Yet their mother had only grief and care.

   Pretty is that yellow oriole
   And pleasant its tune.
   There were sons, seven men,
   Yet none could soothe his mother's heart.

Hsün was a place in Northern Honan. I insert this poem here only because, like the last, it reads to me like a song taken from or connected with a folk-story. The commentators explain it as 'a eulogy on filial sons,' an interpretation which they can only justify by very tortuous means. The bad sons are contrasted with the pretty and innocent bird.

79 THE Kiang parts and joins.
    Our lady went to be married
    And did not take us.
    She did not take us,
    But afterwards she was sorry.

    The Kiang has its islands.
    Our lady went to be married
    And did not bring us.
    She did not bring us,
    But afterwards she found room for us.

    The Kiang divides and joins.
    Our lady that went to be married
    Did not move us with her.
    She did not move us with her,
    But in the end she has let us come.

I call the Yangtze the Kiang, to distinguish it from the
Yellow River, which I call simply 'the River.' This is a
song of bridesmaids who suffered the indignity of being
left behind when the bride removed to her husband's
house. The image of a river dividing and joining again,
as a symbol of temporary parting, occurs in early Japanese
poetry: 'Like the torrent whose course is barred by a
great rock, though now we are parted, in the end I know
that we shall meet,' *warete mo suye ni awamu to zo omou.*[1]
The last line, 'But in the end she has let us come,' is
corrupt, and the sense can only be guessed at.

[1] *Shikwa Wakashū*, Book VII, No. 228.

80 SWOOP flies that falcon;
Dense that northern wood.
Not yet have I seen my lord;
Sore grieves my heart.
What will it be like, what like?
I am sure many will forget me.

On the hill is a clump of oaks
And in the lowlands, the piebald-tree.
Not yet have I seen my lord;
My grief I cannot cure.
What will it be like, what like?
I am sure many will forget me.

On the hill is a clump of plum-trees;
And on the lowlands, planted pear-trees.
Not yet have I seen my lord;
With grief I am dazed.
What will it be like, what like?
I am sure many will forget me.

The theme of the comparisons is that everything in
nature goes its wonted way and is in its proper place; but
I am embarking on a new, unimaginable existence.

81   High spurt the waters of that fountain,
Yet it flows back into the Ch'i.
My love is in Wei,
No day but I think of him.
Dear are my many cousins;[1]
It would be well to take counsel with them:

'On the journey you will lodge at Tzŭ,[2]
You will drink the cup of parting at Ni,
A girl that goes to be married,
Leaving parents, leaving brothers.'
I will ask all my aunts
And next, my elder sister:

'On the journey you will lodge at Kan;
You will drink the cup of parting at Yen,
Grease wheels, look to axle-caps,
And the returning carriages will go their way:
"A quick journey to the Court of Wei,
And may you get there safe and sound."

I think of the Forked Fountain,
Long now I sigh for it.
I think of Mei and Ts'ao,
And how my heart yearns!
Come, yoke the horses, let us drive away,
That I may be rid at last of my pain.

[1] Literally, 'the various female members of the Ch'i clan,' the
speaker's clan. The scene of the poem is northern Honan.
[2] This is their answer; so, too, in verse 3.

82 THERE was a girl with us in our carriage
Whose face was like the mallow-flower.
As we swept along,
Oh, at her belt the bright girdle-gems!
That fair eldest Chiang
Was fair and fine indeed.

There was a girl with us in the same
        carriage-line
Whose face was like the mallow blossom.
As we swept along,
How those girdle-stones jingled!
That lovely eldest Chiang,
All that was told of her is true.

83 COMPANION of her lord till death,
The pins of her wig[1] with their six gems,
Easy and stately,
Like a mountain, a river
Worthy of her blazoned gown.
That our lady is not a fine lady
How can any man say?

Gorgeous in its beauty
Is her pheasant-wing robe,
Her thick hair billows like clouds,
No false side-lock does she need.
Ear-plugs of jade,
Girdle pendants of ivory,
Brow so white.
How comes it that she is like a heavenly one,
How comes it that she is like a god?

[1] Compare No. 98.

Oh, splendid
In her ritual gown!
Rich the crapes and embroideries
That she trails and sweeps.
Clear is our lady's brow,
That brow well-rounded.
Truly such a lady
Is a beauty matchless in the land.

84 GORGEOUS in their beauty
Are the flowers of the cherry.
Are they not magnificent in their dignity,
The carriages of the royal bride?

Gorgeous in her beauty
As flower of peach or plum,
Granddaughter of King P'ing,
Child of the Lord of Ch'i.

Wherewith does she angle?
Of silk is her fishing-line,
This child of the Lord of Ch'i,
Granddaughter of King P'ing.

We know nothing further about this royal marriage,
but it must have taken place about the middle of the
eighth century. Fish, in the *Songs*, are symbols of fertility.
In No. 160 a dream of fishes is interpreted as a promise of
good harvests. In general, the fish that get caught in one's
nets and traps are indications of other blessings that
Heaven will send. Fish (and fishing, as in the present song)
figure in several of the marriage songs. Now in India
fishing was part of the marriage ceremony, and the
fertility and prosperity of the marriage was augured from

the catch. Thus, according to the *Gṛhyasūtra*,[1] the bridal
pair go into the water up to their knees and catch fish in
a new garment. They ask a Brahmin who accompanies
them what he sees, and he replies, 'Children and cattle.'
Similar customs still survive in modern India.[2] A rite of
this kind probably once existed in ancient China; but all
memory of it was forgotten by the time the com-
mentators set to work upon the *Book of Songs*.

85   In the wicker fish-trap by the bridge
Are fish, both bream and roach.
A lady of Ch'i goes to be married;
Her escort is like a trail of clouds.

In the wicker fish-trap by the bridge
Are fish, both bream and tench.
A lady of Ch'i goes to be married;
Her escort is thick as rain.

In the wicker fish-trap by the bridge
The fish glide free.
A lady of Ch'i goes to be married;
Her escort is like a river.

[1] See R. Pischel, *Sitzungsberichte der Akademie der Wissenschaften*,
Berlin, 1905, p. 529.
[2] See W. Crooke, *Religion and Folklore of Northern India*, p. 244
and p. 478. Also Westermarck, *History of Human Marriage*, II, 484,
and W. Logan, *Malabar*: 'Bride and bridegroom stand beside a tub
of water in which several small live fish are placed and by means
of a cloth capture these fish.' Vol. I, p. 128.

86 A SPLENDID woman and upstanding;
Brocade she wore, over an unlined coat,
Daughter of the Lord of Ch'i,
Wife of the Lord of Wei,
Sister of the Crown Prince of Ch'i,
Called sister-in-law by the Lord of Hsing,
Calling the Lord of T'an her brother-in-law.

Hands white as rush-down,
Skin like lard,
Neck long and white as the tree-grub,
Teeth like melon seeds,
Lovely head, beautiful brows.
Oh, the sweet smile dimpling,
The lovely eyes so black and white.

This splendid lady takes her ease;
She rests where the fields begin.
Her four steeds prance,
The red trappings flutter.
Screened by fans of pheasant-feather she is
        led to Court.
Oh, you Great Officers, retire early,
Do not fatigue our lord.

Where the water of the river, deep and wide,
Flows northward in strong course,
In the fish-net's swish and swirl
Sturgeon, snout-fish leap and lash.
Reeds and sedges tower high.
All her ladies are tall-coiffed;
All her knights, doughty men.

This poem celebrates the most famous wedding of
Chinese antiquity, that of Chuang Chiang, daughter of
the Lord of Ch'i (northern Shantung), who married the
Lord of Wei in 757 B.C. Wei centred round the modern

Weihwei in northern Honan. Hsing was farther north, on the borders of Honan and southern Hopeh. T'an was the modern Ch'êng-tzŭ-ai, near Lungshan, in central Shantung. It has become famous because of the excavations carried out there in recent years.[1] One has to bear in mind that the bridegroom and bride are in other parts of the world often treated as though they were a king and queen. It is not impossible that such a song as this, though royal in origin, was afterwards sung at ordinary people's weddings.

87   'FAIR, fair,' cry the ospreys
     On the island in the river.
     Lovely is this noble lady,
     Fit bride for our lord.

     In patches grows the water mallow;
     To left and right one must seek it.
     Shy was this noble lady;
     Day and night he sought her.

     Sought her and could not get her;
     Day and night he grieved.
     Long thoughts, oh, long unhappy thoughts,
     Now on his back, now tossing on to his side.

     In patches grows the water mallow;
     To left and right one must gather it.
     Shy is this noble lady;
     With great zithern and little we hearten her.

[1] See, for example, *Academia Sinica*, IV, 2 (1933), for an article by Tung Tso-pin on the antiquities of the T'an site.

In patches grows the water mallow;
To left and right one must choose it.
Shy is this noble lady;
With gongs and drums we will gladden her.

88 IN the south is an upturning tree;
One cannot shelter under it.
Beyond the Han a lady walks;
One cannot seek her.
Oh, the Han it is so broad,
One cannot swim it,
And the Kiang, it is so rough
One cannot boat it!

Tall grows that tangle of brushwood;
Let us lop the wild-thorn.
Here comes a girl to be married;
Let us feed her horses.
Oh, the Han it is so broad,
One cannot swim it,
And the Kiang, it is so rough
One cannot boat it!

Tall grows that tangle of brushwood;
Let us lop the mugwort.
Here comes a girl to be married;
Let us feed her ponies.
Oh, the Han it is so broad,
One cannot swim it,
And the Kiang, it is so rough
One cannot boat it.

The mention of the Han River and the Yangtze together
fixes the scene of this song somewhere near the modern
Hankow, in east-central Hupeh.

89 Now the magpie had a nest,
    But the cuckoo lived in it.
    Here comes a girl to be married;
    With a hundred coaches we'll meet her.

    Now the magpie had a nest,
    But the cuckoo made a home in it.
    Here comes a girl to be married;
    With a hundred coaches we'll escort her.

    Now the magpie had a nest,
    But the cuckoo filled it.
    Here comes a girl to be married;
    With a hundred coaches we'll gird her.

It is an honour for other birds to rear the cuckoo's young, as we may see by this poem of Tu Fu (eighth century A.D.) on the Small Cuckoo:

    It gets its young reared in many birds' nests,
    And the many birds do not dare complain,
    But continue to care for the feeding of its young
    With mien as reverent as one who serves a god.

Here the bride coming as an honoured stranger into the family is compared to the young cuckoo. I do not think any bird as large as the magpie ever fosters the cuckoo, and it is not impossible that 'magpie' is a mistake for 'sparrow.' The two words have almost the same sound.

90   THICK grows that southernwood;
The falling dew drenches it.[1]
Now that I have seen my lord
My heart is eased.
So peaceably he laughs and talks
That I am happy and at rest.

Thick grows that southernwood;
The falling dew lies heavy upon it.
Now I have seen my lord,
He has become my protector, my light.[2]
May his power[3] have no flaw,
May he live for evermore!

Thick grows that southernwood;
The falling dew dabbles it.
Now that I have seen my lord
I am happy and at peace.
May he bring good to his elder brothers,
            his younger brothers,
May he have magic power and great
            longevity!

Thick grows that southernwood;
The falling dew soaks it.
Now I have seen my lord,
His rein-ends jingling,
His chariot-bells and bridle-bells chiming,
In whom all blessings meet.

[1] Symbol of the bride's tears.
[2] Reading very doubtful.
[3] Wherever the word 'power' occurs in the translations it represents the Chinese word *tê*; see Appendix IV.

91 WIND and rain, chill, chill!
    But the cock crowed kikeriki.
    Now that I have seen my lord,
    How can I fail to be at peace?

    Wind and rain, oh, the storm!
    But the cock crowed kukeriku.
    Now that I have seen my lord,
    How can I fail to rejoice?

    Wind and rain, dark as night,
    The cock crowed and would not stop.
    Now that I have seen my lord,
    How can I any more be sad?

The weather, just how the cock crows, markings on the
horses of the bridegroom's carriage (No. 97)—everything
that happens or is seen on a wedding-day is ominous.
The notes I ascribe to the cock are not exact transcriptions,
but merely convenient equivalents.

92 THE mulberry on the lowland, how graceful!
    Its leaves, how tender!
    Now that I have seen my lord,
    Ah, what delight!

    The mulberry on the lowland, how graceful!
    Its leaves, how glossy!
    Now that I have seen my lord,
    What joy indeed!

    The mulberry on the lowland, how graceful,
    Its leaves, how fresh!
    Now I have seen my lord,
    His high fame holds fast.

Love that is felt in the heart,
Why should it not be told in words?
To the core of my heart I treasure him,
Could not ever cease to love him.

93   ANXIOUSLY chirps the cicada,
Restlessly skips the grasshopper.
Before I saw my lord
My heart was ill at ease.
But now that I have seen him,
Now that I have met him,
My heart is at rest.

I climbed that southern hill
To pluck the fern-shoots.
Before I saw my lord
My heart was sad.
But now that I have seen him,
Now that I have met him,
My heart is still.

I climbed that southern hill
To pluck the bracken-shoots.
Before I saw my lord
My heart was sore distressed.
But now that I have seen him,
Now that I have met him,
My heart is at peace.

94 FAST bundled is the firewood;
The Three Stars[1] have risen.
Is it to-night or which night
That I see my Good Man?
Oh, masters, my masters,[2]
What will this Good Man be like?

Fast bundled is the hay;
The Three Stars are at the corner.[3]
Is it to-night or which night
That shall see this meeting?
Oh, masters, my masters,
What will that meeting be like?

Fast bundled is the wild-thorn;
The Three Stars are at the door.
Is it to-night or which night
That I see that lovely one?
Oh, masters, my masters,
What will that lovely one be like?

[1] The Belt of Orion.
[2] May merely be a meaningless exclamation.
[3] Of the house, as seen from inside.

95 GUESTS: Slim and fine is the axle-pin of a coach,
And lovely the young girl that has come.
Of hunger we made light, of thirst;
For her fair fame had reached us.

HOST: Though I have no fine friends to meet you,
Pray feast and rejoice.

GUESTS: Such shelter gives that wood on the plains
That the pheasants all roost there.
Truly of this great lady
The magic Powers are strong.[1]

HOST: Pray feast and be at ease,
Good friends, of whom I cannot weary.

Although this wine is not good,
Try to drink just a little.
Although these meats are not fine,
Try to eat just a little.
Although I have no Power that I can impart
to you,
Pray sing and dance.

GUESTS: We climbed that high ridge
To cut firewood from the oak-tree,
To cut firewood from the oak-tree.
And ah, its leaves so wet!
But now that in the end we have seen you,
All our sorrows are at rest.

High hills we breasted,
Long ways we went,
Our four steeds prancing,
Six reins like zithern strings.
But the sight of your new bride
Brings good comfort to our hearts.

[1] Her *tê* has drawn us to this place.

96 My lord is all a-glow.
In his left hand he holds the reed-organ,
With his right he summons me to make
        free with him.'
Oh, the joy!

My lord is care-free.
In his left hand he holds the dancing plumes,
With his right he summons me to sport
        with him.
Oh, the joy!

97 THE coach-wheels crunch;
There is one horse with a white forehead.
I have not yet seen my lord;
I am waiting till they send for me.

On the hillside grows the lacquer-tree,
On the lowlands the chestnut-tree.
Now I have seen my lord;
He sits opposite me, playing his zithern:
'If to-day we are not merry,
In time to come we shall be too old.'

On the hillside grows the mulberry-tree,
On the lowlands the willow.
Now I have seen my lord;
He sits opposite me, playing his reed-organ:
'If to-day we are not merry,
In time to come we shall be gone.'

¹ The first Chinese character in *Textual Notes*, p. 14, should be *yu*
('from'), not *yu* ('wander').

Some time after marriage the wife was solemnly pre-
sented to her husband's ancestors. It is this rite, and not the
arrival of the bride from her father's house, which from
the religious point of view really constitutes the wedding.
It is thus the counterpart to what takes place in church
in Western marriage ritual. It will be noticed that the
bride wears a wig or head-covering of false hair. This
was only worn while serving the ancestors. Modern
Jewish brides go further, shaving their heads and wearing
a wig during the whole of their married life.

98   SEE, she gathers white aster
      By the pools, on the little islands.
      See, she uses it
      At the rituals of her prince and lord.

      See, she gathers white aster
      Down in the ravine.
      See, she uses it
      In the ancestral hall of prince and lord.

      Her tall wig nods
      At dawn of night, while she plies her task.
      With tall wig gently swaying
      Here she comes back to her room.

When women were going to have babies they ate plantain in order to secure easy delivery. This plant has always had a high reputation as a drug in the West as well as in the East. In the Highlands it was called the Plant of Healing. It was one of the nine sacred herbs of the Saxons, and Pliny held that it was a cure for hydrophobia. Its use in childbirth is, so far as I know, peculiar to China.

> 99 THICK grows the plantain;
> Here we go plucking it.
> Thick grows the plantain;
> Here we go gathering it.
>
> Thick grows the plantain;
> Here we hold it between the fingers.
> Thick grows the plantain;
> Here we are with handfuls of it.
>
> Thick grows the plantain;
> Here we have our aprons full of it.
> Thick grows the plantain;
> Now apronfuls are tucked in at our
>   belts.

The next few poems deal with separation and difficulties after marriage.

100 My lord is on service;
He did not know for how long.
Oh, when will he come?
The fowls are roosting in their holes,
Another day is ending,
The sheep and cows are coming down.
My lord is on service;
How can I not be sad?

My lord is on service;
Not a matter of days, nor months.
Oh, when will he be here again?
The fowls are roosting on their perches,
Another day is ending,
The sheep and cows have all come down.
My lord is on service;
Were I but sure that he gets drink and food!

101 WILD and windy was the day;
    You looked at me and laughed,
    But the jest was cruel, and the laughter
       mocking.
    My heart within is sore.

    There was a great sandstorm that day;
    Kindly you made as though to come,
    Yet neither came nor went away.
    Long, long my thoughts.

    A great wind and darkness;
    Day after day it is dark.
    I lie awake, cannot sleep,
    And gasp with longing.

    Dreary, dreary the gloom;
    The thunder growls.
    I lie awake, cannot sleep,
    And am destroyed with longing.

102   I RIDE home, I gallop
      To lay my plaint before the lord of Wei,
      I gallop my horses on and on
      Till I come to Ts'ao.
      A great Minister, post-haste![1]
      How sad my heart.

      He[2] no longer delights in me;
      I cannot go back.
      And now, seeing how ill you use me,
      Surely my plan is not far-fetched!

      He no longer delights in me;
      I cannot go back across the river.
      And now, seeing how ill you use me,
      Surely my plan is not rash!

      I climb that sloping mound,
      I pick the toad-lilies.
      A woman of good intent
      Has always the right to go.
      That the people of Hsü should prevent it
      Is childish, nay, mad.

      I walk in the wilderness;
      Thick grows the caltrop.
      Empty-handed in a great land,
      To whom could I go, on whom rely?
      Oh, you great officers and gentlemen,
      It is not I who am at fault;
      All your many plans
      Are not equal to what I propose.

          [1] Sent to bring her back.
          [2] Her husband in Hsü.

The general situation in this poem is quite clear. The speaker is a lady of Wei, unhappily married in Hsü, a small State to the south-east of Wei. She attempts to go back to her own people and home, but is detained by the men of Hsü. She speaks of Hsü as a 'great land' out of conventional courtesy. Tradition says that she was Mu Fu-jên, a Wei princess married to the Lord of Hsü about 671 B.C.

103   O ORIOLE, yellow bird,
Do not settle on the corn,
Do not peck at my millet.
The people of this land
Are not minded to nurture me.
I must go back, go home
To my own land and kin.

O oriole, yellow bird,
Do not settle on the mulberries,
Do not peck my sorghum.
With the people of this land
One can make no covenant.
I must go back, go home
To where my brothers are.

O oriole, yellow bird
Do not settle on the oaks,
Do not peck my wine-millet.
With the people of this land
One can come to no understanding.
I must go back, go home
To where my own men[1] are.

[1] Lit. 'fathers,' i.e. her adult kinsmen, whether father or father's brothers.

104   WE thought you were a simple peasant
Bringing cloth to exchange for thread.
But you had not come to buy thread;
You had come to arrange about me.
You were escorted across the Ch'i
As far as Beacon Hill.
'It is not I who want to put it off;
But you have no proper match-maker.
Please do not be angry;
Let us fix on autumn as the time.'

I climbed that high wall
To catch a glimpse of Fu-kuan,[1]
And when I could not see Fu-kuan
My tears fell flood on flood.
At last I caught sight of Fu-kuan,
And how gaily I laughed and talked!
You consulted your yarrow-stalks[2]
And their patterns showed nothing unlucky.
You came with your cart
And moved me and my dowry.

Before the mulberry-tree sheds its leaves,
How soft and glossy they are!
O dove, turtle-dove,
Do not eat the mulberries![3]
O ladies, ladies,
Do not take your pleasure with men.
For a man to take his pleasure
Is a thing that may be condoned.
That a girl should take her pleasure
Cannot be condoned.

[1] Where her lover was. The scene is northern Honan.
[2] Used in divination. See on No. 145, verse 4.
[3] Which are supposed to make doves drunk.

The mulberry leaves have fallen
All yellow and seared.
Since I came to you,
Three years I have eaten poverty.
The waters of the Ch'i were in flood;
They wetted the curtains of the carriage.[1]
It was not I who was at fault;
It is you who have altered your ways,
It is you who are unfaithful,
Whose favours are cast this way and that.

Three years I was your wife.
I never neglected my work.
I rose early and went to bed late;
Never did I idle.
First you took to finding fault with me,
Then you became rough with me.
My brothers disowned me;
'Ho, ho,' they laughed.
And when I think calmly over it,
I see that it was I who brought all this
    upon myself.

I swore to grow old along with you;
I am old, and have got nothing from you
    but trouble.
The Ch'i has its banks,
The swamp has its sides;
With hair looped and ribboned[2]
How gaily you talked and laughed,
And how solemnly you swore to be true,
So that I never thought there could be a
    change.
No, of a change I never thought;
And that *this* should be the end!

[1] Which was a good omen.
[2] While still an uncapped youth.

105 I WENT into the country;
Deep the shade of the ailanto.
It was as bride and wife
That I came to your house.
But you did not provide for me—
Sent me back to land and home.

I went into the country;
I plucked the dockleaf.
It was as bride and wife
That I came to live with you.
But you did not provide for me—
Back to my home you sent me.

I went into the country;
I plucked the pokeweed.
You thought nothing of the old marriage—
Found for yourself a new mate.
Not for her wealth, oh no!
But merely for a change.[1]

106 DEEP rolls the thunder
On the sun-side of the southern hills.
Why is it, why must you always be away,
Never managing to get leave?
O my true lord,
Come back to me, come back.

Deep rolls the thunder
On the side of the southern hills.
Why is it, why must you always be away,
Never managing to take rest?
O my true lord,
Come back to me, come back.

The last two lines may very likely be corrupt.

Deep rolls the thunder
Beneath the southern hills.
Why is it, why must you be always away,
Never managing to be at home and rest.
O my true lord,
Come back to me, come back.

107 CLOSE the cloth-plant spreads its fibres
Along the banks of the river.
Far from big brothers, from little brothers
I must call a stranger 'Father,'[1]
Must call a stranger 'Father';
But he does not heed me.

Close the cloth-plant spreads its fibres
Along the margin of the river.
Far from big brothers, from little brothers
I must call a stranger 'Mother,'
Must call a stranger 'Mother';
But she does not own me.

Close the cloth-plant spreads its fibres
Along the lips of the river.
Far from big brothers, from little brothers
I must call strangers kinsmen,
Must call strangers kinsmen;
But they do not listen to me.

[1] This sounds more like adoption than marriage.

108 ZIP, zip the valley wind,
Bringing darkness, bringing rain.
'Strive to be of one mind;
Let there be no anger between you.'
He who plucks greens, plucks cabbage
Does not judge by the lower parts.
In my reputation there is no flaw,
I am yours till death.

Slowly I take the road,
Reluctant at heart.
Not far, no, near;
See, you escort me only to the gateway.[1]
Who says that sow-thistle is bitter?
It is sweeter than shepherd's-purse.
You feast your new marriage-kin,
As though they were older brothers, were
        younger brothers.

'It is the Wei that makes the Ching look
        dirty;
Very clear are its shoals.'[2]
You feast your new relations,
And think me no fit company.
'Do not break my dam,
Do not open my fish-traps.
Though for my person you have no regard,
At least pity my brood.'[3]

[1] He hustles her off the premises without courtesy.
[2] It is only in comparison with the new wife that I seem shabby.
These lines are no doubt a proverb; the poem comes from Honan
and not from Shensi. The Ching flows into the Wei to the east of
the old Chou capital in Shensi.
[3] These lines, several times repeated in the *Songs*, must be a
quotation.

Where the water was deep
I rafted it, boated it;
Where the water was shallow
I swam it, floated it.
Whether a thing was to be had or no
I strove always to find it.
When any of your people were in trouble
I went on my knees to help them.

Why do you not cherish me,
But rather treat me as an enemy?
You have spoilt my value;
What is used, no merchant will buy.
Once in times of peril, of extremity
With you I shared all troubles.
But now that you are well-nurtured, well-
    fed,
You treat me as though I were a poison.

I had laid by a good store,
Enough to provide against the winter;
You feast your new kin,
And that provision is eaten up.
Then you were violent, were enraged,
And it gave me great pain.
You do not think of the past;
It is only anger that is left.

109   ZIP, zip the valley wind!
        Nothing but wind and rain.
        In days of peril, in days of dread
        It was always 'I and you.'
        Now in time of peace, of happiness,
        You have cast me aside.

        Zip, zip the valley wind!
        Nothing but wind and duststorms.
        In days of peril, in days of dread
        You put me in your bosom.
        Now in time of peace, of happiness
        You throw me away like slop-water.

        Zip, zip the valley wind
        Across the rocky hills.
        No grass but is dying,
        No tree but is wilting.
        You forget my great merits,
        Remember only my small faults.

110 THE white-flower is twisted into bast,
The white reeds are bound in bundles.
But my lord is estranged from me,
Lets me be all alone.

White clouds spread across the sky,
There is dew on sedge and reed.
Heaven is verging towards calamity;
My lord makes no plan.

The Hu-t'o[1] northward flowing
Wets those paddy fields.
Full of woe is this song I chant,
Thinking of that tall man.

They have gathered that brushwood of the
     mulberry-tree;
High it blazes in the furnace.
To think of that tall man
Truly scorches my heart.

Drums and bells in the house!
One can hear them from outside.
Thinking of you I am in misery—
How you looked at me without love.

There is a pelican on the dam,
A crane in the wood.
Thinking of that big man
Truly frets my heart.

There is a mandarin-duck on the dam;
It folds its left wing.
My lord is not good;
Twofold, threefold he gives his favours.

[1] In eastern-central Shansi.

Lopsided is that stone;
If you tread on it, it goes down.
My lord is estranged from me,
And leaves me to my misery.

In the last verse there are some puns, which I have
explained in my textual notes.

The next piece is a marriage song adapted to celebrate
not the meeting between bride and bridegroom but an
audience given by a feudal superior to his vassal. No
doubt most of the other marriage songs in this book
were often used in the same way; but this is the only one
in which the wording has manifestly been altered to fit
the new purpose. The line which has been changed is the
last in verse 3: 'He gave me a hundred strings of cowries.'
Vast numbers of inscriptions record the giving of
cowries by feudal lords to their vassals, as a reward for
faithful services. There is not the slightest reason to suppose
that a bridegroom ever gave his bride a gift of cowry
shells. 'A hundred' probably only means 'a great many.'
A good account of the use of cowries as currency in
ancient China is given by H. G. Creel in *The Birth of
China*, page 92. Judging by the analogy of numerous
similar songs, the line must originally have run, 'My
spirits rise' (*wo hsin tsê hsing*), or something to that
effect.

111   THICK grows the tarragon
       In the centre of that slope.
       I have seen my lord;
       He was pleased and courteous to boot.

Thick grows the tarragon
In the middle of that island.
I have seen my lord,
And my heart is glad.

Thick grows the tarragon
In the centre of that mound.
I have seen my lord;
He gave me a hundred strings of cowries.

Unsteady is that osier boat;
It plunges, it bobs.[1]
But now that I have seen my lord
My heart is at rest.

In some lands the first visit of the bride to her parents
is a ritual event of great importance. This is so, for
example, among the Manchus. In China it was not made
so much of; but it was a recognized institution, which
had a technical name: *Lai-ning*, 'coming to comfort.'
The domestic excitement aroused by such a visit is
vividly portrayed in that great novel, *The Dream of the
Red Chamber*,'[2] in the passage which describes the return
of Pao-yü's sister from Court.

112   How the cloth-plant spreads
Across the midst of the valley!
Thick grows its leaves.
The oriole in its flight
Perches on that copse,
Its song is full of longing.

[1] I was uneasy about what sort of reception I should get.
[2] Chapter XVIII.

How the cloth-plant spreads
Across the middle of the valley!
Close grow its leaves,
I cut them and steam them,
Make cloth fine and coarse,
For clothes that will not irk me.

I will go to my nurse,
I will tell her I am going home.
Here I sud my shift,
Here I wash my dress.
Which things are clean and which not?
I am going to comfort my parents.

113   BUXOM is the peach-tree;
How its flowers blaze!
Our lady going home
Brings good to family and house.

Buxom is the peach-tree;
How its fruit swells!
Our lady going home
Brings good to family and house.

Buxom is the peach-tree;
How thick its leaves!
Our lady going home
Brings good to the people of her house.

114 SWALLOW, swallow on your flight,
Wing high, wing low.
Our lady that goes home,
Far we escort beyond the fields.
Gaze after her, cannot see her,
And our tears flow like rain.

Swallow, swallow on your flight,
Now up, now down.
Our lady that goes home,
Far we go with her.
Gaze after her, cannot see her,
And stand here weeping.

Swallow, swallow on your flight,
Call high, call low.
Our lady that goes home,
Far we lead towards the south.
Gaze after her, cannot see her,
Sad are our hearts indeed!

A lady T'ai-jên is she,
Her heart so faithful and true!
So gentle, so docile,
Clean and careful of her person,
Mindful of her late lord,
Making provision for his helpless ones.

This, as has always been recognized, is a song about a
lady who, after the death of her husband, returns to her
father's house. In the last verse she is compared to T'ai-
jên, the mother of King Wên,[1] model of womanly
virtues.

[1] Founder of the Chou dynasty, traditionally supposed to have
died in 1122 B.C.

The following is the song of the handmaids in some princely household. They had to leave their master's side before daybreak, to 'fade out' before dawn, and therefore compare themselves to stars; whereas the wife could remain with her lord all night.

115   TWINKLE those small stars,
Three or five in the east.
Shrinking, through the dark we walk
While it is still night in the palace.
Truly, fates are not equal.

Twinkle those small stars,
In Orion, in the Pleiads.
Shrinking, through the dark we walk
Burdened with coverlet and sheet.
Truly, fates are not alike.[1]

I close this group with a song which is said to have been made by a woman who lost her husband in the wars of Duke Hsien of Chin, 676–651 B.C.; and so lead up to the next group, which deals with warriors and war.

116   THE cloth-plant grew till it covered the
thorn bush;
The bindweed spread over the wilds.
My lovely one is here no more.
With whom? No, I sit alone.

[1] For a comparatively modern parallel, see J. K. Shryock, 'Ch'ên Ting's Account of the Marriage Customs of the Chiefs of Yünnan,' *American Anthropologist*, Vol. 36, No. 4, 1934.

The cloth-plant grew till it covered the
    brambles;
The bindweed spread across the borders
    of the field.
My lovely one is here no more.
With whom? No, I lie down alone.

The horn[1] pillow so beautiful,
The worked coverlet so bright!
My lovely one is here no more.
With whom? No, alone I watch till dawn.

Summer days, winter nights—
Year after year of them must pass
Till I go to him where he dwells.
Winter nights, summer days—
Year after year of them must pass
Till I go to his home.

Compare the old Japanese poem quoted above,
Introduction, page 14.

[1] A pillow of wood inlaid with horn?

117   F<small>IRMLY</small> set are the rabbit nets,
       Hammered with a *ting, ting*.
Stout-hearted are the warriors,
Shield and rampart of our elder and lord.

Firmly set are the rabbit nets,
Spread where the paths meet.
Stout-hearted are the warriors,
Good comrades for our elder and lord.

Firmly set are the rabbit nets,
Spread deep in the woods.
Stout-hearted are the warriors,
Belly and heart of our elder and lord.

118   T<small>HE</small> men of Ch'ing are in P'êng,
Their armoured teams very strong.
Two spears, pennon out-topping pennon
Above the river[1] they move at ease.

The men of Ch'ing are in Hsiao,
Their armoured teams very swift.
Two spears, hook topping hook;
Above the river they course at will.

The men of Ch'ing are in Chou,
Their armoured teams move free.
The Left circles its banners, the Right raises them,
While the Centre shouts 'Well done!'

[1] The scene of the song is near K'ai-fêng Fu in Honan, apparently on both banks of the Yellow River. I do not think it is possible to connect it with any definite historical incident, but the traditional date (*c.* 660 B.C.) is quite a likely period. There was probably more point in it than meets the eye. As it stands, the song is singularly flat and uninteresting.

119 HIS furs of lamb's wool so glossy!
Truly he is steadfast and tough.
That great gentleman
Would give his life rather than fail his lord.

His furs of lamb's wool, facings of leopard's fur!
He is very martial and strong.
That great gentleman
Is the upholder of right in this land.

His furs of lamb's wool so splendid,
His three festoons so gay!
That great gentleman
Is the first in all our land.

120 THE small war-chariot with its shallow body,
The upturned chariot-pole, with its five bands,
The slip rings, the flank-checks,
The traces stowed away in their silvered case.
The patterned mat, the long naves,
Drawn by our piebalds, our whitefoots.
To think of my lord,
Gracious as jade,
In his plank hut
Brings turmoil to every corner of my heart.

His four steeds so strong,
The six reins in his hand;
The piebald and the bay with black mane are inside,
The brown horse with black mouth and the deep-
            black horse are outside.
The dragon shields are held touching,
Silvered too the buckle straps.[1]

[1] It was the buckles that were silvered. Inversion for the sake of
rhyme.

My thoughts are of my lord
So gracious at home in the town.
When can I expect him?
How can I endure thus to think of him?

The team lightly caparisoned, perfectly trained,
The trident spear with silvered butt,
The shield many-coloured with its coating of
        feathers,
The tiger-skin quiver with its chiselled collar,
The two bows stretched one against the other
To the bamboo-frame lashed with rattan.
My thoughts are of my lord
Whether I sleep or wake.
Gentle is my good man,
Flawless is his fair name.

121   THEY beat their drums with a loud noise,
       Leaping and prancing weapon in hand,
       Building earth-works at the capital or
              fortifying Ts'ao.
       We[1] alone march to the south.

       We were led by Sun Tzŭ-chung
       To subdue Ch'ên and Sung.
       He does not bring us home;
       My heart is sad within.

       Here we stop, here we stay,
       Here we lose horses
       And here find them again
       Down among the woods.

    [1] The people of Wei, whose capital at the probable date of this
poem was north of the Yellow River; Ch'ên and Sung lay to the
south of the river.

'For good or ill, in death as in life;
This is the oath I swear with you.
I take your hand
As token that I will grow old along with you.'

Alas for our bond!
It has not lasted even for our lifetime.
Alas for our troth!
You did not trust me.

The last verse but one is the wife's marriage-vow. This song, like No. 125, is about a soldier who comes home only to find that his wife has given him up for dead and married again.

122   How few of us are left, how few!
       Why do we not go back?
       Were it not for our prince and his concerns,
       What should we be doing here in the dew?

       How few of us are left, how few!
       Why do we not go back?
       Were it not for our prince's own concerns,
       What should we be doing here in the mud?

123   THE cloth-plant on that high mound,
How its joints stretch on and on!
O my uncles, O my elders,
Why so many days?

Why are you tarrying?
There must be a reason.
Why does it take so long?
There must be a cause.

Our fox-furs are messed and worn;
There is not a waggon that we have not
      brought to the east.
O uncles, O elders,
You do not share our toils with us.

Pretty little creatures
Were the children of the owl;[1]
O uncles and elders
With your ear-plugs[2] so grand!

---

[1] But grow up baleful and hideous; so, too, the uncles and elders fail to come up to expectation.

[2] For ear-plugs, see No. 15. There is the suggestion that they stop up their ears and do not listen to our appeal.

124 I CLIMB that wooded hill
And look towards where my father is.
My father is saying, 'Alas, my son is on service;
Day and night he knows no rest.
Grant that he is being careful of himself,
So that he may come back and not be left behind!'

I climb that bare hill
And look towards where my mother is.
My mother is saying, 'Alas, my young one is on
    service;
Day and night he gets no sleep.
Grant that he is being careful of himself,
So that he may come back, and not be cast away.'

I climb that ridge
And look towards where my elder brother is.
My brother is saying, 'Alas, my young brother
    is on service;
Day and night he toils.
Grant that he is being careful of himself,
So that he may come back and not die.'

125 I WENT to the eastern hills;
Long was it till I came back.
Now I am home from the east;
How the drizzling rain pours!
I am back from the east,
But my heart is very sad.
You made for me that coat and gown
'Lest my soldier should go secret ways.'[1]
Restless the silkworm that writhes
When one puts it on the mulberry-bush;
Staunch I bore the lonely nights,
On the ground, under my cart.

I went to the eastern hills;
Long, long was it till I came back.
Now I am home from the east;
How the drizzling rain pours!
The fruit of the bryony
Has spread over the eaves of my house.
There are sowbugs in this room;
There were spiders' webs on the door.
In the paddock were the marks of wild deer,
The light of the watchman[2] glimmers.
These are not things to be feared,
But rather to rejoice in.[3]

I went to the eastern hills;
Long, long was it till I came back.
When I came from the east,
How the drizzling rain did pour!
A stork was crying on the ant-hill;
That means a wife sighing in her chamber.

---

[1] Be untrue.   [2] The 'night-goer,' i.e. the glow-worm.
[3] All these things can be interpreted as good omens. For example,
lu, 'deer,' suggests *lu*, 'luck.' The spider is called 'happy son' and
other such names.

'Sprinkle and sweep the house,
We are back from our campaign.'
There are the gourds piled up,
So many, on the firewood cut from the
    chestnut-tree.
Since I last saw them
Till now, it is three years!

I went to the eastern hills;
Long, long was it till I came back.
When I came from the east,
How the drizzling rain did pour!
'The oriole is in flight,
Oh, the glint of its wings!
A girl is going to be married.
Bay and white, sorrel and white are her
    steeds.
Her mother has tied the strings of her
    girdle;
All things proper have been done for her.'
This new marriage is very festive;
But the old marriage, what of that?

This song is a typical 'elliptical ballad,' in which
themes are juxtaposed without explanation. Thus 'the
oriole . . .' down to 'all things proper have been done
for her,' is a marriage-song theme, which lets us know
that during the soldier's absence his wife has assumed his
death and married again.

126 THE wild geese are flying;
       Suk, suk go their wings.
       The soldiers are on the march;
       Painfully they struggle through the wilds.
       In dire extremity are the strong men;
       Sad are their wives, left all alone.

       The wild geese are flying;
       They have lighted in the middle of the marsh.
       The soldiers are walling a fort;
       The hundred cubits[1] have all risen.
       Though they struggle so painfully,
       At last they are safely housed.

       The wild geese are flying;
       Dolefully they cry their discontent.
       But these were wise men
       Who urged us in our toil,
       And those were foolish men
       Who urged us to make mischief and rebel.

127 MINISTER of War,
       We are the king's claws and fangs.
       Why should you roll us on from misery to
              misery,
       Giving us no place to stop in or take rest?

       Minister of War,
       We are the king's claws and teeth.
       Why should you roll us from misery to
              misery,
       Giving us no place to come to and stay?

---

[1] Cubit-square frames held the earth in position when the walls
were being built.

Minister of War,
Truly you are not wise.
Why should you roll us from misery to
misery?
We have mothers who lack food.

128 TENDER and pretty[1] are the yellow orioles
Perching on the side of the hill.
The way is long;
I am so tired. What will become of me?
'Let him have a drink, let him have some food,
Give him a lesson, scold him,
But bid that hind coach
Call to him and pick him up.'

Tender and pretty are the yellow orioles
Perching on the corner of the hill.
How dare I shirk marching?
But I fear I cannot keep up.
'Let him have a drink, let him have some food,
Give him a lesson, scold him,
But bid that hind coach
Call to him and pick him up.'

Tender and pretty are the yellow orioles
Perching on the side of the hill.
How dare I shirk marching?
But I fear I shall not hold out.
'Let him have a drink, let him have some food,
Give him a lesson, scold him,
But bid that hind coach
Call to him and pick him up.'

---

[1] *Mien-man* also suggests 'on and on.' The orioles find their perch;
but the soldier is allowed no rest.

129 JAGGED are the rocks.
     Oh, how high!
     These hills and rivers go on and on.
     Oh, how toilsome!
     But soldiers fighting in the east
     Have no time to pause.

     Jagged are the rocks.
     Oh, how steep!
     These hills and rivers go on and on.
     It seems as though they would never end.
     But soldiers fighting in the east
     Have no time to halt.

     We met swine with white trotters
     Plunging in a herd through the waves.
     The moon is caught in the Net.[1]
     There will be deluges of rain.
     Soldiers fighting in the east
     Have no time to rest.

---

[1] The Net, i.e. the Hyades, connected by the Chinese, as by us,
with rain. Swine with white trotters are also an omen of rain.
Rain falling looks like a net cast over the landscape. The characters
for 'net' and 'rain' are in their oldest forms very similar.

130 WHAT plant is not faded?
What day do we not march?
What man is not taken
To defend the four bounds?

What plant is not wilting?
What man is not taken from his wife?
Alas for us soldiers,
Treated as though we were not fellow-men!

Are we buffaloes, are we tigers
That our home should be these desolate
        wilds?
Alas for us soldiers,
Neither by day nor night can we rest!

The fox bumps and drags
Through the tall, thick grass.
Inch by inch move our barrows
As we push them along the track.

The next four poems deal with or mention the campaigns of the Chou people against the fierce Hsien-yün tribes. The two Chinese generals, Nan-chung, in No. 132, and Chi-fu, in No. 133, are both traditionally placed in King Hsüan's reign (827–782 B.C.). Of the Hsien-yün we know very little. All that we can be certain of is that they were a dreaded foe who invaded Shensi, the home-country of the Chou, and were driven back in a series of campaigns some of which took place round about 800 B.C.

131   WE plucked the bracken, plucked the bracken
While the young shoots were springing up.
Oh, to go back, go back!
The year is ending.
We have no house, no home
Because of the Hsien-yün.
We cannot rest or bide
Because of the Hsien-yün.

We plucked the bracken, plucked the bracken
While the shoots were soft.
Oh, to go back, go back!
Our hearts are sad,
Our sad hearts burn,
We are hungry and thirsty,
But our campaign is not over,
Nor is any of us sent home with news.

We plucked the bracken, plucked the bracken;
But the shoots were hard.
Oh, to go back, go back!
The year is running out.
But the king's business never ends;
We cannot rest or bide.
Our sad hearts are very bitter;
We went, but do not come.

What splendid thing is that?
It is the flower of the cherry-tree.
What great carriage is that?
It is our lord's chariot,
His war-chariot ready yoked,
With its four steeds so eager.
How should we dare stop or tarry?
In one month we have had three alarms.

We yoke the teams of four,
Those steeds so strong,
That our lord rides behind,
That lesser men protect.
The four steeds so grand,
The ivory bow-ends, the fish-skin quiver.
Yes, we must be always on our guard;
The Hsien-yün are very swift.

Long ago, when we started,
The willows spread their shade.
Now that we turn back
The snowflakes fly.
The march before us is long,
We are thirsty and hungry,
Our hearts are stricken with sorrow,
But no one listens to our plaint.

132 WE bring out our carts
On to those pasture-grounds.
From where the Son of Heaven is
Orders have come that we are to be here.
The grooms are told
To get the carts loaded up.
The king's service brings many hardships;
It makes swift calls upon us.

We bring out our carts
On to those outskirts.
Here we set up the standards,
There we raise the ox-tail banners,
The falcon-banner and the standards
That flutter, flutter.
Our sad hearts are very anxious;
The grooms are worn out.

The king has ordered Nan-chung
To go and build a fort on the frontier.
To bring out the great concourse of chariots,
With dragon banners and standards so bright.
The Son of Heaven has ordered us
To build a fort on that frontier.
Terrible is Nan-chung;
The Hsien-yün are undone.

Long ago, when we started,
The wine-millet and cooking-millet were in
    flower.
Now that we are on the march again
Snow falls upon the mire.
The king's service brings many hardships.
We have no time to rest or bide.
We do indeed long to return;
But we fear the writing on the tablets.[1]
    [1] The king's command.

'Dolefully cry the cicadas,
Hop and skip go the grasshoppers.
Before I saw my lord
My heart was full of grief.
But now that I have seen my lord
My heart is still.'[1]
Terrible is Nan-chung;
Lo, he has stricken the warriors of the West!

The spring days are drawn out;
All plants and trees are in leaf.
Tuneful is the oriole's song.
The women gather aster[2] in crowds.
We have bound the culprits;[3] we have
            captured the chieftains,
And here we are home again!
Terrible is Nan-chung;
The Hsien-yün are levelled low.

[1] Bridal-hymn formula, spoken by the wives.
[2] For use in the ancestral temple.
[3] For trial. Enemies are criminals and their instigators must be tried at law, like criminals. It was the same sentiment which after the Great War led to the demand that the Kaiser should be 'tried.' See additional notes.

133   IN the sixth month all is bustle,
      We put our war-chariots in order,
      Our four steeds are in good fettle,
      We load our bow-cases and quivers.
      The Hsien-yün are ablaze,
      We have no time to lose.
      We are going out to battle,
      To set aright the king's lands.

      Our team of blacks is well-matched,
      A pattern of perfect training.
      It is the sixth month;
      We have finished all our field-work,
      We have finished all our field-work
      Throughout the thirty leagues.[1]
      We are going out to battle
      To help the Son of Heaven.

      Our four steeds are tall and broad,
      Hugely high they stand.
      We fall upon the Hsien-yün,
      We do great deeds,
      So stern, so grim
      We fulfil the tasks of war,
      Fulfil the tasks of war
      That the king's lands may be at rest.

      The Hsien-yün were scornful of us,
      They encamped at Chiao-huo.[2]

[1] Compare No. 155. A league was three hundred paces.
[2] Generally supposed to have been near the modern Fu-fêng,
west of the Chou capital. The meaning of Hao and Fang is very
uncertain. It would be rash to build geographical theories on the
order in which the places are mentioned, for this may be dictated
by the necessities of rhyme.

They invaded Hao and Fang.
As far as the north banks of the Ching.
With woven pattern of bird blazonry
Our silken banners brightly shone.
Big chariots, ten of them,
Went first, to open up a path.

Those war-chariots were well balanced
As though held from below, hung from
    above.
Our four steeds were unswerving,
Unswerving and obedient.
We smote the Hsien-yün
As far as the great plain.[1]
Mighty warrior[2] is Chi-fu,
A pattern to all the peoples.

Chi-fu feasts and is happy;
He has received many blessings from Heaven:
'Here I am, back from Hao;
I have been away a long time
And must give a drinking-party to my
    friends,
With roast turtle and minced carp.'
And who was with him?
Chang Chung, pious[3] and friendly.

---

[1] Probably not the modern T'ai-yüan in Shansi.
[2] Or 'mighty in peace and war'; see Appendix IV.
[3] To his ancestors. But the 'pious and friendly' may easily be a
corruption of another personal name.

134 Lo, we were plucking the white millet
In that new field,
In this fresh-cleared acre,
When Fang-shu arrived
With three thousand chariots
And a host of guards well-trained.
Yes, Fang-shu came
Driving his four dappled greys,
Those dappled greys so obedient,
In his big chariot painted red,
With his awning of lacquered bamboo and
       his fish-skin quiver,
His breast-buffers[1] and metal-headed reins.

Lo, we were plucking the white millet
In that new field,
In this middle patch,
When Fang-shu arrived
With three thousand chariots,
With banners shining bright.
Yes, Fang-shu came
With leather-bound nave and metal-studded
       yoke,
His eight bells jingling,
Wearing his insignia—
The red greaves so splendid,
The tinkling onion-stones at his belt.

Swoop flew that hawk
Straight up into the sky,
Yet it came here to roost.
Fang-shu has come
With three thousand chariots
And a host of guards well-trained.

[1] Pear-shaped buffers which hung from the horse's shoulder-girth.

Yes, Fang-shu has come
With his bandsmen beating the drums,
Marshalling his armies, haranguing his hosts.
Illustrious truly is Fang-shu,
Deep is the roll of the drums,
Shaking the hosts with its din.

Foolish were you, tribes of Ching,[1]
Who made a great nation into your foe.
Fang-shu is old in years,
But in strategy he is at his prime.
Fang-shu has come,
He has bound culprits, captured chieftains.
His war-chariots rumble,
They rumble and crash
Like the clap of thunder, like the roll of
      thunder.
Illustrious truly is Fang-shu,
It was he who smote the Hsien-yün,
Who made the tribes of Ching afraid.

[1] The people later called Ch'u. At this period they were between
the Han River and the Yangtze, in northern Hupeh.

We have seen from the last poem that simultaneously
with the attacks of the Hsien-yün, the Chou had trouble
on their southern frontier. As an ally against their
southern enemies they made friends with the chieftain
of Shên,[1] and King Hsüan's successor, the last king of
western Chou,[2] married a Shên princess. The Lord of
Shao, a fief near the Chou capital, was sent with an
army to the south, to fortify Hsieh, a stronghold of the
Shên people. During the same period great campaigns,
of which we hear much in the bronze inscriptions, were
carried on against the tribes of the Huai Valley.

135   LUSTY is the young millet;
       Copious rains have fattened it.
       Long, long was our march to the south;
       But the Lord of Shao has rewarded it.

       Oh, our loads, our barrows,
       Our waggons, our oxen!
       But now the marching is over
       And at last we are going home.

       Oh, our footmen, our chariot-drivers,
       Our armies, our hosts!
       But now our marching is over
       And at last we are going back.

       Noble is the palace at Hsieh;
       The Lord of Shao planned it.
       Glorious was the army on its march;
       The Lord of Shao gave it victory.

       The highlands and the lowlands were
           made safe;
       The springs and streams cleared.
       The Lord of Shao has vanquished,
       And the king's heart is at rest.

[1] In southern Honan.   [2] King Yu, 781–772 B.C.

136 THE Kiang and the Han sweep by;
The warriors march on and on.
No peace, no play;
The tribes of the Huai are mustering.
All our chariots are out,
All our standards set.
No peace, no rest;
The tribes of the Huai are attacking.

The Kiang and the Han spread far;
The warriors march far and wide.
They secure the frontiers on every side;
They tell the king of their victory.
On every frontier there is peace;
The king's lands are all secure.
No longer is there any strife;
The king's heart can be at rest.

'On the banks of Kiang and Han'
(Such was the king's command to the Lord
     of Shao)
'You are to make new fields on every side;
You are to tithe my lands.'
Then without delay, without haste
The king's domains were marked out,
They were divided and duly ordered
All the way to the southern seas.

The king charged Hu of Shao
(And his charge was published far and wide)[1]
'When Wên and Wu received their mandate
The Duke of Shao was their support.

[1] A mandate to this lord of Shao, couched in similar terms, will
be found on the bronze inscription Karlgren, B. 104.

Do not say "I am a lesser descendant";
You have equalled the Duke of Shao.[1]
You have been zealous in deeds of war
And therefore I grant you a boon.

'I bestow upon you a jade sceptre and a jade
        goblet,
And a bowl of black mead.
Announce it to the Mighty Ones
That I give you hills, lands and fields;
That the charge which you receive from the
        house of Chou
Is as that which your ancestor received.'
Then Hu did obeisance and bowed his head
Saying, 'Long live the Son of Heaven.'

Hu did obeisance and bowed his head,
Then in commemoration of the king's bounty
He made the Duke of Shao's urn.[2]
The Son of Heaven—may he live for ever!
Illustrious is he, the Son of Heaven,
Famous for ever,
Spreading the Power of his governance
Everywhere throughout the lands.

[1] Great supporter and possibly half-brother of the second Chou
king, Wu Wang.
[2] Not necessarily the same one as Karlgren, B. 104.

137 MIGHTIEST of all heights is the Peak[1]
Soaring up into the sky.
The Peak sent down a Spirit
Which bore Fu and Shên.[2]
Now Shên and Fu
Became the sure support of Chou;
A fence to screen the homelands,
A wall to guard the four sides.

Diligent was the Lord of Shên
In the service of the royal successors,
Having his castle in Hsieh,
A model to the lands of the south.
The king bid the Lord of Shao:
'Make secure the Lord of Shên's home,
Let him receive this southern land,
Let his heirs for ever have charge of it.'

The king[3] charged the Lord of Shên:
'Go to this southern country,
Approach these people of Hsieh,
Make there your appanage.'
The king charged the Lord of Shao:
'Tithe the Lord of Shên's lands and fields.'
The king charged his stewards:
'Shift his lordship's own men.'

The Lord of Shên's palace
By the Lord of Shao was planned.
Stout were its walls,
And when the Hall of Ancestors was
          complete,

[1] North of Têng-fêng hsien, near Honan Fu. Also called Sung-shan and 'Middle Peak.'
[2] Fu was a sister-state, just to the east of Shên. This is a type of origin legend which is very unusual in the Far East.
[3] King Yu (781–772)?

Complete in all its majesty,
The king gave the Lord of Shên
Four steeds high-stepping
And breast-buffers very splendid.

The king sent to the Lord of Shên
A state coach and a team of horses;
'I have considered where you should live:
There is nowhere like the southern land.
I give you a great sceptre
To be your treasure.
Go, O father of the royal bride,
And guard the southern clime.'

Then the Lord of Shên indeed went.
The king drank the parting cup in Mei,[1]
And the Lord of Shên went back to the
　　　south,
To Hsieh he duly returned.
The king charged the Lord of Shao:
'Tithe the Lord of Shên's lands.
That he may be furnished with a store of
　　　grain,
And speed him on his way.'

The Lord of Shên, hale and venerable,
Has made his entry into Hsieh
With followers stout-hearted, both riding
　　　and afoot.
There is joy throughout the lands of Chou;
If war comes, they have a safe protection.
Glorious is the Lord of Shên,
The king's eldest father-in-law,
A pattern of valour and might.

---

[1] This may be corrupt, as Mei was to the west of the capital, and not on the direct route to the south.

The Lord of Shên's nature
Is mild, kindly, and upright;
His gentleness to all the lands
Is famous on every side.
So Chi-fu made this ballad,
Its words very grand,
Its tune long and lovely,
As a present to the Lord of Shên.

Chi-fu is a very common type of name, and it does not follow that this Chi-fu is the same as the Chi-fu who fought against the Hsien-yün.

138   YOUNG and tender is this sweet pear-tree;
Do not lop it or knock it,
For the Lord of Shao took shelter under it.

Young and tender is this sweet pear-tree;
Do not lop or harm it,
For the Lord of Shao rested under it.

Young and tender is this sweet pear-tree;
Do not lop it or uproot it,
For the Lord of Shao reposed beneath it.

This song is supposed to have been made by the people of the south, in grateful memory of the Lord of Shao's services to their country.

139 THE king, majestic and glorious,
Charged his minister
Nan-chung Ta-tsu
And his Grand Leader Huang-fu:
'Set in order my six armies,
Repair my war-chariots,
With due caution, with due care
Extend my favour to these southern lands.'

The king told his officer
To charge Hsiu-fu, Lord of Ch'êng:[1]
'Marshal the ranks to right and left;
Prepare my hosts and battalions,
Go along the shores of the Huai,
Destroy this land of Hsü.'
And without loiter or delay
These three ministers went about their
        task.

Majestic, terrible,
Very splendid, a Son of Heaven,
Our king quietly set to work,
Not idling nor loitering.
The land of Hsü was mightily shaken;
Startled as by an earthquake was the land
        of Hsü.
As at a roll of thunder, as by a clap of
        thunder
The land of Hsü was startled, and quaked.

The king spread his war-might,
He thundered and raged.
Forward went his tiger slaves,[2]
Fierce as ravening tigers.

[1] Ch'êng was a fief in Shensi; another Ch'êng near Loyang in Honan also claimed to be the site of Hsiu-fu's fief. The historian Ssŭ-ma Ch'ien believed himself to be descended from him.
[2] Military officers.

Everywhere he garrisoned the banks of the
    Huai,
Again and again took chieftains and captives.
He cleared those banks of Huai;
The king's armies encamped there.

The king's hosts swept along
As though flying, as though winged,
Like the river, like the Han,
Steady as a mountain,
Flowing onward like a stream,
Rank on rank, in serried order,
Immeasurable, unassailable;
Mightily they marched through the land
    of Hsü.

The king's plans have been faithfully effected,
All the regions of Hsü have submitted,
All the regions of Hsü are at one;
It was the Son of Heaven's deed.
In the four quarters all is peace;
The peoples of Hsü come in homage.
The regions of Hsü no longer disobey;
The king goes back to his home.

The Hsü people, who lived along the Huai Valley both
in Shantung and Anhui, had been a great power in the
early days of the Chou dynasty. A remarkable number of
Hsü bronzes has been found.

140   THE fourth month was summer weather;
The sixth month, blistering heat.
Have our ancestors no compassion
That they can bear to see us suffer?

The autumn days were bitterly cold;
All plants and grasses withered.
I am sick of turmoils and troubles;
When shall we go home?

The winter days were stormy and wild;
The whirlwinds, blast on blast!
Other people are all in comfort;
Why should we alone be harmed?

On the hill were lovely trees,
Both chestnut-trees and plum-trees.
Cruel brigands tore them up;
But no one knew of their crime.

Look at that spring water;
Sometimes clear, sometimes foul.
But we every day meet fresh disaster.
How can we be expected to feed?[1]

On flow the Kiang and the Han,
Main-threads of this southern land.
We are worn out with service;
Why does no one heed us?

Would that I were an eagle or a falcon
That I might soar to heaven.
Would I were a sturgeon or snout-fish
That I might plunge into the deep.

[1] Our parents.

On the hill grows the bracken,
In the lowlands, the red-thorn.
A gentleman made this song
That his sorrows might be known.

There has been a good deal of discussion about the
social status of the people who wrote the songs. In this
case, at any rate, it would seem that we have definite
information: 'A gentleman (*chün-tzŭ*) made this song.'
But I would not be too sure. European pamphlets that
claimed to be by 'a person of quality' were certainly not
always the work of veritable *chün-tzŭ*.

141   DRUMS and bells jingle
       Where the Huai flows broad.
       Sad is my heart and sore;
       That good man, my lord—
       I long for him and cannot forget.

       The drums and bells blend their sound;
       The waters of the Huai sweep on.
       Sad is my heart and wretched.
       That good man, my lord—
       In his power no flaw.

       Bells play, the great drum is beaten;
       The Huai has three islands.
       Sad is my heart and shaken.
       That good man, my lord—
       In his power no fault.

       Din of drums and bells,
       Sound of the small zithern, the great.
       Reed-organ and stone chimes make music
              together.
       There are songs of the capital, songs of
              the south,
       And flute unfaltering.

It is possible that this song is a lament for someone
who lost his life during the southern campaigns of the
late western Chou. But this is very uncertain.

142 THE people of our race were created by
Heaven
Having from the beginning distinctions and
rules.[1]
Our people cling to customs,
And what they admire is seemly behaviour.
Heaven, looking upon the land of Chou,
Sent a radiance to earth beneath.
To guard this Son of Heaven
It created Chung Shan Fu.[2]

In his nature Chung Shan Fu
Is a pattern of mildness and blessedness.
Good is his every attitude and air,
So cautious, so composed!
Following none but ancient teachings,
Striving only for dignity and good
deportment,
Obedient to the Son of Heaven,
Whose glorious commands he spreads
abroad.

The king commanded Chung Shan Fu:
'Be a pattern to all the officers of Court,
Continue the work of your ancestors,
Protect the royal person,
Go out and in with the royal commands,
Be the king's throat and tongue,
Spread his edicts abroad
That through all the land men may be
stirred.'

[1] 'When asked whether the customs were still performed . . .
a woman said: "How should they not be performed? Were we not
created with them?" ' From Monica Hunter's book on the Bantu
tribe Pondo (*Reaction to Conquest*), p. 537.

[2] Who appears in the *Kuo Yü* 'Stories of the Kingdoms,' as an
adviser of King Hsüan. His career probably began under Li (878–
842).

With due awe of the king's command
Did Chung Shan Fu effect it.
If in the land anything was darkened
Chung Shan Fu shed light upon it.
Very clear-sighted was he and wise.
He assured his own safety;[1]
But day and night never slackened
In the service of the One Man.

There is a saying among men:
'If soft, chew it;
If hard, spit it out.'
But Chung Shan Fu
Neither chews the soft,
Nor spits out the hard;
He neither oppresses the solitary and the
      widow,
Nor fears the truculent and strong.

There is a saying among men:
'Inward power is light as a feather;
Yet too heavy for common people to raise.'
Thinking it over,
I find none but Chung Shan Fu that could
      raise it;
For alas! none helped him.
When the robe of state was in holes
It was he alone who mended it.

When Chung Shan Fu went forth
His four steeds quivered;
His warriors so nimble,

---

[1] To assure one's own safety ('guard oneself') was one of the
main avowed objects of Chou morality. The phrase occurs on
numerous bronze inscriptions. One assures one's safety by pleasing
one's ancestors.

Each determined to keep his place.[1]
His four steeds so strong,
The eight harness-bells tinkling.
The king charged Chung Shan Fu
To fortify that eastern land.[2]

His four steeds so fine,
The eight harness-bells chiming,
Chung Shan Fu went to Ch'i,
And swift was his return.
Chi-fu made this ballad
Gentle as a clean breeze.
Chung Shan Fu has long been burdened
    with care;
May this calm his breast.

143   Oh, bright Heaven high above,
Shining down upon the earth below,
Our march to the west
Has led us to the desert wilds!
It was in the early days of the second month;[3]
We have suffered cold and heat.
Oh, the sadness of my heart,
Its poison is very bitter.
Thinking of those who nurtured me
My tears fall like rain.
Of course I long to come home,
But I fear the meshes of crime.

Long ago when we set out
The days and months[4] were just becoming
    mild.

---

[1] In the line of chariots. Literally 'not to be caught up.'
[2] Perhaps to help the people of Ch'i to fortify their new capital at Lin-tzŭ, 859 B.C.
[3] That we got here.   [4] i.e. the weather.

When shall I get back?
The year is drawing to its close.
When I think I am single-handed
And my affairs very many,
Oh, the sadness of my heart!
Truly, I cannot get leave.
Thinking of those that nurtured me,
Full of longing I turn and gaze.
Indeed, I long to come home,
But I am afraid of the wrath that would
     ensue.

Long ago when we set out
The days and months were just becoming
     warm.
When shall I get back?
The affairs of the campaign press upon me
     more and more.
The year is drawing to its close;
They are plucking southernwood, cutting the
     beans.
Oh, the sadness of my heart!
I only make myself miserable by thinking.
When I remember those who nurtured me
I rise and leave the place where I lie.
Indeed, I am longing to go home;
But I dread the commotion that would follow.

Listen to that, you gentlemen,
And do not forever take your ease.
Fulfil the duties of your station;
God sides with the upright and straight.
The spirits, they are listening
And will give good to you.
Listen to that, you gentlemen,
And do not forever take your rest.

Fulfil the duties of your station.
God loves the upright and straight.
The spirits, they are listening
And will give you blessings for evermore.[1]

The next piece is not a war-song; but I include it here,
as it fits in well with the others in the group. If you look
up 'Han' in any topographical dictionary, you will find
that the Han of this song is in Hopeh, near Peking.
There is, however, no real evidence that such a place
existed. It has been invented by scholars who could not
bear to think of the people of Yen coming right across
two provinces, when they helped to fortify Han. But the
Lord of Shao brought his people much farther to fortify
Hsieh; and Chung Shan Fu went all the way from
Shensi to Shantung to fortify Ch'i.

In the opening words,[2] the king giving his commands
is compared to the Great Yü who gave the streams and
hills their present form. The Mount Liang of ancient
legend was the range on each side of the 'Dragon Gate';[3]
through these mountains Yü cut an outlet for the Yellow
River. Han was a feudal State which lay chiefly in
south-western Shansi, near where the Fên runs into the
Yellow River; but also partly across the Yellow River;
in eastern Shensi.

[1] The word 'God' in this verse is not expressed, but it or
'Heaven' must be understood as the subject of the sentence. In the
last verse the minstrel addresses his audience.

[2] Compare the opening of No. 200.

[3] The northern Lung-mên, not the one in Honan.

144   MIGHTY is Mount Liang,
It was Yü who fashioned it;
High aloft are its paths.
The Lord of Han received a charge;
The king in person delivered it:
'Continue the work of your ancestors,
Do not neglect this my charge,
Day and night never idle,
Steadfastly fulfil the duties of your rank;
My orders cannot be slighted.
Lead unsubmissive lands
To the assistance of your sovereign lord.'

With four steeds so splendid,
Very tall and broad,
The Lord of Han came to audience;
Bearing his great sceptre of office
He had audience with the king.
And the king gave to the Lord of Han
An embroidered banner, with blazonry of
        pennons,
An awning of lacquered bamboo, a
        carved cross-bar,
A dark-red robe, crimson slippers,
A breast-buffer, a chiselled frontlet,
Leather-work for his front-rail, a short-
        haired skin-rug,
Metal-headed reins and metal yokes.

The Lord of Han went forth,
Went forth and lodged in T'u.
Hsien-fu gave the farewell party—
A hundred cups of clear wine.
And what were the meats?
Roast turtle and fresh fish.
And what were the vegetables?
Bamboo-shoots and reed-shoots.

And what did he get as presents?
A team of horses and a big chariot.
The trays and dishes were neatly laid;
My lord and his people feasted and were at
    ease.

The Lord of Han took a wife,
Niece of the king at Fên,[1]
Daughter of Chüeh-fu.
The Lord of Han went to meet her
In Chüeh's domain,
With a hundred teams of steeds very strong,
The eight bells tinkling,
Glorious the brightness,
The bridesmaids that were with her
Thronging like clouds.
The Lord of Han surveyed them;
Their splendour filled the gates.

Chüeh-fu was a great warrior;
There was not a land he had not reached.
But thinking of a place for his daughter
    Han Chi[2]
He could think of nowhere pleasanter than
    Han.
Very pleasant the land of Han,
Its rivers and pools so large,
Its bream and tench so fat,
Its deer so plentiful,
And black bears and brown,
Wild cats and tigers.

[1] This almost certainly means King Li, who *c.* 842 was driven
out of his capital and took refuge at Chih, in southern-central
Shansi, on the banks of the Fên River.

[2] This is an odd way to speak of her, for she did not become
Han Chi ('girl of the Chi clan married to the Lord of Han') until
after her marriage.

Without mishap she reached this lovely
    dwelling-place;
Han-chi rested and was at peace.

Wide was that castle wall of Han
Completed by the hosts of Yen.[1]
Because of the charge given to his ancestor
He sheltered all the tribes of Muan.
And the king gave to the Lord of Han
The Chui tribes and the Mo;
He received all the northern lands
And ruled them as their lord.
He built walls, he dug ditches,
He divided the land and apportioned it.
He sent to Court skins of the white wolf,
Of red panther and brown bear.

[1] In Hopei, near Peiping. Muan (I write it thus to distinguish it
from the English word Man) and Mo were both very general
names for barbarian tribes, irrespective of their locality. I doubt if
these Mo are in any way connected with the Wei-mo of Korea in
Han times. The Chui are unknown.

In 771 B.C. the Chou capital was sacked by barbarian tribes, and the Western Chou dynasty came to an end. A new capital was set up near Lo-yang in Honan, but henceforward the Chou (now known as Eastern Chou) ceased to have any real political power, the Chou king becoming merely the religious head of the affiliated States. The strong States of Ch'in and Chin kept the barbarians in check to the north and west. The real danger to the diminished Chou kingdom came from the rising power of the Ch'u people in the south. In No. 150 we find the king's soldiers defending Shên, Fu, and Hsü in southern Honan. In No. 152 we find the people of Ts'ao in south-western Shantung lamenting the decline of Chou and ready to march to its assistance.

145   WIFE: Tall grows that pear-tree,
                Its fruit so fair to see.[1]
                The king's business never ends;
                Day in, day out it claims us.
   CHORUS: In spring-time, on a day so sunny—
                Yet your heart full of grief?
                The soldiers have leave!

   WIFE: Tall grows that pear-tree,
                Its leaves so thick.
                The king's business never ends;
                My heart is sick and sad.
   CHORUS: Every plant and tree so leafy,
                Yet your heart sad?
                The soldiers are coming home!

---

[1] 'The tree flowers in its season; but the soldiers cannot lead a natural existence' (earliest commentator). This use of contrast was completely misunderstood by later interpreters.

SOLDIER: I climb that northern hill
          To pluck the boxthorn.
          The king's business never ends;
          What will become of my father, of
              my mother?
CHORUS: Their wickered chariots drag painfully
              along,
          Their horses are tired out.
          But the soldiers have not far to go.

WIFE: If he were not expected and did not
              come
          My heart would still be sad.
          But he named a day, and that day is
              passed,
          So that my torment is great indeed.
CHORUS: The tortoise and the yarrow-stalks
              agree;
          Both tell glad news.
          Your soldier is close at hand.

The tortoise and the yarrow-stalks represent two
methods of divination. The first consisted in heating the
carapace of a tortoise and 'reading' the cracks that
appeared; the second, in shuffling stalks of the Siberian
milfoil. For the former, see note on No. 240.

146 My four steeds are weary,
    The high road is very far.
    Indeed, I long to come home;
    But the king's business never ends.
    My heart is sick and sad.

    My four steeds are weary,
    They pant, those white steeds with black
        manes.
    Indeed, I long to come home,
    But the king's business never ends;
    I have no time to tarry or stay.

    See how they fluttered, those doves,[1]
    Now rising, now dropping;
    Yet they settled on the bushy oaks.
    But the king's business never ends;
    I have no time to feed my father.

    See how they fluttered, those doves,
    Now rising, now hovering.
    Yet they settled on the bushy boxthorn.
    But the king's business never ends;
    I have no time to feed my mother.

    I must yoke my white horses with black
        manes,
    I must gallop at top speed.
    Indeed, I long to come home.
    That is why I made this song,
    To tell how I long to feed my mother.

---

[1] The turtle dove is supposed to be very assiduous in feeding its parents. But I think the meaning here is simply that the dove rests at last; whereas the soldier gets no rest.

147   I GO along the high banks of the Ju[1]
Cutting faggots from the bough.
I have not yet seen my lord;
I feel a pang as of morning hunger.

I go along the high banks of the Ju
Cutting boughs that have been lopped and
    grown again.
At last I have seen my lord;
He has not left me for ever.

'The bream has a red tail;
The royal house is ablaze.
But though it is ablaze,
My father and mother are very dear.'

[1] Tributary of the Huai, south-eastern Honan. In the last verse
the returning husband speaks. A fish with a bleeding tail, floating
helplessly downstream, is the symbol of a ruined kingdom, as we
may see from a passage in the *Tso Chuan* chronicle (Duke Ai. 17th
year).

148 How can you plead that you have no wraps?
I will share my rug with you.
The king is raising an army;
I have made ready both axe and spear;
You shall share them with me as my comrade.

How can you plead that you have no wraps?
I will share my under-robe with you.
The king is raising an army,
I have made ready both spear and halberd;
You shall share them with me when we start.

How can you plead that you have no wraps?
I will share my skirt[1] with you.
The king is raising an army,
I have made ready both armour and arms;
You shall share them with me on the march.

[1] As a rug at night.

149 No breeze stirs,
     No cartwheel grates.
     I gaze down the highway
     And my heart is sad within.

     No breeze blows,
     No cartwheel whirrs.
     I gaze down the highway
     And my heart within is sore.

     If there is anyone who offers to cook
          the fish
     One is glad to wash the cauldrons for
          him.
     If anyone will make cause with the
          west,[1]
     That's a tune I'll gladly join in!

     [1] This song is attributed to the people of Kuei, which lay imme-
     diately to the east of the new Chou capital. The singer, I think,
     wanted to make cause with Chou instead of with Ch'i.

150 THE spraying of the waters
Cannot float away firewood that is bundled.[1]
Yet those fine gentlemen
Are not here with us defending Shên.[2]
Oh, the longing, the longing!
In what month shall we get home?

The spraying of the waters
Cannot float away thornwood that is
        bundled.
Yet those fine gentlemen
Are not here with us defending Fu.
Oh, the longing, the longing!
In what month shall we get home?

The spraying of the waters
Cannot float away osiers that are
        bundled.
Yet those fine gentlemen
Are not here with us defending Hsü.
Oh, the longing, the longing!
In what month shall we get home?

[1] Image of cohesion.
[2] The three places mentioned are all in southern Honan. See
No. 137.

151   *Suk, suk* go the bustard's plumes;
It has settled on the oak clump.
But the king's business never ends;
I cannot plant my cooking-millet and wine-
    millet.
Where can my father and mother look to for
    support?
O blue Heaven so far away,
When will this all be settled?

Suk suk, go the bustard's wings;
It has settled on the thorn-bushes.
But the king's business never ends;
I cannot plant my wine-millet and cooking-
    millet.
What, then, are my father and mother to eat?
O blue Heaven so far away,
When will it all end?

Suk, suk goes that row of bustards;
They have settled on the mulberry clump.
But the king's business never ends;
I cannot plant my rice and spiked millet.
Then how shall my father and mother be fed?
O blue Heaven so far off,
When will things go back to their wonted
    ways?

152 SPLASH, that falling spring
Soaks that clustering henbane.
With a groan I start from my sleep
When I think of the city of Chou.

Splash, that falling spring
Soaks that clustering southernwood.
With a groan I start from my sleep
When I think of Chou and its city.

Splash, that falling spring
Soaks that clustering yarrow.
With a groan I start from my sleep
When I think of the city camp.

Strong grow the millet shoots;
Heavy rains have fattened them.
All the lands must march;
The Lord of Hsün[1] will reward them.

[1] Duke Wên, of Chin, who was acclaimed as Duke by the troops
at Hsün, in southern Shansi, after his return from exile in 636. In
632 he organized a federation of States pledged to support the king
of Chou. The people of Ts'ao, to whom this song is attributed,
belonged to the confederacy.

Agriculture

NEW ground was prepared for agriculture by felling trees, tearing out bushes, and setting fire to the debris. The charred remains helped to fertilize the soil. No other kind of manure is mentioned in the Songs. New agricultural land was divided up into plots separated by balks upon which vegetables were grown. A famous inscription[1] about an assignment of land at a date round about the ninth century reads exactly like an English medieval land-charter. That is to say, the holding described appears to consist of numerous strips of land scattered over a wide area, and it seems that something analogous to our strip-cultivation (open-field system) must have existed in China. Part of each holding was cultivated by the common people for the benefit of the lord who held this holding in fief; part (the 'private fields') was cultivated by the people for their own benefit. It seems that hilly ground facing south or east was often chosen. Work on the southern fields is always spoken of as being done first, presumably because these fields ripened quickest.

After being cultivated for a time, land was allowed to lie fallow. 'New fields' were fallow land that had just been put under cultivation again.

It is very likely that excavation of tombs will before long settle exactly what crops the Chou people grew, and I will not speculate on this subject. It is clear that there were two kinds of millet, one used for eating and one chiefly for making wine.[2] The two terms are generally translated 'common

---

[1] The Nieh-jên *p'an*. Kuo Mo-jo, *Ta Hsi K'ao Shih*, folio 129. 'On across such and such a stream; up to the side of the willow-tree . . . a plot on the T'ung road . . . a plot on the Chou road,' is the type of assignment.

[2] Using the word in a very loose sense, as I do throughout this book. For Chinese rice-wine (Japanese *sake*) is very unlike grape-wine.

millet' and 'glutinous millet.' I am, however, informed at Kew that this distinction, though applicable to rice, has no meaning when applied to millet. I must leave all these questions to experts. My only contribution is to eliminate the term maize, used by some previous translators. This is certainly an anachronism.

Thirty leagues (a league was three hundred paces) is mentioned as the area of cultivation. We do not know exactly what this means. Beyond the cultivated area lay *yeh*, 'the waste,' a term that could presumably be applied to bush or steppe. Probably it was not applied to forests.

No. 200, included among sacrificial poems, deals largely with agriculture.

The first three poems are among those (about a dozen in all) which follow a system of rhyme less strict than that observed in other parts of the book. This may merely mean that they were recitations, not songs. It certainly does not prove (as has often been supposed) that they are earlier in date.

153   MIGHTY are you, Hou Chi,[1]
Full partner in heaven's power.
That we, the thronging peoples, were
        raised up
Is all your doing.
You gave us wheat and barley
In obedience to God's command.
Not to this limit only or to that frontier,
But near, far and for ever throughout
        these lands of Hsia.[2]

154   Ho, ho, my servants and officers!
Be zealous at your tasks.
The king will reward your achievements;
Come and take counsel, come and take
        thought.
Ho, ho, guardians and protectors,[3]
The spring is at its close.
What more do you look for?
How goes the new field?
Oh, royal the wheat and barley!
You shall gather in its bright grain;
Brightly has shone God on high
Till yours now is a rich harvest.
Call all my men saying, 'Get ready your
        spades and hoes;
Have a look, all of you, to your sickles
        and scythes.'

[1] Ancestor of the Chou people; inventor of agriculture. See
No. 238.   [2] i.e. China.
[3] i.e. of the people. I think this is only a name for the king's
officers. But much in this song is uncertain and obscure.

155 COME now! the victorious kings[1]
Are shedding their light upon you.
Lead those farm labourers
To scatter the many grains.
Work your private lands to the full,
The whole thirty leagues;[2]
And labour with your ploughs,
Ten thousand of you in pairs.

156 ABUNDANT is the year, with much millet, much
        rice;
But we have tall granaries,
To hold myriads, many myriads and millions
        of grain.
We make wine, make sweet liquor,
We offer it to ancestor, to ancestress,
We use it to fulfil all the rites,
To bring down blessings upon each and all.

[1] The spirits of former kings. I do not think one king in particular
is meant.
[2] Compare No. 133 and p. 159.

157 THEY clear away the grass, the trees;
Their ploughs open up the ground.
In a thousand pairs they tug at weeds and
　　roots,
Along the low grounds, along the ridges.
There is the master and his eldest son,
There the headman and overseer.
They mark out, they plough.
Deep the food-baskets that are brought;
Dainty are the wives,
The men press close to them.
And now with shares so sharp
They set to work upon the southern acre.
They sow the many sorts of grain,
The seeds that hold moist life.
How the blade shoots up,
How sleek, the grown plant;
Very sleek, the young grain!
Band on band, the weeders ply their task.
Now they reap, all in due order;
Close-packed are their stooks—
Myriads, many myriads and millions,
To make wine, make sweet liquor,
As offering to ancestor and ancestress,
For fulfilment of all the rites.
'When sweet the fragrance of offering,
Glory shall come to the fatherland.
When pungent the scent,
The blessed elders are at rest.'[1]
Not only here is it like this,
Not only now is it so.
From long ago it has been thus.

---

[1] Or, 'are reassured'; *ning* is technical of visits to 'reassure' the
anxious. The two sayings have the form of proverbs.

158 VERY sharp, the good shares,
At work on the southern acre.
Now they sow the many sorts of grain,
The seeds that hold moist life.
Here come provisions for you,
Carried in baskets, in hampers.
Their dinner is fine millet,
Their rush-hats finely plaited,
Their hoes cut deep
To clear away thistle and smartweed:
'Where thistle and smartweed lie rotting,
Millet grows apace.'
It rustles at the reaping,
Nods heavy at the stacking,
It is piled high as a wall,
Is as even as the teeth of a comb.
All the barns are opened:
'When all the barns are brim full,
Wife and child will be at peace.'
We kill this black-muzzled bull.
Oh, crooked[1] is its horn!
We shall succeed, we shall continue,
Continue the men of old.

---

[1] The crumpled horn suggests 'hooking on' one generation to another.

The piece which follows is not a calendar but a song made out of sayings about 'works and days,' about the occupations belonging to different seasons of the year. There is no attempt to go through these in their actual sequence. 'Seventh month,' 'ninth month,' and so forth, means the seventh and ninth months of the traditional, popular calendar, which began its year in the spring; whereas 'days of the First,' 'days of the Second' means, according to the traditional explanation, the days of the first and second months in the Chou calendar, which began its year round about Christmas, that is to say, at the time of the winter solstice. 'The Fire ebbs' is explained as meaning 'Scorpio is sinking below the horizon at the moment of its first visibility at dusk.' Did this happen in northern China round about September during the eighth and seventh centuries B.C., the probable period of this song? That is a question which I must leave to astronomers.

159   In the seventh month the Fire ebbs;
       In the ninth month I hand out the coats.
       In the days of the First, sharp frosts;
       In the days of the Second, keen winds.
       Without coats, without serge,
       How should they finish the year?
       In the days of the Third they plough;
       In the days of the Fourth out I step
       With my wife and children,
       Bringing hampers to the southern acre
       Where the field-hands come to take good cheer.

       In the seventh month the Fire ebbs;
       In the ninth month I hand out the coats.
       But when the spring days grow warm
       And the oriole sings
       The girls take their deep baskets
       And follow the path under the wall
       To gather the soft mulberry-leaves:

'The spring days are drawing out;
They gather the white aster in crowds.
A girl's heart is sick and sad
Till with her lord she can go home.'

In the seventh month the Fire ebbs;
In the eighth month they pluck the rushes,
In the silk-worm month they gather the
    mulberry-leaves,
Take that chopper and bill
To lop the far boughs and high,
Pull towards them the tender leaves.
In the seventh month the shrike cries;
In the eighth month they twist thread,
The black thread and the yellow:
'With my red dye so bright
I make a robe for my lord.'

In the fourth month the milkwort is in spike,
In the fifth month the cicada cries.
In the eighth month the harvest is gathered,
In the tenth month the boughs fall.
In the days of the First we hunt the racoon,
And take those foxes and wild-cats
To make furs for our Lord.
In the days of the Second is the great Meet;
Practice for deeds of war.
The one-year-old[1] we keep;
The three-year-old we offer to our Lord.

In the fifth month the locust moves its leg,
In the sixth month the grasshopper shakes its
    wing,
In the seventh month, out in the wilds;
In the eighth month, in the farm,
In the ninth month, at the door.

[1] Boar.

In the tenth month the cricket goes under
    my bed.
I stop up every hole to smoke out the rats,
Plugging the windows, burying the doors:
'Come, wife and children,
The change of the year is at hand.
Come and live in this house.'

In the sixth month we eat wild plums and
    cherries,
In the seventh month we boil mallows and
    beans.
In the eighth month we dry the dates,
In the tenth month we take the rice
To make with it the spring wine,
So that we may be granted long life.[1]
In the seventh month we eat melons,
In the eighth month we cut the gourds,
In the ninth month we take the seeding hemp,
We gather bitter herbs, we cut the ailanto for
    firewood,
That our husbandmen may eat.

In the ninth month we make ready the stack-
    yards,
In the tenth month we bring in the harvest,
Millet for wine, millet for cooking, the early
    and the late,
Paddy and hemp, beans and wheat.
Come, my husbandmen,
My harvesting is over,
Go up and begin your work in the house,
In the morning gather thatch-reeds,
In the evening twist rope;

[1] Wine increases one's *tê* (inner power) and consequently increases the probability of one's prayers being answered. That is why we drink when we wish people good luck.

Go quickly on to the roofs.
Soon you will be beginning to sow your
    many grains.

In the days of the Second they cut the ice
    with tingling blows;
In the days of the Third they bring it into
    the cold shed.
In the days of the Fourth very early
They offer lambs and garlic.
In the ninth month are shrewd frosts;
In the tenth month they clear the stack-
    grounds.
With twin pitchers they hold the village feast,
Killing for it a young lamb.
Up they go into their lord's hall,
Raise the drinking-cup of buffalo-horn:
'Hurray for our lord; may he live for ever
    and ever!'

160   Who says you have no sheep?
    Three hundred is the flock.
    Who says you have no cattle?
    Ninety are the black-lips.
    Here your rams come,
    Their horns thronging;
    Here your cattle come,
    Their ears flapping.

    Some go down the slope,
    Some are drinking in the pool,
    Some are sleeping, some waking.
    Here your herdsmen come

In rush-cloak and bamboo-hat,
Some shouldering their dinners.
Only thirty brindled[1] beasts!
Your sacrifices will not go short.

Your herdsman comes,
Bringing faggots, bringing brushwood,
With the cock-game, with hen-game.
Your rams come,
Sturdy and sound;
None that limps, none that ails.
He beckons to them with raised arm;
All go up into the stall.

Your herdsman dreams,
Dreams of locusts and fish,
Of banners and flags.
A wise man explains the dreams:
'Locusts and fishes
Mean fat years.
Flags and banners
Mean a teeming house and home.'[2]

People performing a ritual, such as that of offering or
sacrifice, often call the things connected with the ritual
by 'kennings,' substitute names of an allusive kind. Thus,
according to the Book of Rites (*Li Chi*), in the ancestral
temple the bull is called First Great Warrior; the pig,
Fatty; the hare, Bright Look. Other words are 'semi-
tabooed,' by having a fixed epithet. Thus jade is called
'blessed jade.' Compare our 'semi-taboo' when we feel the
necessity of putting the epithet 'poor' in front of the name

[1] i.e. the rest are whole-coloured and therefore suitable for
sacrifice.
[2] This helps to explain why flag-waving plays such a prominent
part in the fertility-rites of peasant Europe.

of dead people whom we mention. In No. 161 'The Thing Purified' is probably the bowl, and 'The Thing Bright' ('bright' being the stock epithet of things connected with the spirits) is the grain brought in the bowl. The sacrificer himself has a kenning. He is called 'the descendant' (it is only later that the word means specifically 'great-grandson') in his relationship to offerings in general and to the offerings of harvest ritual in particular. The Field Grandad is defined as meaning 'the previous harvest.'[1] Agriculturalists in many parts of the world believe that the virtue of the crop is concentrated in the last sheaf to be cut. This sheaf, known in England as 'The Old 'Un' and in Germany as 'Der alte Mann,' is kept till next year (it is often nailed to a cowshed) and imparts its virtue to the fresh crop.

In Morocco young locusts, not yet able to fly, are dealt with by putting straw in their path and setting fire to it. Perhaps the last sheaf was used in China in the same way (No. 162, verse 2).

161 'FAR it stretches, that big field;
   Every year we take ten thousand.
   I take last year's crop
   And feed my labourers.
   For a long time we have had good harvests,
   And now they are off to the southern acres,
   Some weeding, some banking.
   The wine-millet and cooking-millet are as
     lusty
   As we prayed for, as we willed.
   Fine, my chosen men!'

[1] In later times the meaning of this phrase was no longer understood. The 'Field Grandfather' was identified with the culture hero Shên Nêng, who belongs to a very different circle of ideas. Compare *Chou Li*, Chapter XLVI, folio 51.

'With the Thing Purified, the Thing Bright,
With our bullocks for sacrifice, and our
    sheep
We come to honour the Earth Spirit, to
    honour the quarters.
For our fields have all done well,
The labourers have had luck.
We twang zitherns, beat drums
To serve Field Grandad,
To beg for sweet rain,
So that our millet may be blessed,
Our men and girls well fed.'

Here comes the Descendant,
With his wife and children,
Bringing dinner to the southern acres.
The labourers come to take good cheer,
Break off a morsel here, a morsel there,
To see what tastes good:
'On the crop-balks and the long acre
All is fine and plentiful.
I don't think the Descendant will find fault;
The labourers have worked hard.'

The Descendant's crops
Are thick as thatch, tall as a shaft;
The Descendant's stacks
Are high as cliffs, high as hills.
We shall need thousands of carts,
Shall need thousands of barns,
For millet, rice, and spiked millet;
The labourers are in luck.
'Heaven reward you with mighty blessings!
Long life to you, age unending!'

162 THE big field brings a heavy crop.
We have chosen the seed, have seen to our
    tools;
We have got everything ready for you.[1]
With our sharp ploughs
Let us begin on the southern acre.
Now we sow our many crops;
They grow straight and tall;
The Descendant is well pleased.

There are no bare patches, everywhere our
    crops sprout,
They are firm, they are good,
There is no foxtail, no weeds.
Avaunt, all earwigs and pests,
Do not harm our young crops.
The Field Grandad has holy power,
He can take you and offer you to the
    flaming fire.

A damp air comes chill,
Brings clouds that gather,
Raining on our lord's fields
And then on our private plots.
There stand some backward blades that were
    not reaped,
Here some corn that was not garnered,
There an unremembered sheaf,
Here some littered grain—
Gleanings for the widowed wife.

Here is the Descendant
With his wife and children
Bringing dinner to the southern acres.
The labourers come to take good cheer.

      [1] The bailiff.

Then he makes offering to the quarters,
Smoke-offering and sacrifice,
With his red bull and his black,
With his wine-millet and cooking-millet,
Makes offering and sacrifice,
That blessings may be ours for evermore.

Blessings on Gentle Folk

163   In the south is a tree with drooping boughs;
The cloth-creeper binds it.
Oh, happy is our lord;
Blessings and boons secure him!

In the south is a tree with drooping boughs;
The cloth-creeper covers it.
Oh, happy is our lord;
Blessings and boons protect him!

In the south is a tree with drooping boughs;
The cloth-creeper encircles it.
Oh, happy is our lord;
Blessings and boons surround him!

164   The locusts' wings say 'throng, throng';
Well may your sons and grandsons
Be a host innumerable.

The locusts' wings say 'bind, bind';
Well may your sons and grandsons
Continue in an endless line.

The locusts' wings say 'join, join';[1]
Well may your sons and grandsons
Be forever at one.

[1] The three noises that the locusts' wings make are punned upon and interpreted as omens.

165 THE cuckoo is on the mulberry-tree;
Her young go astray;
But good people, gentle folk—
Their ways are righteous.
Their ways are righteous,
Their thoughts constrained.

The cuckoo is on the mulberry-tree;
Her young on the plum-tree.
Good people, gentle folk—
Their girdles are of silk.
Their girdles are of silk,
Their caps of mottled fawn.

The cuckoo is on the mulberry-tree;
Her young amid the thorns.
Good people, gentle folk—
Their ways are faultless.
Their ways are faultless,
They shape our land from end to end.

The cuckoo is on the mulberry-tree,
Her young on the hazel.
Good people, gentle folk—
Shape the people of this land.
Shape the people of this land,
And may they do so for ten thousand
    years!

166 THE wolf may catch in its own dewlap
Or trip up upon its tail.
But this nobleman, so tall and handsome,
In his red shoes stands sure.

The wolf may trip upon its tail
Or be caught in its dewlap.
But this nobleman, so tall and handsome—
In his fair fame is no flaw.

167 MAY Heaven guard and keep you
In great security,
Make you staunch and hale;
What blessing not vouchsafed?
Give you much increase,
Send nothing but abundance.

May Heaven guard and keep you,
Cause your grain to prosper,
Send you nothing that is not good.
May you receive from Heaven a hundred
    boons,
May Heaven send down to you blessings
    so many
That the day is not long enough for them all.

May Heaven guard and keep you,
Cause there to be nothing in which you do
    not rise higher,
Like the mountains, like the uplands,
Like the ridges, the great ranges,
Like a stream coming down in flood;
In nothing not increased.

Lucky and pure are your viands of sacrifice
That you use in filial offering,
Offerings of invocation, gift-offerings, offering
  in dishes and offering of first-fruits
To dukes and former kings.
Those sovereigns say: 'We give you
Myriad years of life, days unending.'

The Spirits are good,
They will give you many blessings.
The common people are contented,
For daily they have their drink and food.
The thronging herd, the many clans[1]
All side with you in deeds of power.

To be like the moon advancing to its full,
Like the sun climbing the sky,
Like the everlastingness of the southern hills,
Without failing or falling,
Like the pine-tree, the cypress in their
  verdure—
All these blessings may you receive!

[1] Into which the Chou overlords were divided.

168 THE fish caught in the trap
Were yellow-jaws and sand-eels.
Our lords have wine
Good and plentiful.

The fish caught in the trap
Were bream and tench.
Our lords have wine
Plentiful and good.

The fish caught in the trap
Were mud-fish and carp.
Our lords have wine
Good and to spare.

Things they have in plenty,
Only because their ways are blessed.
Things they have that are good,
Only because they are at peace with one
        another.
Things they have enough and to spare,
Only because their ways are lovely.

169   In the south there are lucky fish,
In their multitudes they leap.
Our lord has wine;
His lucky guests shall feast and rejoice.

In the south there are lucky fish,
In their multitudes they glide.
Our lord has wine;
His lucky guests shall feast and be merry.

In the south there is a tree with drooping
    boughs;
The sweet gourds cling to it.
Our lord has wine;
His lucky guests shall be feasted and
    comforted.

Winging, winging, the doves
In their flocks they come.[1]
Our lord has wine;
His lucky guests shall be feasted, shall be
    surfeited.

---

[1] Birds are the messengers of Heaven; when they come in flocks,
it means that Heaven will send many blessings.

170   On the southern hills grows the nutgrass;
On the northern hills the goosefoot.
Happiness to our lord
That is the groundwork of land and home!
Happiness to our lord!
May he live for evermore.

On the southern hills the mulberry;
On the northern hills the willow.
Happiness to our lord,
That is the light of land and home.
Happiness to our lord!
May he live for ever and ever.

On the southern hills the aspen;
On the northern hills the plum-tree.
Happiness to our lord
That is the father and mother of his people.
Happiness to our lord!
May his fair fame be for ever.

On the southern hills the cedrela;
On the northern hills the privet.
Happiness to our lord,
Yes, and life long-lasting!
Happiness to our lord!
May his fair fame never droop.

On the southern hills the box-thorn;
On the northern hills the catalpa.
Happiness to our lord,
Yes, till locks are seer and face is grey!
Happiness to you, our lord!
To your descendants, safety and peace!

171 How it chirrups, the mulberry-finch!
Beautifully mottled its wing.
Our lord is happy and at ease;
He has received the blessings of heaven.

How it chirrups, the mulberry-finch!
Beautifully mottled its throat.
Our lord is happy and at ease,
He, the shelterer of all the lands.

The shelter, the prop,
A pattern to the many chieftains;
Peaceable and mild,
Receiver of blessings innumerable.

His drinking horn high-curving,
His good wine so soft;
No self-glory, no pride,[1]
So that all blessings he wins.

[1] There are many variants.

172   ALL happiness to our lord!
May he show forth his inward power,
Bring good to the common people and to
    the men of Chou,
He shall get rewards from heaven;
Safety, succour are ordained for him,
From heaven held out to him.

Seeking rewards, a hundred blessings,
Getting sons and grandsons in their
    thousands,
Solemn and majestic,
Bringing good to lords and princes,
Never erring or forgetting,
Following faithfully the old statutes.

Grave in deportment,
Of reputation consistent,
Without malice or hate,
Following the way of all his peers,
Receiving blessings limitless,
Chain-thread and master-strand of all the
    lands.

Their chain-thread, master-strand;
A comfort to his friends,
To all princes and ministers;
Loved by the Son of Heaven,
Never slackening at his task,
He in whom the common people put
    their trust.

173 FAR off at that wayside pool we draw;
Ladle there and pour out here,
And with it we can steam our rice.
All happiness to our lord,
Father and mother of his people.

Far off at that wayside pool we draw;
Ladle there and pour out here,
And with it we can rinse our earthen bowls.
All happiness to our lord,
Refuge of his people.

Far off at that wayside pool we draw;
Ladle there and pour out here,
And with it we can rinse our lacquer bowls.
All happiness to our lord,
Support of his people.

The meaning of the comparison is, I think, that though
our lord is far above us, we are all able to share in his *tê*.

174 THROUGH a bend in the hillside
A gust of wind came from the south.
All happiness to our lord.
We come to sport, we come to sing,
To spread his fame.

Carefree shall be your sport,
Pleasant and diverting your time of rest.
All happiness to our lord.
May your life be prolonged
That you may continue in the ways of
    former dukes.

Great and glorious are your domains,
And mightily secure.
All happiness to our lord.
May your life be prolonged,
You whom all the spirits serve.

Long will last the charge you have
    received,
In blessings and rewards you shall be at
    peace.
All happiness to our lord.
May your life be prolonged,
Deep bliss be yours for ever.

Flourishing, majestic,
Of great piety and inner power,
You shall be continued, protected.
All happiness to our lord,
A model to all the lands.

Raised aloft, exalted.
Like a jade sceptre, like a token of jade,
Of good repute, of good fame.
All happiness to our lord,
Chain-string of all the lands.

The phoenix[1] is in flight,
Clip, clip go its wings;
It is here that it alights.
In their multitude swarm the king's good
    men;
But it is our lord that is chosen to serve,
For by the Son of Heaven he is loved.

The phoenix is in flight,
Clip, clip go its wings;
It is to Heaven that it soars.
In their multitudes swarm the king's good
    men;
But it is only to our lord that a charge is
    given,
For he is loved by all the men of Chou.

The phoenix sings
On that high ridge;
The dryandra grows
Where it meets the early sun.
Thick-leaved the tree,
Melodious the bird.

Our lord's chariots
Are many in number;
Our lord's horses,
Well trained and swift.
So I have put together many verses
To make this song.

---

[1] The *fêng-huang*, afterwards classified as a mythical bird; but it would not seem to be so in this song.

175 MANDARIN ducks were in flight;
We netted them, snared them.
Long life to our lord,
Well may blessings and rewards be his!

There are mandarin ducks on the dam,
Folding their left wings.[1]
Long life to our lord,
Well may blessings forever be his!

When there is a team of horses in the stable
We give it fodder, give it grass.
Long life to our lord,
May all blessings nurture him!

When there is a team of horses in the stable
We give it grass, give it fodder.
Long life to our lord,
May all blessings safely bind him!

[1] Wing folded on wing portends blessing heaped upon blessing.

176   WHEN one gathers beans, gathers beans,
       One puts them in baskets square or round.
       The princes have come to Court;
       With what gift can I present them?
       Although this is nothing to give them,
       It shall be a great coach and four.
       What besides this shall I give them?
       Black robe and broidered skirt.

       High spurts that fountain;
       Come, pluck the cress that grows by it.
       The princes have come to Court;
       Let us look at their banners.
       Their banners flutter, flutter,
       Their harness bells ring.
       Driving teams of three, teams of four,
       The princes arrive.

       Red greaves on their legs,
       Cross-laced below.
       Not that they are wanton or loose;
       These are what the Son of Heaven gave.
       Oh, happy princes,
       To whom the Son of Heaven gave his
            charge!
       Oh, happy princes,
       Before whom all blessings were spread!

       The branches of the oak,
       Their leaves cluster close.
       Oh, happy princes
       That guard the Son of Heaven's land!
       Oh, happy princes,
       In whom all blessings unite!
       On this side and that, to left and right,
       We join in your procession.

It was adrift, that willow boat;
Now to our tow-line we have tied it.
Oh, happy princes,
Whom the Son of Heaven measures.[1]
Oh, happy princes,
May all blessings shelter them!
Let us play, let us sport;
For the princes have come.

[1] Probably corrupt. We need a meaning parallel to 'tied.'

Welcome

177 FLOCK the egrets in their flight
　　To that western moat.
My guest has come,
He too with like movements.
They there find no harm;
Of him here we shall never weary.
Through the day, into the night,
May he long keep holiday!

178 A GUEST, a guest,
And white his horse.
Rich in adornment, finely wrought
The carving and chiselling of his spear-
　　　shafts.

A guest so venerable,
A guest of great dignity.
Come, give him a tether
To tether his team.

Here we follow him,
To left and right secure him.
Prodigal is he in his courtesies;
He will bring down blessings very
　　　joyful.

179   HIGH rise the pole-banners
In the outskirts of Chün,[1]
With white bands braided.
Oh, fine horses, four abreast!
Such great gentlemen,
What can we offer them?

High rise the pole-banners
By the gate-house of Chün,
With white bands bound.
Oh, fine horses, five abreast!
Such great gentlemen,
What can we give them?

High rise the pole-banners
By the walls of Chün,
With white bands plaited.
Oh, fine horses, six abreast![2]
Such great gentlemen,
How can we feed them?

[1] Near the capital of the Wei State, in northern Honan.
[2] Evidence of six horses having drawn one chariot has been found in excavations of Chou tombs.

180   TALL is the pear-tree
That is on the left side of the road.
Ah, that good lord
At last[1] has deigned to visit me.
To the depths of my heart I love him.
Had I but drink and food for him!

Tall is the pear-tree
That is at the turn of the road.
Ah, that good lord
At last is willing to come and play with me.
To the depths of my heart I love him.
Had I but drink and food for him!

181   ON Mount Chung-nan[2] what is there?
There are peach-trees, plum-trees.
My lord has come
In damask coat, in fox furs,
His face rosy as though rouged with
        cinnabar.
There is a lord for you indeed!

On Mount Chung-nan what is there?
The boxthorn, the wild plum-tree.
My lord has come
In brocaded coat, embroidered skirt,
The jades at his girdle tinkling.
Long may he live, long be remembered!

[1] Play of words on 'tall' and 'at last'? Both approximately *died*
in Archaic Chinese.
[2] South of Hsi-an Fu, Shensi

182 WHAT of the night?
The night is not yet spent.
The torches in the courtyard are
alight.
But my lord has come;
Tinkle, tinkle go his harness-bells.

What of the night?
The night is not yet old.
The torches in the courtyard are
bright.
But my lord has come;
Twit, twit go the bells.

What of the night?
The night nears dawn.
The torches in the courtyard gleam.
My lord has come;
I can see his banners.

183   Yu, yu, cry the deer
      Nibbling the black southernwood in the
            fields.
      I have a lucky guest.
      Let me play my zithern, blow my reed-
            organ,
      Blow my reed-organ, trill their tongues,
      Take up the baskets of offerings.
      Here is a man that loves me
      And will teach me the ways of Chou.

      Yu, yu, cry the deer
      Nibbling the white southernwood of the
            fields.
      I have a lucky guest,
      Whose fair fame is very bright.
      He sees to it that the common people do
            not waver,
      Of all gentlemen he is the pattern and
            example.
      I have good wine;
      Let my lucky guest now feast and play.

      Yu, yu, cry the deer
      Nibbling the wild garlic of the fields.
      I have a lucky guest.
      I play my zitherns, small and big,
      Play my zitherns, small and big.
      Let us make music together, let us be merry,
      For I have good wine
      To comfort and delight the heart of a lucky
            guest.

   For the 'luckiness' of guests, compare *Odyssey*, VI, 207,
'All guests and beggars are envoys of Zeus.'

184 THE red bow is unstrung,
     When one is given it, one puts it away.
     I have a lucky guest;
     To the depths of my heart I honour him.
     The bells and drums are all set;
     The whole morning I feast him.

     The red bow is unstrung,
     When one is given it, one stores it.
     I have a lucky guest;
     To the depths of my heart I delight in him.
     The bells and drums are all set;
     The whole morning I ply him.

     The red bow is unstrung,
     When one is given it, one puts it in its
          press.
     I have a lucky guest;
     To the depths of my heart I love him.
     The bells and drums are all set;
     The whole morning I drink pledges with
          him.

185 UNSULLIED the white colt
     Eating the young shoots of my stack-
          yard.[1]
     Keep it tethered, keep it tied
     All day long.
     The man whom I love
     Here makes holiday.

     Unsullied the white colt
     Eating the bean leaves of my stack-
          yard.
     Keep it tethered, keep it tied
     All night long.
     The man whom I love
     Is here, a lucky guest.

     Unsullied the white colt
     That came so swiftly.
     Like a duke, like a lord
     Let your revels have no end.
     Prolong your idle play,
     Protract your leisure.

     Unsullied the white colt
     In that deserted valley,
     With a bundle of fresh fodder.
     'Though you, its master, are fair as jade
     Do not let the news of you be rare as
          gold or jade,
     Keeping your thoughts far away.'

[1] Used as a vegetable garden when not required for stacking crops.

186 Look there at the Lo[1] River,
Its waters so deep and wide.
Our lord has come,
Blessings heaped upon him thick as
       thatch;
In his madder knee-caps so red
He is raising the king's six hosts.

Look there at the Lo River,
Its waters so deep and wide.
Our lord has come,
With his scabbard-gems that blaze.
May our lord for ten thousand years
Keep safe his house and home.

Look there at the Lo River,
Its waters so deep and wide.
Our lord has come,
In whom all blessings join.
May our lord for ten thousand years
Keep safe his home and land.

[1] We cannot tell whether the Lo in Shensi or the Lo in Honan is
meant.

187   GAY the flower,
Lush its leaves.
I have seen my lord,
And my heart is at rest,
My heart is at rest.
Small wonder that he is praised!

Gay the flower,
Gorgeous its yellow.
I have seen my lord,
And magnificent he is,
Magnificent he is.
Small wonder that he is blessed!

Gay the flower,
With its yellow and white.
I have seen my lord
Driving white horses with black manes,
Four white horses with black manes,
And six reins all glossy.

Put them to the left, to the left,
And gentlemen do what is best.
Put them to the right, to the right;
Gentlemen know what to do.
And knowing so well what to do,
Small wonder that they continue!

188   I ESCORTED my mother's brother
       As far as the north of the Wei.
       What present did I give him?
       A big chariot and a team of bays.

       I escorted my mother's brother;
       Far my thoughts followed him.
       What present did I give him?
       A lovely ghost-stone,[1] a girdle-pendant
           of jade.

[1] So the word is written; but the ghost' element may merely be
phonetic.

Feasting

189 FLUTTER, flutter go the gourd leaves;
We pluck them and boil them.
Our lord has wine;
He fills his cup and tastes it.

Here is a rabbit with a white head;[1]
Come, bake it, roast it.
Our lord has wine;
He fills a cup and proffers it.

Here is a rabbit with a white head;
Come, roast it, broil it.
Our lord has wine;
We fill a cup and hand it to him.

Here is a rabbit with a white head;
Come, roast it or bake it.
Our lord has wine;
We fill a cup and pledge with it.

[1] I should think a rabbit with a white head was lucky, because it meant that one would live till one's hair went white.

190   THE FEASTERS: The cricket is in the hall,
                                      The year is drawing to a close.
                                      If we do not enjoy ourselves now,
                                      The days and months will have
                                            slipped by.
  THE MONITOR: Do not be so riotous
                                      As to forget your homes.
                                      Amuse yourselves, but no wildness!
                                      Good men are always on their guard.

THE FEASTERS: The cricket is in the hall,
The year draws to its end.
If we do not enjoy ourselves now,
The days and months will have
    gone their way.
THE MONITOR: Do not be so riotous
As to forget the world beyond.
Amuse yourselves, but no wildness!
Good men are always on the watch.

THE FEASTERS: The cricket is in the hall,
Our field-waggons are at rest.
If we do not enjoy ourselves now,
The days and months will have
    fled away.
THE MONITOR: Do not be so riotous
As to forget all cares.
Amuse yourselves, but no wildness!
Good men are always demure.

191   On the mountain is the thorn-elm;
      On the low ground the white elm-tree.
      You have long robes,
      But do not sweep or trail them.
      You have carriages and horses,
      But do not gallop or race them.
      When you are dead
      Someone else will enjoy them.

      On the mountain is the cedrela;
      On the low ground the privet.
      You have courtyard and house,
      But you do not sprinkle or sweep them.
      You have bells and drums,
      But you do not play on them, beat them.
      When you are dead
      Someone else will treasure them.

      On the mountain is the varnish-tree;
      On the low ground the chestnut.
      You have wine and meat;
      Why do you not daily play your zithern,
      And perhaps once in a way be merry,
      Once in a way sit up late?
      When you are dead
      Someone else will enter into your house.

192 SOPPING lies the dew;
Not till the sun comes will it dry.
Deep we quaff at our night-drinking;
Not till we are drunk shall we go home.

Sopping lies the dew
On that thick grass.
Deep we quaff at our night-drinking,
Here at the clan-gathering we will carry
      it through.[1]

Sopping lies the dew
On those boxthorns and brambles.
Renowned are you, our guests,
None of you failing in noble power.

Those oil-trees, those pawlovnias,
Their fruits hang thick.
Blessed and happy are you, my lords,
None failing in noble ways.

[1] Meaning doubtful.

193   THE fish are at home, at home among their
             water-plants,
      Beautifully streaked are their heads.
      The king is at home, at home in Hao,[1]
      Content and happy he drinks his wine.

      The fish are at home, at home among their
             water-plants,
      Very pliant are their tails.
      The king is at home, at home in Hao,
      Drinking his wine, happy and content.

      The fish are at home, at home among their
             water-plants,
      Snuggling close to their reeds.
      The king is at home, at home in Hao,
      Very soft he lies.

---

[1] Said to have been the capital of Chou in the early days of the
dynasty. When this poem was written, Hao had probably become
a pleasure-palace, a sort of Versailles. We do not know at what
date the later conception of a 'capital' began. When we discuss
where the earliest kings had their 'capital,' we are perhaps com-
mitting an anachronism. Possibly in early times the centre of
government was where the king was at the moment.

The Clan Feast

194   The flowers of the cherry-tree,
     Are they not truly splendid?
Of men that now are,
None equals a brother.

When death and mourning affright us
Brothers are very dear;
As 'upland' and 'lowland' form a pair,
So 'elder brother' and 'younger brother'
     go together.

There are wagtails[1] on the plain;
When brothers are hard pressed
Even good friends
At the most do but heave a sigh.

Brothers may quarrel within the walls,
But outside they defend one another from
     insult;
Whereas even good friends
Pay but short heed.

But when the times of mourning or
     violence are over,
When all is calm and still,
Even brothers
Are not the equal of friends.

Set out your dishes and meat-stands,
Drink wine to your fill;
All you brothers are here together,
Peaceful, happy, and mild.

     [1] Symbols of agitation.

Your wives and children chime as well
As little zithern with big zithern.
You brothers are in concord,
Peaceful, merry, in great glee.

Thus you bring good to house and home,
Joy to wife and child.
I have deeply studied, I have pondered,
And truly it is so.

195   TING, ting goes the woodman's axe;
Ying, ying cry the birds,
Leave the dark valley,
Mount to the high tree.
'Ying' they cry,
Each searching its mate's voice.

Seeing then that even a bird
Searches for its mate's voice,
How much the more must man
Needs search out friends and kin.
For the spirits are listening
Whether we are all friendly and at peace.

'Heave ho,' cry the woodcutters.
I have strained my wine so clear,
I have got a fatted lamb
To which I invite all my fathers.[1]
Even if they choose not to come
They cannot say I have neglected them.

Spick and span I have sprinkled and swept,
I have set out the meats, the eight dishes
        of grain.

[1] Paternal uncles.

I have got a fatted ox,
To which I invite all my uncles,
And even if they choose not to come
They cannot hold me to blame.

They are cutting wood on the bank.
Of strained wine I have good store;
The dishes and trays are all in rows.
Elder brothers and younger brothers, do
　　　not stay afar!
If people lose the virtue that is in them,
It is a dry throat that has led them astray.

When we have got wine we strain it, we!
When we have none, we buy it, we!
Bang, bang we drum, do we!
Nimbly step the dance, do we!
And take this opportunity
Of drinking clear wine.

196   A CAP so tall,
      What is it for?
      Your wine is good,
      Your viands, blessed.
      Why give them to other men?
      Let it be to brothers and no one else.
      Do not the mistletoe and the dodder
      Twine themselves on cypress and pine?
      Before I saw my lord[1]
      My sad heart had no rest;
      But now that I have seen my lord,
      What happiness is mine!

      A cap so tall,
      What is it for?
      Your wine is good,
      Your viands, blessed.
      Why give them to other men?
      Your brothers must all come.
      Do not mistletoe and dodder
      Twine about the top of the pine?
      Before I saw my lord
      My sad heart knew no peace;
      But now I have seen my lord,
      What good times are at hand!

      A cap so tall
      Is for putting on the head.
      Your wine is good,
      Your viands high heaped.
      Why give them to other men?
      Send for brothers, nephews, uncles.
      When a snowstorm is coming
      Sleet falls in its van.
      But death and loss may come any day;
      Not for long are we together.
      Enjoy wine to-night;
      Our lord holds feast!

              [1] Bridal-song formula.

197 THEY are sprouting, those wayside reeds.
Let not the oxen or sheep trample them.
They are forming stem-shoots, they are branching;
Now the leaves are clustering.
Tender to one another should brothers be,
None absenting himself, all cleaving together.

Spread out the mats for them,
Offer them stools.
Spread the mats and the over-mats,
Offer the stools with shuffling step.[1]
Let the host present the cup, the guest return it;
Wash the beaker, set down the goblet.

Sauces and pickles are brought
For the roast meat, for the broiled,
And blessed viands, tripe and cheek;
There is singing and beating of drums.

The painted bows are strong,
The four arrows well balanced.
They shoot, all with like success;
The guests are arranged according to their merits.[2]

The painted bows are bent,
The four arrows, one after another, are aimed.
The four arrows are as though planted;
The guests must be arranged according to their
        deportment.

[1] A sign of respect. Literally with 'joined progress,' i.e. never letting the heel of one foot get beyond the toes of the other.

[2] They are asked, 'Have you ever run away in battle?' etc., and arranged accordingly. Compare *Li Chi*, section on shooting.

It is the descendant of the ancestors who presides;
His wine and spirits are potent.
He deals them out with a big ladle,
That he may live till age withers him,

Till age withers him and back is bent;
That his life may be prolonged and protected,
His latter days be blessed;
That he may secure eternal blessings.

198   'How do you manage to be in Chu-lin?'
       'We are the escort of Hsia Nan.
       He has come to Chu-lin;
       We are the escort of Hsia Nan.

       We drove our four horses;
       We did not pause till the outskirts of Chu.
       We drove our four colts,
       And were in time for breakfast at Chu.'

The mention of 'breakfast' is the only justification for
including in this group a song which it would otherwise
be hard to classify. Hsia Nan was a grandee of the Ch'ên
State, in east-central Honan; his castle was at Chu-lin,
not far from the Ch'ên capital. The satirical intention
which the commentators attribute to the song does not
fit in with its wording. In any case the date is about
600 B.C., or somewhat earlier.

Sacrifice

THE only unfamiliar conception in the sacrificial songs is the 'Dead One.' The word (*shih*) literally means to 'lay out' and consequently can be applied to 'laying' meals (as in No. 127), or to the 'laying out' of the dead. It is thus a euphemism, a softened word, less direct than our word corpse. At Chinese sacrifices a young man, usually the grandson of the sacrificer, impersonated the ancestor to whom the sacrifice was being made. For the time being the spirit of the ancestor entered into him. It was, however, no frenzied 'possession,' like that of the Siberian Shaman; on the contrary, the demeanour of the Dead One was extremely quiet and restrained.

199   THICK grows the star-thistle;
        We must clear away its prickly clumps.
        From of old, what have we been doing?
        We grow wine-millet and cooking-millet,
        Our wine-millet, a heavy crop;
        Our cooking-millet doing well.
        Our granaries are all full,
        For our stacks were in their millions,
        To make wine and food,
        To make offering, to make prayer-offering,
        That we may have peace, that we may
            have ease,
        That every blessing may be vouchsafed.

        In due order, treading cautiously,
        We purify your oxen and sheep.
        We carry out the rice-offering, the harvest
            offering,
        Now baking, now boiling,

Now setting out and arranging,
Praying and sacrificing at the gate.
Very hallowed was this service of offering;
Very mighty the forefathers.
The Spirits and Protectors[1] have accepted;
The pious descendant shall have happiness,
They will reward him with great blessings,
With span of years unending.

We mind the furnaces, treading softly;
Attend to the food-stands so tall,
For roast meat, for broiled meat.
Our lord's lady hard at work
Sees to the dishes, so many,
Needed for guests, for strangers.
Healths and pledges go the round,
Every custom and rite is observed,
Every smile, every word is in place.
The Spirits and Protectors will surely come
And requite us with great blessings,
Countless years of life as our reward.

Very hard have we striven
That the rites might be without mistake.
The skilful recitant conveys the message,
Goes and gives it to the pious son:
'Fragrant were your pious offerings,
The Spirits enjoyed their drink and food.
They assign to you a hundred blessings.
According to their hopes, to their rules,
All was orderly and swift,
All was straight and sure.
For ever they will bestow upon you good
        store;
Myriads and tens of myriads.'

[1] Generally understood by modern scholars as being a title of
the Dead One. I think it means the Ancestors; but there is not much
difference; for the time being the Impersonator *is* an Ancestor.

The rites have all been accomplished,
The bells and drums are ready.
The pious son goes to his seat
And the skilful recitant conveys the message:
'The Spirits are all drunk.'
The august Dead One then rises
And is seen off with drums and bells;
The Spirits and Protectors have gone home.
Then the stewards and our lord's lady
Clear away the dishes with all speed,
While the uncles and brothers
All go off to the lay feast.

The musicians go in and play,
That after-blessings may be secured.
Your viands are passed round;
No one is discontented, all are happy;
They are drunk, they are sated.
Small and great all bow their heads:
'The Spirits,' they say, 'enjoyed their drink
    and food
And will give our lord a long life.
He will be very favoured and blessed,
And because nothing was left undone,
By son's sons and grandson's grandsons
Shall his line for ever be continued.'

200   TRULY, those southern hills—
It was Yü[1] who fashioned them;
Those level spaces, upland and lowland—
The descendant tills them.
We draw the boundaries, we divide the plots,
On southern slopes and eastern we set out
        acres.

A great cloud covers the heavens above,
Sends down snows thick-falling.
To them are added the fine rains of spring.
All is swampy and drenched,
All is moistened and soft,
Ready to grow the many grains.

The boundaries and balks are strictly drawn;
The wine-millet and cooking-millet give good
        yield,
To be harvested by the descendant;
That he may have wine and food
To supply the Dead One and the guests,
And so get life long-lasting.

In the midst of the field are the huts;
Along the boundaries and balks are gourds.
He dries them, pickles them,
And offers them to his great forefathers.
So shall the descendant live long,
Receiving Heaven's favour.

He makes libation with clear wine,
Then follows with the Ruddy Male,[2]
Offering it to the forefathers, to the ancients.
He holds the bell-knife
To lay open the hair;
He takes the blood and fat.

[1] See No. 144.   [2] Kenning for the bull.

So he offers the fruits, offers the flesh
So strong-smelling, so fragrant.
Very hallowed was this service of offering,
Very mighty his forefathers.
They will reward him with great blessings,
With span of years unending.

201   Look at the foothills of Mount Han
With hazel and redthorn so thick.
Here's happiness to my lord,
A happy quest for blessings.[1]

Fair is that jade-handled spoon[2]
And the yellow flood within.
Happiness to my lord,
On whom all blessings shall descend.

The kite flies up to Heaven;
The fish leaps in its pool.
Happiness to my lord,
And a portion[3] for his people.

The clear wine is brought,
The Ruddy Male is ready
For offering, for sacrifice,
That great blessings may be vouchsafed.

So thick grow those oaks
That the people never lack for firewood.
Happiness to our lord!
May the Spirits always have rewards for
    him.

[1] Pun on *Han lu,* 'foothills of Han,' and *han lu,* 'quest for
blessings.' Mount Han is in south-western Shensi.
[2] A libation-ladle with a straight handle of jade.
[3] Reading very doubtful.

Dense grows the cloth-creeper,
Spreading over branches and boughs.
Happiness to our lord!
In quest of blessings may he never fail.

202 WE are drunk with wine,
We are sated with power.
Here's long life to you, our lord;
May blessings be vouchsafed to you for
     ever.

We are drunk with wine,
All the dishes have gone the round.
Here's long life to you, our lord;
May their Shining Light[1] be vouchsafed
     to you.

May their Shining Light beam mildly upon
     you;
High fame and good end to all you do.
That good end is well assured;
The impersonator of the Ancient tells a
     lucky story.

And what is his story?
'Your bowls and dishes are clean and
     good;
The friends that helped you
Helped with perfect manners.

Their manners were irreproachable;
My lord will have pious sons,
Pious sons in good store.
A good thing is given you for ever.'

[1] See note on p. 226.

And what is this good thing?
'Your house shall be raised,
My lord shall have long life,
Blessed shall be his inheritance for ever.'

And what is this inheritance?
'Heaven will cover you with rewards.
My lord shall live long,
Have long life, and a gift as well.'

And what is this gift?
'He gives to you a girl.
He gives to you a girl,
That you may in due time have grandsons
          and sons.'

203 THE wild-duck are on the Ching;[1]
     The ducal Dead[2] reposes and is at peace.
     Your wine is clear,
     Your food smells good.
     The Dead One quietly drinks;
     Blessings are in the making.

     The wild-duck are on the sands;
     The Dead One is calm and well disposed.
     Your wine is plentiful,
     Your food is good.
     The Dead One quietly drinks;
     Blessings are being made.

[1] Tributary of the Wei, in Shensi.
[2] Impersonator of a former Duke or ruler. I have omitted the
adjective in the remaining verses.

The wild-duck are on the island;
The Dead One is calm and at rest.
Your wine is well strained,
Your food well sliced.
The Dead One quietly drinks;
The blessings are coming down.

The wild-duck are where the streams meet;
The Dead One is calm, is at ease.
The feast is set in the clan-temple,
The place to which blessings descend.
The Dead One drinks quietly,
While blessings go on heaping up.

The wild-duck are in the ravine;
The Dead One is resting, overcome.
The good wine was delicious;
Roast meat and broiled, most savoury.
The Dead One is quietly drinking;
We shall have no cares in time to come.

204 Ah, the glorious ancestors—
Endless their blessings,
Boundless their gifts are extended;
To you, too, they needs must reach.
We have brought them clear wine;
They will give victory.
Here, too, is soup well seasoned,
Well prepared, well mixed.
Because we come in silence,
Setting all quarrels aside,
They make safe for us a ripe old age,
We shall reach the withered cheek, we shall
        go on and on.
With our leather-bound naves, our bronze-
        clad yokes,
With eight bells a-jangle
We come to make offering.
The charge put upon us is vast and mighty,
From heaven dropped our prosperity,
Good harvests, great abundance.
They come,[1] they accept,
They send down blessings numberless.
They regard the paddy-offerings, the offerings
        of first-fruits
That T'ang's[2] descendant brings.

[1] The ancestors.
[2] This is a song of the Sung people, who counted themselves as descendants of the Shang (predecessors of Chou). The Sung people told much the same stories about their founder, T'ang the Victorious, as did the Chou about King Wên. T'ang is supposed to have come to the throne in 1766 B.C.

Music and Dancing

THE songs which I have grouped together as connected
with music and dancing do not, of course, include all
the dance-songs in the book; No. 9, for example, seemed
to go better with the Songs of Courtship. No doubt many
of the other pieces, particularly those in the Courtship
and Marriage group, were used as dance-songs. Several
of the 'dynastic songs' (216, 226, 234–237) are traditionally
associated with dances; but the connection is very
uncertain, and I have preferred to class them with the
other short dynastic pieces.

205   BLIND men, blind men[1]
In the courtyard of Chou.
We have set up the cross-board, the stand,
With the upright hooks, the standing plumes.
The little and big drums are hung for beating;
The tambourines and stone-chimes, the mallet-
    box and scraper.
All is ready, and they play.
Pan-pipes and flute are ready and begin.
Sweetly blend the tones,
Solemn the melody of their bird-music.
The ancestors are listening;
As our guests they have come,
To gaze long upon their victories.[2]

[1] Musicians were generally blind men.
[2] As re-enacted in our pantomime.

206   THE unicorn's hoofs!
      The duke's sons throng.
      Alas for the unicorn!

      The unicorn's brow!
      The duke's kinsmen throng.
      Alas for the unicorn!

      The unicorn's horn!
      The duke's clansmen throng.
      Alas for the unicorn!

That this was a dance-song is shown by its extreme
likeness to No. 207, which we know to have been a
dance-song. There is a 'unicorn-dance' in Annam. It
takes place at the full moon of the eighth month.[1] Masked
dances sometimes end by the chief mask being set up
and shot at.[2] That, I think, is what is happening here.
The archers shoot away first its hoofs, then its brow,
then its horn.

[1] Van Huyen, *Les Chants Alternés . . . en Annam*, p. 18.
'L'homme qui sait bien danser avec une tête de licorne. . . .'

[2] F. E. Williams, 'Mask Ceremonies on the Papuan Gulf,'
Congrès International des Sciences Anthropologiques, *Compte
Rendu* (1934), p. 274.

207   STRONG grow the reeds;
At one shot I kill five swine.
Alas for the Tsou-yü!

Strong grows the wormwood;
At one shot I kill five hogs.
Alas for the Tsou-yü!

In the section on music in the *Book of Rites* it is said that
in the pantomime which represented the victory of King
Wu of Chou over Shang, at the end of the dance, 'to
the left they shoot the Wild Cat's Head and to the
right the Tsou-yü,' which was a mythological animal,
parallel to the unicorn. Here we have the song that the
archers, boasting of their prowess, sing while they
'shoot the Tsou-yü.' Heroes in Russian epics shoot through
thirty trees, so that we need not be surprised to find these
bowmen claiming incredible feats.

The Confucians were in the habit of concocting a sort
of pseudo-history by investing mythological figures,
both animal and human, with bureaucratic functions.
Thus in the first[1] book of the *Shu Ching*, various monsters
such as the dragon are enrolled into the civil service.
The same thing happened to the Tsou-yü, who already
in the *Book of the Lord Shang* (third century B.C.) appears
as Keeper of the King's Paddocks. Some commentators
have taken the name Tsou-yü in this song as the name of
an official!

---

[1] Or second, according to the current arrangement.

208 So grand, so tall
He is just going to do the Wan dance;[1]
Yes, just at noon of day,
In front of the palace, on a high place,
A big man, so warlike,
In the duke's yard he dances it.

He is strong as a tiger,
He holds chariot reins as though they
        were ribbons.
Now in his left hand he holds the flute,
In his right, the pheasant-plumes;
Red is he, as though smeared with ochre.
The duke hands him a goblet.

'On the hills grows a hazel-tree;
On the low ground the liquorice.
Of whom do I think?
Of a fair lady from the West.
That fair lady
Is a lady from the West.'[2]

[1] Despite all that commentators have written on the subject, I do
not think that we really know what 'Wan' means. See Appendix II.
[2] This is the song that accompanies the dance.

209 THE nutgrass still grows on the hill;
On the low ground the lotus flower.
But I do not see Tzu-tŭ;
I only see this madman.

On its hill the tall pine stands;
On the low ground the prince's-feather.
But I do not see Tzŭ-ch'ung;
I see only a mad boy.

The 'madmen' were young men dressed up in black jackets and red skirts who 'searched in the houses and drove out pestilences.'[1] In order to do this they must have been armed, for disease-demons are attacked with weapons, just like any other enemy. It is therefore not surprising that the *Chou Li*[2] lists them among various categories of armed men. Their nearest European equivalents are the Căluşari dancers of Rumania, who created such a stir in London when they attended the International Folk Dance Festival in 1935. Professor Vuia describes[3] the dance of the Căluşari as having originally been 'a dance with arms, intended to drive away demons of ill-health.' Closely analogous were the famous 'Flower Boys' of Korea, who reached their zenith in the sixth century A.D.

The *yu-lung* of verse 2 has been identified as *Polygonum orientale* ('prince's-feather').

This is presumably the song with which the people of the house greeted the exorcists.

[1] Commentary on *Tso Chuan* chronicle; Duke Min, second year. For the medley garb of these 'wild men,' see *Kuo Yü*, the story of Prince Shên-shêng of Chin.
[2] Chapter 54.
[3] *Journal of the English Folk Dance and Song Society*, 1935, p. 107, where a note by me on the Korean parallel is also printed.

210   FALLEN leaves, fallen leaves,
       The wind, he blows you.
       O uncles, O elders,
       Set the tune and I will sing with you.

       Fallen leaves, fallen leaves,
       The wind, he buffets you.
       O uncles, O elders,
       Set the tune and I will follow you.

211   How you make free,
       There on top of the hollow mound!
       Truly, a man of feeling,
       But very careless of repute.

       Bang, he beats his drum
       Under the hollow mound.
       Be it winter, be it summer,
       Always with the egret feathers in his hand.

       Bang, he beats his earthen gong
       Along the path to the hollow mound.
       Be it winter, be it summer,
       Always with the egret plumes in his hand.

212 Oh, stalwart, stalwart,
     Stalwart that team of browns!
     At dawn of night in the palace,
     In the palace that is growing light,
     There throng the egrets,[1]
     Egrets that sink down.
     The drum goes din, din.
     They are drunk and dance.
     Heigh, the joys we share!

     Oh, stalwart, stalwart,
     Stalwart those four steeds!
     At dawn of night in the palace,
     In the palace, drinking wine,
     There throng the egrets,
     Egrets in flight.
     The drum goes din, din.
     They are drunk and must go home.
     Heigh, the joys we share!

     Oh, stalwart, stalwart,
     Stalwart that team of greys!
     At dawn of night in the palace,
     In the palace a feast is set.
     From this day as beginning
     Every harvest shall have surplus,
     Our lord shall have corn
     To give to grandsons and sons.
     Heigh, the joys we share!

[1] As we have seen above (No. 211), dancers held egret plumes in their hands, and 'the egrets' here mean the dancers. They are compared to strong steeds; it is possible that they wore horse-masks or were in some way accoutred as hobby-horses. Not, however, quite in the way familiar to us; for the ancient Chinese drove horses, but did not ride them.

213 OH, fine, oh, lovely!
     We set up our tambourines and drums.
     We play on the drums loud and strong,
     To please our glorious ancestors.
     The descendant of T'ang[1] has come;
     He has secured our victories.
     There is a din of tambourines and drums;
     A shrill music of flutes,
     All blent in harmony
     With the sound of our stone chimes.
     Magnificent the descendant of T'ang;
     Very beautiful his music.
     Splendid are the gongs and drums;
     The Wan dance, very grand.
     We have here lucky guests;
     They too are happy and pleased.
     From of old, in days gone by,
     Former people began it,
     Meek and reverent both day and night,
     In humble awe discharging their tasks.
     May they heed our burnt-offerings, our
              harvest offerings,
     That T'ang's descendants bring.

[1] This, like No. 204, is a song of the Sung people.

Dynastic Songs

214 SOLEMN the hallowed temple,
     Awed and silent the helpers,[1]
Well purified the many knights
That handle their sacred task.
There has been an answer in heaven;
Swiftly they[2] flit through the temple,
Very bright, very glorious,
Showing no distaste towards men.

The spirits of the dead, in these hymns[3] as in the bronze inscriptions, are 'very bright'; a dazzling radiance surrounds them. The same conception, extended to living monarchs, dominates early Iranian religion, and was taken over by the Buddhists, Manicheans, and Nestorians, to be embodied in the nimbi and haloes of their divinities. It is still currently expressed in the haloes of Christian saints.

[1] Feudal lords in attendance at the sacrifice
[2] The Spirits.
[3] I write 'hymn' and 'song' for convenience, since they are metrical. But possibly these were recited, not sung.

215 THE charge that Heaven gave
      Was solemn, was for ever.
      And ah, most glorious
      King Wên in plenitude of power!
      With blessings he has whelmed us;
      We need but gather them in.
      High favours has King Wên[1] vouchsafed
           to us;
      May his descendants hold them fast.

Kings rule in virtue of a charge (*ming*), an appointment assigned to them by Heaven, just as barons hold their fiefs in virtue of a *ming* from their overlord.

216 CLEAR and glittering bright
      Are the ordinances of King Wên.
      He founded the sacrifices
      That in the end gave victory,
      That are the happy omens of Chou.

These are said to be the words of a mime-dance (*hsiang-wu*) which enacted the battles of King Wên. This type of tradition is, however, very unreliable. The piece reads like a sacrificial hymn.

[1] Father of King Wu, who conquered the Yin. The standard chronology puts his accession in 1134 B.C. The twenty-six kings from 770 to 249 B.C. had an average reign-length of twenty years. If we apply this average to the twelve kings who preceded them, the date 1134 works out as a hundred years too early. For the conquest of the Yin (also called Shang) see p. 251.

217 RENOWNED and gracious are those rulers, those
  sovereigns
That bestow upon us happy blessings.
Their favour towards us is boundless;
May sons and grandsons never forfeit it!
There are no fiefs save in your land;
It is you, O kings, who set them up.
Never forgetting what your valour won
May we continue it in our sway!
None are strong save the men of Chou,
Every land obeys them.
Nothing so glorious as their power,
All princes imitate them.
Ah, no! The former kings do not forget us.

218 HEAVEN made a high hill;
The Great King laid hand upon it.
He felled the trees;
King Wên strengthened it.
He cleared the bush;
Mount Ch'i has level ways.
May sons and grandsons keep it!

Mount Ch'i is about seventy miles west of Sianfu,
the capital of Shensi, on the north side of the Wei River.
The 'Great King' is Tan-fu, grandfather of Wên (the first
Chou king).

219   HIGH heaven had a firm charge;
      Two monarchs received it.
      Nor did King Ch'êng stay idle,
      Day and night he buttressed that charge
      By great endeavours.
      Ah! The Bright Splendours
      Hardened his will;
      Therefore he could establish it.

The 'two monarchs' are Wen and his son Wu, who conquered the Shang. Ch'êng (1115–1079 B.C., standard chronology), as his name implies, completed their work. The bright splendours are what the early Persians would have called the *hvarenô*, the magic halo of the former kings. See on No. 214.

220   WE bring our offerings,
      Our bulls and sheep;
      May Heaven bless them!
      Our ritual is patterned
      On the rules of King Wên.
      Daily we bring peace to frontier lands.
      See, King Wên blesses us;
      He has approved and accepted.
      Now let us day and night
      Fear Heaven's wrath,
      And thus be shielded.

Heaven's 'charge,' as we shall see constantly in the songs which follow, is 'changeable.' Just as the king can withdraw the *ming* which entitles a baron to hold his fief, so Heaven when displeased can in a moment withdraw its dynastic charge.

221   HE goes through his lands;
       May high Heaven cherish him!
       Truly the succession is with Chou.
       See how they tremble before him!
       Not one that fails to tremble and quake.
       Submissive, yielding are all the Spirits,
       Likewise the rivers and high hills.
       Truly he alone is monarch.
       Bright and glorious is Chou;
       It has succeeded to the seat of power.
       'Then put away your shields and axes,
       Then case your arrows and bows;
       I have store enough of good power
       To spread over all the lands of Hsia.'[1]
       And in truth, the king protected them.

222   TERRIBLE in his power was King Wu;
       None so mighty in glory.
       Illustrious were Ch'êng and K'ang
       Whom God on high made powerful.
       From the days of that Ch'êng, that K'ang,[2]
       All the lands were ours.
       Oh, dazzling their brightness!
       Let bell and drum blend,
       Stone-chime and pipes echo,
       That rich blessings may come down,
       Mighty blessings come down.
       Every act and posture has gone rightly,
       We are quite drunk, quite sated;
       Blessings and bounties shall be our reward.

[1] China in general.   [2] 1078-1053 B.C. (standard chronology).

223 OH, the Ch'i and the Chü[1]
     In their warrens have many fish,
     Sturgeons and snout-fish,
     Long-fish, yellow-jaws, mud-fish and carp,
     For us to offer, to present,
     And gain great blessings.

224 HE comes in solemn state,
     He arrives in all gravity
     By rulers and lords attended,
     The Son of Heaven, mysterious:
     'Come, let us offer up the Broad Male![2]
     Help me to set out the sacrifice.
     Approach, O royal elders,
     To succour me, your pious son.
     None so wise in all things as the men of our
          tribe
     Or so skilled in peace and war as their
          kings,
     Who now repose at august Heaven's side
     And can lend lustre to their posterity.
     May they grant us long life,
     Vouchsafe to us manifold securities.
     May they help us, the glorious elders;
     May they help us, the mighty mothers.'

[1] Northern tributaries of the Wei. They join and flow into the
Wei about half-way between Sianfu and Weinan.
[2] Compare the kennings in No. 161.

225 So they appeared before their lord the king
To get from him their emblems,
Dragon-banners blazing bright,
Tuneful bells tinkling,
Bronze-knobbed reins jangling—
The gifts shone with glorious light.
Then they showed them to their shining
    ancestors
Piously, making offering,
That they might be vouchsafed long life,
Everlastingly be guarded.
Oh, a mighty store of blessings!
Glorious and mighty, those former princes
    and lords
Who secure us with many blessings,
Through whose bright splendours
We greatly prosper.

226 OH, great were you, King Wu!
None so doughty in glorious deeds.
A strong toiler was King Wên;
Well he opened the way for those that
    followed him.
As heir Wu received it,
Conquered the Yin, utterly destroyed them.[1]
Firmly founded were his works.

This and Nos. 234–237 are said to be words of the
mime dance which enacted the victories of King Wu.
They may ultimately have been used for that purpose,
but I doubt if they originally belonged to the war-dance.
There is a pun on the word I have translated 'toiler' and
the name of King Wên. One must read the first *wên* with
the 'heart' radical underneath.

[1] Usually interpreted 'put an end to the slaughters.' The Con-
fucians created a myth that King Wu conquered by goodness and
not by force. But compare *Shu Ching* (Legge, *Chinese Classics*,
Vol. III, p. 482), 'He exterminated his enemies.'

227 PITY me, your child,
       Inheritor of a House unfinished,
       Lonely and in trouble.
       O august elders,
       All my days I will be pious,
       Bearing in mind those august forefathers
       That ascend and descend in the courtyard.
       Yes, I your child,
       Early and late will be reverent.
       O august kings,
       The succession shall not stop!

Nos. 227–231 are all songs from the legend of King
Ch'êng. It is said that when he came to the throne he was
a mere child and had to be helped in his rule by his uncle,
the Duke of Chou. He also had wicked uncles, who
rebelled against him, making common cause with the
son of the last Shang king. The story in its main features
is probably historical. But the part played by the Duke
of Chou has perhaps been exaggerated by the Confucians,
who made the duke into a sort of patron saint of their
school.

228 HERE, then, I come,
       Betake myself to the bright ancestors:
       'Oh, I am not happy.
       I have not yet finished my task.
       Help me to complete it.
       In continuing your plans I have been idle.
       But I, your child,
       Am not equal to the many troubles that
              assail my house.
       You that roam in the courtyard,[1] up and down,
       You that ascend and descend in His house,
       Grant me a boon, august elders!
       Protect this my person, save it with your
              light.'

              [1] Of God.

229   REVERENCE, reverence!
By Heaven all is seen;
Its charge is not easy to hold.
Do not say it is high, high above,
Going up and down about its own business.
Day in, day out it watches us here.
I, a little child,
Am not wise or reverent.
But as days pass, months go by,
I learn from those that have bright
    splendour.
O Radiance, O Light,
Help these my strivings;
Show me how to manifest the ways of
    power.

230   I WILL take warning,
Will guard against ills to come.
Never again will I bump myself and bang
    myself
With bitter pain for my reward.
Frail was that reed-warbler;
It flew away a great bird.
I, not equal to the troubles of my house,
Must still perch upon the smartweed.

When the reed-warbler grows up it turns into an
eagle. Till then it perches in a nest precariously hung
between the stems of reeds or other water-plants, liable
to be hurled to disaster at the first coming of wind or
rain. So the boy king, when he gets older, will pounce
upon his enemies. But for the present he must be content
to 'perch upon the smartweed,' i.e. put up with his
troubles.

231 OH, kite-owl, kite-owl,
     You have taken my young.
     Do not destroy my house.
     With such love, such toil
     To rear those young ones I strove!

     Before the weather grew damp with rain
     I scratched away the bark of that mulberry-
          tree
     And twined it into window and door.
     'Now, you people down below,
     If any of you dare affront me. . . .'

     My hands are all chafed
     With plucking so much rush flower;
     With gathering so much bast
     My mouth is all sore.
     And still I have not house or home!

     My wings have lost their gloss,
     My tail is all bedraggled.
     My house is all to pieces,
     Tossed and battered by wind and rain.
     My only song, a cry of woe!

This poem is traditionally associated with the legend of
King Ch'êng and his protector, the Duke of Chou. It
figures in the *Metal-clasped Box*,[1] a fairly late work which,
however, incorporates a good deal of early legend. The
song is said to have been given to King Ch'êng by his
good uncle. Naturally the kite-owl, always classed as a
'wicked bird' by the Chinese, symbolizes the wicked,
rebellious uncles. The persecuted bird, who is the speaker
in the poem, would seem most naturally to be the
Duke of Chou, and the young whom the bird had
reared with such love and care would then be the boy

     [1] One of the books of the *Shu Ching*.

king. But the allegory does not work out very closely, and it is possible that the song had a quite different origin, and was only later utilized as an ornament to the legend of King Ch'êng.

232　BROKEN were our axes
　　And chipped our hatchets.[1]
　　But since the Duke of Chou came to the
　　　　East
　　Throughout the kingdoms all is well.
　　He has shown compassion to us people,
　　He has greatly helped us.

　　Broken were our axes
　　And chipped our hoes.
　　But since the Duke of Chou came to the
　　　　East
　　The whole land has been changed.
　　He has shown compassion to us people,
　　He has greatly blessed us.

　　Broken were our axes
　　And chipped our chisels.
　　But since the Duke of Chou came to the
　　　　East
　　All the kingdoms are knit together.
　　He has shown compassion to us people,
　　He has been a great boon to us.

[1] i.e. the whole State was in a bad way. The Duke of Chou was sent to rule in Lu, the southern part of Shantung.

233 In silk robes so spotless,
In brown caps closely sewn,
From the hall we go to the stair-foot,
From the sheep to the bulls,
With big cauldrons and little.
Long-curving the drinking-horn;
The good wine so soft.
No noise, no jostling;
And the blessed ancestors will send a
     boon.

234 Oh, gloriously did the king lead;
Swift was he to pursue and take.
Unsullied shines his light;
Hence our great succour,
We all alike receive it.
Valiant were the king's deeds;
Therefore there is a long inheritance.
Yes, it was your doing;
Truly, you it was who led.

This is perhaps the most difficult poem in the whole
book, and I am not confident that I have understood it
correctly.

235 He brought peace to myriad lands,
And continual years of abundance.
Heaven's bidding he never neglected.
Bold was King Wu,
Guarded and aided by his knights
He held his lands on every side.
Firmly he grounded his House.
Bright he shines in heaven,
Helping those that succeed him.

236   IT was King Wên that laboured;
       We, according to his work, receive.
       He spread his bounties;
       Ours now to make secure
       The destiny of this Chou.
       Oh, his bounties!

237   MIGHTY this people of Chou!
       It climbed those high hills,
       The narrow ridges, towering peaks;
       Followed gully and wide stream.
       To all that is under heaven
       Is linked as compeer
       The destiny of Chou.

Dynastic Legends

THE legend which follows becomes more interesting if we connect its main features with parallels that, though they are familiar, may not immediately spring to the mind of the reader.

The hero is born of a mother whose barrenness is removed by a miracle. We are reminded of another 'mother of nations,' Sarah of the Bible, and of numerous folk-stories which begin with a king and queen who are glorious in every other way, but have no child. They always end by having a child, who becomes the hero of the story.

Hou Chi's mother obtains a child by treading on the mark of God's big toe. We could, instead of God, translate *ti* by ancestor, meaning the spirit of a former king. Other versions of the story say 'a giant's tracks.' We are at once reminded that till recently childless women tried to remedy their condition by sitting upon the prehistoric figures of big men traced on chalky hills in various parts of England. The footprints of gods figure in many religions. Colossal footprints of Buddha were shown in several parts of North-Western India. Treading on a big toe can actually form part of the ritual of marriage, as, for example, among the Arapesh in New Guinea.[1]

The singularity of the hero is established by the fact that he was born of a barren or even of a virgin mother. It is confirmed by the fact that successive attempts to destroy him in infancy completely fail. Among famous infants upon whose lives fruitless attempts were made, either by exposure or other means, were Gilgamesh, Krishna, Moses, Cyrus, Oedipus, Ajātaśatru, Semiramis Queen of Assyria, and Pao Ssŭ, Queen of Chou.

[1] See Margaret Mead, *Sex and Temperament*, p. 95. For the bride to tread on the bridegroom's toe used to be a sort of ritual joke at German peasant weddings.

In our legend there are three successive attempts to get rid of the hero. This part of the stock heroic birth-legend was completely standardized and appears in almost identical sequence and rhythm in very widely separated parts of the world. Thus, to take a stray example, Prince Lal, a hero of a primitive Indian tribe, the Gonds, is put in the buffalo-shed. 'They hoped the buffaloes would trample upon him. But a buffalo suckled him, so they took him to the goat-shed,' and so on.[1] A first-century writer[2] tells how Tung-ming, hero of the Kokurye people in northern Korea, was 'thrown into the pigsty, but the pigs breathed upon him and he remained alive. Then they moved him to the stable, hoping that the horses would trample upon him; but the horses breathed upon him, and he did not die.'

In all such stories birds and animals (in our legend, sheep, oxen, and birds) help the child. They may even, as in the case of Romulus and Remus, act as foster-parents. But often there are also helpful humans, such as the woodcutters in our legend or Spaco and her husband in the Herodotean version of the Cyrus legend. Sometimes the human and animal foster-parents become confused. 'Spaco' is explained to mean bitch; yet in Herodotus' narrative she figures as a woman. Hou Chi, however, was more miraculous than Cyrus. He did not need foster-parents, but provided in the most enterprising way for his own needs.

[1] *Songs of the Forest*, Shamrad Hivale and Verrier Elwin, 1936.
[2] Wang Ch'ung in *Lun Hêng*, Chapter 100.

238 SHE who in the beginning gave birth to the
          people,
     This was Chiang Yüan.
     How did she give birth to the people?
     Well she sacrificed and prayed
     That she might no longer be childless.
     She trod on the big toe of God's footprint,
     Was accepted and got what she desired.
     Then in reverence, then in awe
     She gave birth, she nurtured;
     And this was Hou Chi.[1]

     Indeed, she had fulfilled her months,
     And her first-born came like a lamb
     With no bursting or rending,
     With no hurt or harm.
     To make manifest His magic power
     God on high gave her ease.
     So blessed were her sacrifice and prayer
     That easily she bore her child.

     Indeed, they put it in a narrow lane;
     But oxen and sheep tenderly cherished it.
     Indeed, they[2] put it in a far-off wood;
     But it chanced that woodcutters came to
          this wood.
     Indeed, they put it on the cold ice;
     But the birds covered it with their wings.
     The birds at last went away,
     And Hou Chi began to wail.

     Truly far and wide
     His voice was very loud.
     Then sure enough he began to crawl;

[1] 'Lord Millet.'
[2] The ballad does not tell us who exposed the child. According
to one version it was the mother herself; according to another, her
husband.

Well he straddled, well he reared,
To reach food for his mouth.
He planted large beans;
His beans grew fat and tall.
His paddy-lines were close set,
His hemp and wheat grew thick,
His young gourds teemed.

Truly Hou Chi's husbandry
Followed the way that had been shown.[1]
He cleared away the thick grass,
He planted the yellow crop.
It failed nowhere, it grew thick,
It was heavy, it was tall,
It sprouted, it eared,
It was firm and good,
It nodded, it hung—
He made house and home in T'ai.[2]

Indeed, the lucky grains were sent down to us,
The black millet, the double-kernelled,
Millet pink-sprouted and white.
Far and wide the black and the double-
        kernelled
He reaped and acred;[3]
Far and wide the millet pink and white
He carried in his arms, he bore on his back,
Brought them home, and created the sacrifice.

Indeed, what are they, our sacrifices?
We pound the grain, we bale it out,
We sift, we tread,
We wash it—soak, soak;

[1] By God. Compare No. 153, line 6.
[2] South-west of Wu-kung Hsien, west of Sianfu. Said to be
where his mother came from.
[3] The yield was reckoned per acre (100 ft. square).

We boil it all steamy.
Then with due care, due thought
We gather southernwood, make offering of fat,
Take lambs for the rite of expiation,
We roast, we broil,
To give a start to the coming year.

High we load the stands,
The stands of wood and of earthenware.
As soon as the smell rises
God on high is very pleased:
'What smell is this, so strong and good?'
Hou Chi founded the sacrifices,
And without blemish or flaw
They have gone on till now.

Hou Chi's son Pu-k'u retired to the 'land of the barbarians,' which presumably means that he settled farther north of the Wei. Pu-k'u's grandson, Liu the Duke,[1] brought the descendants of Hou Chi back to Pin.[2] The place-names on which I make no comment are, in my opinion, unidentifiable. Many expressions like 'wide plain,' 'southern ridge,' and so on, may in reality be place-names. I should like to quote here what a very distinguished Chinese geographer of the sixth century A.D., Li Tao-yüan,[3] wrote concerning the place-names of this district: 'Unfamiliar names of rivers and places are currently explained in a variety of different ways. Research in the classics and histories shows that these explanations could all be supported by one ancient authority or another. My own knowledge is too shallow, my experience too superficial to justify me in deciding such questions.'

> 239   STALWART was Liu the Duke,
> Not one to sit down or take his ease.
> He made borders, made balks,
> He stacked, he stored,
> He tied up dried meat and grain
> In knapsacks, in bags;
> Far and wide he gathered his stores.
> The bows and arrows he tested,
> Shield and dagger, halberd and battle-axe;
> And then began his march.
>
> Stalwart was Liu the Duke;
> He surveyed the people,
> They were numerous and flourishing,

[1] I write it thus to show that the title and the name are in the reverse of the usual order.

[2] This is usually placed to the north of the Ching; near Sanshui. But I think the word has a much wider sense and means the territory between the Ching and the Wei.

[3] A.D. 467–527.

He made his royal progress, proclaimed his
    rule;
There were no complaints, no murmurings
Either high up in the hills
Or down in the plains.
What did they carve for him?
Jade and greenstone
As pairs[1] and ends for his sheath.
Stalwart was Liu the Duke.
He reached the Hundred Springs
And gazed at the wide plain,
Climbed the southern ridge,
Looked upon the citadel,
And the lands for the citadel's army.
Here he made his home,
Here he lodged his hosts,
Here they were at peace with one another,
Here they lived happily with one another.

Stalwart was Liu the Duke
In his citadel so safe.
Walking deftly and in due order
The people supplied mats, supplied stools.
He went up to the dais and leant upon a stool.
Then to make the pig-sacrifice
They took a swine from the sty;
He poured out libation from a gourd,
Gave them food, gave them drink;
And they acknowledged him as their prince
    and founder.

Stalwart was Liu the Duke.
In his lands broad and long
He noted the shadows and the height of the
    hills,

    [1] Stones that hung in pairs.

Which parts were in the shade, which in the
    sun,
Viewed the streams and the springs.
To his army in three divisions
He allotted the low lands and the high,
Tithed the fields that there might be due
    provision,
Reckoning the evening sunlight,
And took possession of his home in Pin.

Stalwart was Liu the Duke.
He made his lodging in Pin,
But across the Wei River he made a ford,
Taking whetstones and pounding-stones.
He fixed his setttlement and set its boundaries;
His people were many and prosperous
On both sides of the Huang Valley,
And upstream along the Kuo Valley.
The multitudes that he had settled there
    grew dense;
They went on to the bend of the Jui.[1]

A large part of the human race believes that mankind
is descended from melon seeds. Dr. Alfred Kühn, in his
excellent book on the origin-myths of Indo-China,[2] men-
tions some twenty peoples who in one form or another
hold this belief. A quite superficial search supplied me
with two African examples.[3] I am told that the same
belief existed in North America. The general form of the
story in Indo-China is summarized by N. Matsumoto in

[1] The modern Black Water River, which flows into the Ching
from the west.

[2] *Berichte über den Weltanfang bei den Indochinesen*, Leipzig, 1935.

[3] Among the Shilluk of the Sudan and the Songo tribe of the
Congo. See H. Baumann, *Schöpfung und Urzeit des Menschen im
Mythus der Afrikanischen Völker.*

his *Mythologie Japonaise* as follows: 'The human race is destroyed by a flood. The only survivors are a brother and sister, miraculously saved in a pumpkin. Very reluctantly the brother and sister marry, and have as their offspring sometimes a pumpkin, whose seeds sown in mountain and plain give birth to the different races of man, sometimes a mass of flesh, which the man divides into 360 parts. . . .'

In ancient China, as in modern Indo-China, gourds were commonly used as lifebelts, and it is clear that in all these stories the gourd is merely a primitive equivalent to Noah's Ark.

The first line of the song which follows has always been taken as a simile, and no doubt it functions as one to-day. But in view of the facts mentioned above, it is most likely that imbedded in this line is an allusion to a forgotten belief that 'the people when they were first brought into being' were gourd seeds or young gourds. One has the impression, when reading the opening of this poem, that Tan-fu is an independent culture-hero, a rival, in fact, to Hou Chi. But tradition makes him a descendant of Hou Chi. He leads the people away from Pin, where their security is menaced by savage tribes, to Mount Ch'i, farther west.

The 'as yet they had no houses' of verse 1 does not mean that they were incapable of making houses, but that till their houses were ready they lived in loess-pits, as many inhabitants of Shensi still do permanently. Compare No. 294, last verse, where a migration is also referred to.

240 THE young gourds spread and spread.
The people after they were first brought into being
From the River Tu[1] went to the Ch'i.[2]

[1] i.e. the Wei.
[2] Not the Ch'i of No. 223, but another Lacquer River in western Shensi.

Of old Tan-fu the duke
Scraped shelters, scraped holes;
As yet they had no houses.

Of old Tan-fu the duke
At coming of day galloped his horses,
Going west along the river[1] bank
Till he came to the foot of Mount Ch'i.[2]
Where with the lady Chiang
He came to look for a home.

The plain of Chou was very fertile,
Its celery and sowthistle sweet as rice-cakes.
"Here we will make a start; here take
    counsel,
Here notch our tortoise."[3]
It says, "Stop," it says, "Halt.
Build houses here."

So he halted, so he stopped.
And left and right
He drew the boundaries of big plots and
    little,
He opened up the ground, he counted the
    acres
From west to east;
Everywhere he took his task in hand.

Then he summoned his Master of Works,
Then he summoned his Master of Lands
And made them build houses.
Dead straight was the plumb-line,
The planks were lashed to hold the earth;
They made the Hall of Ancestors, very
    venerable.

[1] The Wei.   [2] See No. 218.
[3] For taking omens with the tortoise, see W. Perceval Yetts: 'The Shang-Yin Dynasty and the An-yang Finds,' *Journal of the Royal Asiatic Society*, July 1933.

They tilted in the earth with a rattling,
They pounded it with a dull thud,
They beat the walls with a loud clang,
They pared and chiselled them with a faint
    p'ing, p'ing;
The hundred cubits all rose;
The drummers could not hold out.[1]

They raised the outer gate;
The outer gate soared high.
They raised the inner gate;
The inner gate was very strong.
They raised the great earth-mound,
Whence excursions of war might start.[2]

And in the time that followed they did not
    abate their sacrifices,
Did not let fall their high renown;
The oak forests were laid low,
Roads were opened up.
The K'un[3] tribes scampered away;
Oh, how they panted!

The peoples of Yü and Jui[4] broke faith,
And King Wên harried their lives.
This I will say, the rebels were brought to
    allegiance,
Those that were first were made last.
This I will say, there were men zealous in
    their tasks,
There were those that kept the insolent at
    bay.

[1] The drummers were there to set a rhythm for the workmen.
But they tired more quickly than the indefatigable builders.

[2] The shrine where the soldiers were 'sworn in' for the combat,
just as the Spanish rebels took vows at the tomb of the Cid before
marching upon Madrid.

[3] The same as the Dog Barbarians?   [4] In western Shensi.

241   KING WÊN is on high;
Oh, he shines in Heaven!
Chou is an old people,
But its charge is new.
The land of Chou became illustrious,
Blessed by God's charge.
King Wên ascends and descends
On God's left hand, on His right.

Very diligent was King Wên,
His high fame does not cease;
He spread his bounties in Chou,
And now in his grandsons and sons,
In his grandsons and sons
The stem has branched
Into manifold generations,
And all the knights of Chou
Are glorious in their generation.

Glorious in their generation,
And their counsels well pondered.
Mighty were the many knights
That brought this kingdom to its birth.
This kingdom well they bore;
They were the prop of Chou.
Splendid were those many knights
Who gave comfort to Wên the king.

August is Wên the king;
Oh, to be reverenced in his glittering light!
Mighty the charge that Heaven gave him.
The grandsons and sons of the Shang,[1]
Shang's grandsons and sons,
Their hosts were innumerable.
But God on high gave His command,
And by Chou they were subdued.

[1] The people overthrown by the Chou.

By Chou they were subdued;
Heaven's charge is not for ever.
The knights of Yin, big and little,
Made libations and offerings at the capital;
What they did was to make libations
Dressed in skirted robe and close cap.
O chosen servants of the king,
May you never thus shame your ancestors!

May you never shame your ancestors,
But rather tend their inward power,
That for ever you may be linked to Heaven's
  charge
And bring to yourselves many blessings.
Before Yin[1] lost its army
It was well linked to God above.
In Yin you should see as in a mirror
That Heaven's high charge is hard to keep.

The charge is not easy to keep.
Do not bring ruin on yourselves.
Send forth everywhere the light of your good
  fame;
Consider what Heaven did to the Yin.
High Heaven does its business
Without sound, without smell.
Make King Wên your example,
In whom all the peoples put their trust.

[1] Another name for the Shang.

242   MIGHTY is God on high,
Ruler of His people below;
Swift and terrible is God on high,
His charge has many statutes.
Heaven gives birth to the multitudes of the
        people,
But its charge cannot be counted upon.
To begin well is common;
To end well is rare indeed.

King Wên said, "Come!
Come, you Yin and Shang!
Why these violent men,
Why these slaughterers—
Why are they in office, why are they in power?
Heaven has sent down to you an arrogant
        spirit;
What you exalt is violence."

King Wên said, "Come!
Come, you Yin and Shang,
And hold fast to what is seemly and fitting;
Your violence leads to much resentment.
Slanders you support and further,
To brigands and thieves you give entry,
Who curse, who use evil imprecations,
Without limit or end."

King Wên said, "Come!
Come, you Yin and Shang!
You rage and seethe in the Middle Kingdom,
You count the heaping up of resentment as
        inward power;
You do not make bright your power,
So that none backs you, none is at your side.
No, your merit does not shine bright,
So that none cleaves to you nor comes to you."

King Wên said, "Come!
Come, you Yin and Shang!
Heaven did not flush you with wine.[1]
Not good are the ways you follow;
Most disorderly are your manners.
Not heeding whether it is dawn or dusk
You shout and scream,
Turning day into night."

King Wên said, "Come!
Come, you Yin and Shang!
You are like grasshoppers, like cicadas,
Like frizzling water, like boiling soup;
Little and great you draw near to ruin.
Men long to walk in right ways,
But you rage in the Middle Kingdom,
And as far as the land of Kuei."[2]

King Wên said, "Come!
Come, you Yin and Shang!
It is not that God on high did not bless you;
It is that Yin does not follow the old ways.
Even if you have no old men ripe in
        judgment,
At least you have your statutes and laws.
Why is it that you do not listen,
But upset Heaven's great charge?"

King Wên said, "Come!
Come, you Yin and Shang!

[1] The charge of drunkenness is continually brought against the
Shang. Possibly the Chou only used wine for sacrificial purposes,
whereas the Shang used it as an everyday beverage.
[2] In eastern Kansu?

There is a saying among men:
'When a towering tree crashes,
The branches and leaves are still unharmed;
It is the trunk that first decays.'
A mirror for Yin is not far off;
It is the times of the Lord of Hsia.''[1]

[1] The Yin destroyed the Hsia because of their wickedness, just as the Chou are now destroying the Yin.

It may be convenient here to give a table of Tan-fu's descendants, excluding those who are not mentioned in the songs.

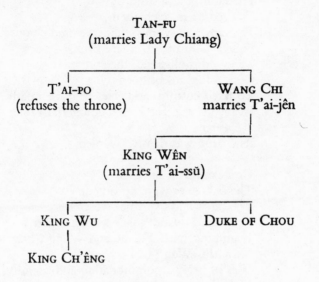

TAN-FU
(marries Lady Chiang)

T'AI-PO
(refuses the throne)

WANG CHI
marries T'ai-jên

KING WÊN
(marries T'ai-ssŭ)

KING WU

DUKE OF CHOU

KING CH'ÊNG

243   GOD on high in sovereign might
Looked down majestically,
Gazed down upon the four quarters,
Examining the ills of the people.
Already in two kingdoms[1]
The governance had been all awry;
Then every land
He tested and surveyed.
God on high examined them
And hated the laxity of their rule.
So he turned his gaze to the west
And here made his dwelling-place.

       [1] Hsia and Yin.

Cleared them, moved them,[1]
The dead trees, the fallen trunks;
Trimmed them, levelled them,
The clumps and stumps;
Opened them, cleft them,
The tamarisk woods, the stave-tree woods;
Pulled them up, cut them back,
The wild mulberries, the cudranias.
God shifted his bright Power;
To fixed customs and rules he gave a path.
Heaven set up for itself a counterpart on
        earth;
Its charge was firmly awarded.

God examined his hills.
The oak-trees were uprooted,
The pines and cypresses were cleared.
God made a land, made a counterpart,[2]
Beginning with T'ai-po and Wang Chi.
Now this Wang Chi
Was of heart accommodating and friendly,
Friendly to his elder brother,
So that his luck was strong.
Great were the gifts that were bestowed upon
        him,
Blessings he received and no disasters,
Utterly he swayed the whole land.

Then came King Wên;
God set right measure to his thoughts,
Spread abroad his fair fame;
His power was very bright,
Very bright and very good.
Well he led, well lorded,

[1] The subject of these verbs is 'the people of Chou.' Possibly
there is a lacuna in the text.
[2] i.e. a king below, as God is King above.

Was king over this great land.
Well he followed, well obeyed,
Obeyed—did King Wên.
His power was without flaw.
Having received God's blessing
He handed it down to grandsons and sons.

God said to King Wên:
'This is no time to be idle,
No time to indulge in your desires.
You must be first to seize the high places.
The people of Mi[1] are in revolt.
They have dared to oppose the great
    kingdom.
They have invaded Yüan and Kung.'
The king blazed forth his anger;
He marshalled his armies,
To check the foe he marched to Lü,[2]
He secured the safety of Chou,
He united all under Heaven.

They drew near to the capital,
Attacking from the borders of Yüan.
They began to climb our high ridges;
But never did they marshal their forces on
    our hills,
Our hills or slopes,
Never did they drink out of our wells,
Our wells, our pools.
The king made his dwelling in the foothills
    and plains,
Dwelt in the southern slopes of Mount Ch'i,
On the shores of the River Wei,
Pattern to all the myriad lands,
King of his subject peoples.

---

[1] In eastern Kansu.   [2] In eastern Kansu?

God said to King Wên,
'I am moved by your bright power.
Your high renown has not made you put on
    proud airs,
Your greatness has not made you change
    former ways,
You do not try to be clever or knowing,
But follow God's precepts.'
God said to King Wên,
'Take counsel with your partner states,
Unite with your brothers young and old,
And with your scaling ladders and siege-
    platforms
Attack the castles of Ch'ung.'[1]

The siege-platforms trembled,
The walls of Ch'ung towered high.
The culprits were bound quietly,
Ears were cut off[2] peacefully.
He made the sacrifice to Heaven and the
    sacrifice of propitiation.[3]
He annexed the spirits of the land, he secured
    continuance of the ancestral sacrifices,
And none anywhere dared affront him.
The siege-platforms shook,
So high were the walls of Ch'ung.
He attacked, he harried,
He cut off, he destroyed.
None anywhere dared oppose him.

[1] In Shênsi? But this is now disputed.

[2] To offer to the ancestors. We are told that the character means 'ears cut off'; but I suspect that, as its form would suggest, it originally meant 'heads cut off.'

[3] To the spirits of the soil over which he rode. Compare No. 262.

The Magic Tower was built by King Wên near his capital at Hao, close to the modern Sianfu. The Moated Mound was a holy place surrounded by water, where the sons of the Chou royal house were trained in the accomplishments of manhood. We have no reason to suppose that the young men were ever segregated there or that the Moated Mound in any way corresponds to the Men's Houses and Initiation Houses of contemporary primitives. Manhood initiation in ancient China was, so far as we have any knowledge of it, a very mild affair, not unlike Christian confirmation. An inscription[1] describes an early Chou king as boating on the waters of the Moated Mound, where he shoots a large wild-goose. The Lord of Hsing, who follows him in a 'boat with red banners,' gives the bird a *coup de grâce*, which suggests that the king had only managed to wing it.

244 WHEN he built the Magic Tower,
      When he planned it and founded it,
      All the people worked at it;
      In less than a day they finished it.

      When he built it, there was no goading;
      Yet the people came in their throngs.
      The king was in the Magic Park,
      Where doe and stag lay hid.

      Doe and stag at his coming leapt and
           bounded;
      The white herons gleamed so sleek.
      The king was by the Magic Pool,
      Where the fish sprang so lithe.

[1] Karlgren, B. 14.

On the upright posts and cross-beams with
    their spikes
Hang the big drums and gongs.
Oh, well-ranged are the drums and gongs,
And merry is the Moated Mound.

Oh, well-ranged are the drums and gongs!
And merry is the Moated Mound.
Bang, bang go the fish-skin drums;
The sightless and the eyeless[1] ply their skill.

245   GREAT dignity had T'ai-jên,
The mother of King Wên;
Well loved was Lady Chiang of Chou,
Bride of the high house.
And T'ai-ssŭ carried on her fair name,
Bearing a multitude of sons.

He[2] was obedient to the ancestors of the
    clan,
So that the Spirits were never angry;
So that the Spirits were never grieved.
He was a model to his chief bride;
A model to his brothers old and young,
And in his dealings with home and land.

Affable was he in the palace,
Reverent in the ancestral hall,
Glorious and regarded by Heaven,
Causing no discontent, protected by Heaven.
Therefore war and sickness did not destroy,
Nor plague nor witchcraft work havoc.

[1] i.e. blind musicians.
[2] King Wu, traditional date 1122–1116 B.C.

Without asking, he knew what was the rule;
Without being admonished, he admitted.[1]
Therefore grown men could use their Inward
     Power,
And young people could find work to do.
The ancient were well content;
And the doughty well employed.

246   BRIGHT they shone on earth below,
Majestic they blaze on high.
Heaven cannot be trusted;
Kingship is easily lost.
Heaven set up a foe to match the Yin;
Did not let them keep their frontier lands.

Chung-shih Jên of Chih[2]
From those Yin and Shang
Came to marry in Chou,
To be a bride in the capital,
And with Chi the king[3]
She joined in works of power.

Ta'i-jên became big with child;
She bore this King Wên.
Now this King Wên
Was very circumspect and reverent,
Toiled to serve God on high.
He received many blessings,
His inward power never failed
To protect his frontiers, his realms.

---

[1] The wise to his counsel? But the whole verse is probably corrupt.

[2] T'ai-jên. She was presumably the daughter of a Shang grandee.

[3] Wang Chi.

Heaven gazed below;
Saw that its charge had been fulfilled,
King Wên had begun his task.
Heaven made for him a match,
To the north of the River Ho,
On the banks of the Wei.

King Wên was blessed.
A great country had a child,
A great country had a child
Fair as a sister of Heaven.
King Wên fixed on a lucky day
And went himself to meet her at the Wei;
He joined boats and made of them a bridge;
Very dazzling their splendour.

There came a command from Heaven
Ordering this King Wên
In Chou, in his capital,
To give the succession to a Lady Hsin,[1]
The eldest of her family;
Who bravely bore King Wu.
'Heaven's protection and help are allotted to
    you
To assail the great Shang.'

The armies of Yin and Shang—
Their catapults were like the trees of a
    forest.
They marshalled their forces at Mu-yeh:[2]
A target set up for us.
'God on high is watching you;
Let no treachery be in your hearts.'

---

[1] Or Shên; near Ho-yang, eastern Shensi. To give her succession
as queen.
[2] In northern Honan, near the Shang capital.

The field of Mu-yeh spread far,
The war chariots gleamed,
The team of white-bellies was tough,
The captain was Shang-fu;[1]
Like an eagle he uprose.[2]
Ah, that King Wu
Swiftly fell upon Great Shang,
Who before daybreak begged for a truce.

247 RENOWNED was King Wên,
Yes, high was his renown.
He united, he gave peace;
Manifold were his victories.
Oh, glorious was King Wên!

King Wên received Heaven's bidding
To do these deeds of war.
He attacked Ch'ung;
He made his capital in Fêng.[3]
Oh, glorious was King Wên!

He built his castle within due boundaries,
He made Fêng according to the ancient plan.
He did not fulfil his own desires,
But worked in pious obedience to the dead.
Oh, glorious our sovereign and king!

Splendid were the works of the king.
Within the walls of Fêng
All the peoples came together.
A sure buckler was our sovereign and king.
Oh, glorious our sovereign and king!

[1] Known also as T'ai Kung Wang; one of the companions of
King Wu.
[2] Very likely corrupt.   [3] West of Sianfu, Shensi.

The Fêng River flowed to the East
In the course made for it by Yü,[1]
Meeting-place for all the peoples.
A pattern was our great king.
Oh, glorious our great king!

To the capital at Hao, to the Moated Mound,
From west, from east,
From south, from north—
There were none that did not surrender.
Oh, glorious the great king!

Omens he took, our king,
Before the building of the capital at Hao;
The tortoise[2] directed it;
King Wu perfected it.
Oh, glorious was King Wu!

By the Fêng River grew white millet.[3]
How should King Wu not be continued?
He bequeathed his teachings and counsels
That they might give peace and protection
        to his sons.
Oh, glorious was King Wu!

[1] See No. 144.   [2] Cf. No. 240.
[3] I should imagine that it grew unplanted and was a portent.
There are many similar portents in Chinese legend.

248 CHOU it is that continues the footsteps here
    below.
From generation to generation it has had wise
    kings.
Three rulers are in Heaven,
And the king[1] is their counterpart in his
    capital.

He is their counterpart in his capital,
The power of generations he has matched;
Long has he been mated to Heaven's command
And fulfilled what is entrusted to a king.

Has fulfilled what is entrusted to a king,
A model to all on earth below;
Forever pious towards the dead,
A very pattern of piety.

Loved is this One Man,
Meeting only with docile powers;[2]
Forever pious towards the dead,
Gloriously continuing their tasks.

Yes, gloriously he steps forward
Continuing in the footsteps of his ancestors.
'For myriads of years
May you receive Heaven's blessing!

Receive Heaven's blessing!'
So from all sides they come to wish him well.
'For myriads of years
May your luck never fail!'

[1] If we count Wên, Wu, and Ch'êng as the three kings, then
this is K'ang (1078-53). But I doubt if the song is as early as that.
[2] With obedient *tê*; i.e. with obedience.

249 THICK grow the oak clumps;
We make firewood of them, we stack them.
Great is the magnificence of the lord king;
On either hand are those that speed for him.

Great is the magnificence of the lord king;
On either hand are those that hold up
        sceptres before him,
Hold up sceptres in solemn state,
As befits doughty knights.

Spurt goes that boat on the Ching;
A host of oarsmen rows it.
When the King of Chou goes forth,
His six armies are with him.

How it stands out, the Milky Way,
Making a blazon in the sky!
Long life to the King of Chou,
And a portion for his people![1]

Chiselled and carved are his emblems,
Of bronze and jade are they made.
Ceaseless are the labours of our king
Fashioning the network of all the lands.

[1] Cf. No. 201.

250 OH, merry the waves of the P'an;
Come, pluck the water-cress.
The Lord of Lu has come;
See, there are his banners.
His banners flutter,
His bells tinkle.
Both little and great
Follow our duke on his way.

Oh, merry the waves of the P'an;
Come, pluck the water-grass.
The Lord of Lu has come
With his steeds so strong.
His steeds so strong,
His fame so bright.
He glances, he smiles,
Very patiently he teaches us.

Oh, merry the waves of the P'an;
Come, pluck the water-mallows.
The Lord of Lu has come,
By the P'an he is drinking wine.
He has drunk the sweet wine
That will give him youth unending;
Following those fixed ways
He assembles the thronging herds.[1]

Reverent is the Lord of Lu,
Scrupulously he keeps his power bright,
Attentively he carries out every attitude
and pose,

[1] Of his guests? Meaning very uncertain. Comparison with No. 262, verse one, suggests that they must be animals; or war-captives?

This is a song of the people of Lu, Confucius's home land. The next six pieces are imitations of the Chou ballads and with the exception of No. 252 make very heavy reading.

A model to his people.
In peace truly admirable and in war,
Casting radiance on his noble ancestors,
Pious towards them in all things,
Bringing upon himself nought but blessings.

Illustrious is the Lord of Lu,
Well he causes his power to shine.
He has made the palace on the P'an,
Where the tribes of Huai come to submit.
Valiant the tiger-slaves[1]
At P'an, offering the severed ears;
Our lord questions skilfully as Kao-yao,[2]
While at P'an they offer the captives.

Magnificent the many knights
Who well have spread the power of his
          desires,
Valiant on the march
They trimmed the tribes of the south-east.
Doughty and glorious,
Yet not bragging or boasting,
Not sharp in contention
By the P'an they announce their deeds.

'Our horn[3] bows were springy,
Our sheaves of arrows whizzed;
Our war-chariots were very steady,
Foot-soldiers and riders were untiring.
We have quite conquered the tribes of Huai;

---

[1] Military officers.
[2] Legendary judge, whose portrait in after days was hung in law-courts. His name means 'drum,' or 'drum-post.'
[3] This expression evidently implies that horn entered into the composition of the bow; but whether as a strengthening to the tip or as part of the substance of the arc we do not know.

They are very quiet, they have ceased to
 resist.
We have carried out your plans;
The tribes of Huai have all been dealt with.'

Fluttering, that owl on the wing
Has roosted in the woods of P'an;
It is eating our mulberry fruits,
Drawn by the lure of our fame.
From afar those tribes of Huai
Come with tribute of their treasures,
Big tortoises, elephant-tusks,
And great store of southern gold.[1]

251   HOLY is the Closed Temple,
Vast and mysterious;
Glorious was Chiang Yüan,
Her power was without flaw.
God on high succoured her;
Without hurt, without harm,
Fulfilling her months, but not late,
She bore Hou Chi,
Who brought down many blessings,
Millet for wine, millet for cooking, the early
 planted and the late planted,
The early ripening and the late ripening,
 beans and corn.
He took possession of all lands below,
Setting the people to husbandry.
They had their millet for wine, their millet
 for cooking,
Their rice, their black millet.

[1] 'Chin' may well not mean 'gold.' But archaeological evidence
is not at present so complete that we can exclude all possibility of
'gold' being mentioned *circa* 650, the probable date of this poem.

He took possession of all the earth below,
Continuing the work of Yü.[1]

Descendant of Hou Chi
Was the Great King
Who lived on the southern slopes of Mount
      Ch'i
And began to trim the Shang.
Till at last came King Wên and King Wu,
And continued the Great King's task,
Fulfilled the wrath of Heaven
In the field of Mu:
'No treachery, no blundering!
God on high is watching you.'
He overthrew the hosts of Shang,
He completed his task.
The king said, 'Uncle,[2]
Set up your eldest son,
Make him lord in Lu;
Open up for yourself a great domain,
To support the house of Chou.'

So he caused the Duke of Lu
To be lord of the east,
Gave him the hills and streams,
Lands, fields, dependencies.
The descendant of the Duke of Chou,
Son of Duke Chuang[3]
With dragon-painted banners made smoke-
      offering and sacrifice,
His six reins so glossy,
At spring and autumn most diligent,
In offering and sacrifice never failing:
'Very mighty is the Lord God,
A mighty ancestor is Hou Chi.'

[1] See No. 144.   [2] The Duke of Chou.   [3] Duke Hsi, 659–627 B.C.

Of a tawny bull we make offering;
It is accepted, it is approved,
Many blessings are sent down.
The Duke of Chou is a mighty ancestor;
Surely he will bless you.
In autumn we offer the first-fruits;
In summer we bind the thwart[1]
Upon white bull and upon tawny.
In many a sacrificial vase
Is roast pork, mince, and soup.
The vessels of bamboo and of wood are on
    the great stand;
The Wan dance is very grand.
To the pious descendant comes luck;
The ancestors have made you blaze, made
    you glorious,
Long-lived and good;
Have guarded that eastern realm.
The land of Lu shall be for ever,
Shall not crack or crumble,
Shall not shake or heave.
In long life you shall be Orion's peer,[2]
Steady as the ridges and hills.
A thousand war-chariots has the duke,
Red tassels, green lashings,
The two lances, bow lashed to bow,
His footmen thirty thousand;
Their helmets hung with shells on crimson
    strings.
Many footmen pressing on
Have faced the tribes of Jung and Ti,[3]

[1] A bar placed on the horns, to mark the animals as sacrificial.

[2] Similar formulae are very common on bronze inscriptions. See additional notes.

[3] The Jung tribes raided the Chou capital in 649; the Ti attacked Central China at a number of different points towards the middle of the seventh century.

Have given pause to Ching and Hsü,[1]
None dares resist us.
The ancestors shall make you glorious, shall
    make you blaze,
Shall make you long-lived and rich,
Till locks are sear and back is bent;
An old age easy and agreeable.
They shall make you glorious and great,
Make you settled and secure,
For thousands upon ten thousands of years;
Safe you shall live for evermore.

To Mount T'ai that towers so high
The land of Lu reaches.
He took Kuei and Mêng,[2]
Then he laid hands on the Greater East,[3]
As far as the coast lands.
The tribes of the Huai River came to terms,
There were none that did not obey.
Such were the deeds of the Lord of Lu.

In his protection are Fu and I;[4]
In his hold the realms of Hsü
As far as the coast lands.
The tribes of Huai, the Muan, and the Mo,
And those tribes of the south—
There are none that do not obey,
None that dare refuse assent.
All have submitted to the Lord of Lu.

----

[1] Ching are the southern people known later as Ch'u. The Hsü (in south-west Shantung and Anhui) were regarded as non-Chinese; but at this period often fought in alliance with the Chinese. We know from the *Tso Chuan* that Duke Hsi took part in an expedition against Ch'u in 656 B.C.

[2] Two hills near the T'ai-shan. 'He' is Duke Hsi.

[3] See on No. 284.

[4] Hills in southern-central Shantung.

Heaven gives the duke its deepest blessings.
In hoary age he has protected Lu,
He has made settlements in Ch'ang and Hsü,[1]
Restored the realm of the Duke of Chou.
Let the Lord of Lu feast and rejoice,
With his noble wife, his aged mother,
Bringing good to ministers and commoners,
Prosperity to his land and realm.
Very many blessings he has received;
In his time of sere locks he has cut new
  teeth!

The pines of Mount Ch'u-lai,[2]
The cypresses of Hsin-fu[3]
Were cut, were measured
Into cubits, into feet.
The roof-beams of pine-wood stick far out,
The great chamber is very vast,
The new shrine very large,
That Hsi-ssŭ made;
Very long and huge;
Whither all the peoples come in homage.

 This, too, is a ballad of the people of Lu, the home of
Confucius. Some critics make out that the last line but
two must be interpreted 'Hsi-ssŭ made this song.' Such a
meaning can only be got by altering the text. Hsi-ssŭ was
a son of Huan, Duke of Lu (711–694 B.C.). This is a
Court poem and very much exaggerates the military and
political importance of Lu at this time.

[1] Western Shantung.
[2] Hills near the present Taian Fu.
[3] Also near Taian Fu.

The next song is traditionally supposed to have been made by K'o, Grand Scribe of Lu, who flourished about 609 B.C., but lived on a considerable time later. The most natural explanation of it is to suppose that the Lu people had received a gift of horses (possibly from the Chou State), just as the people of Wei received such a gift from Duke Huan of Ch'i, as we shall see in No. 256.

252   STOUT and strong our stallions
In the paddock meadows;
Look what strong ones!
There is piefoot and brownie,
Blackie and bay,
Fine horses for the chariot.
O that for ever
We may have horses so good!

Stout and strong our stallions
In the paddock meadows;
Look what strong ones!
Brown and white, grey and white,
Chestnut, dapple-grey,
Sturdy horses for the chariot.
O that for all time
We may have horses of such fettle!

Stout and strong our stallions
In the paddock meadows;
Look what strong ones!
Scaly coat, white with black mane,
Roan with black mane, darkie with white
    mane,
Fleet horses for the chariot.
O untiring
May these horses breed!

Stout and strong our stallions
In the paddock meadows;
Look what strong ones!
Grey and white, ruddy and white,
White shank, wall-eye,
Powerful horses for the chariot.
O without slip
May these horses sire!

The next three ballads were made about the seventh century B.C. by the people of Sung, who were regarded as the descendants of the Shang. That the Shang were fundamentally different in origin from the Chou is suggested by the fact that they had a quite different type of origin myth. The Shang were descended from a lady called Chien Ti, into whose mouth the 'dark bird' (the swallow) dropped an egg. This is the typical eastern Chinese origin myth. The ruling family of Ch'in, which came from eastern China, gave an almost identical account of their origin. In the origin story of the Manchus a magpie drops a red fruit. In some Korean stories the egg is exposed just as the child is in the story of Hou Chi, and in succession dogs, pigs, cattle, horses, birds, so far from doing it injury, vie with one another in guarding and fostering it.

253   HEAVEN bade the dark bird
To come down and bear the Shang,
Who dwelt in the lands of Yin so wide.
Of old God bade the warlike T'ang[1]
To partition the frontier lands.
To those lands was he assigned as their lord;
Into his keeping came all realms.

[1] Legendary date, c. 1760 B.C.

The early lords of Shang
Received a charge that was never in peril.
In the time of Wu Ting's[1] grandsons and
    sons,
Wu Ting's grandsons and sons,
Warlike kings ever conquered,
With dragon-banners and escort of ten
    chariots.
Great store of viands they offered,
Even their inner domain was a thousand
    leagues;
In them the people found sure support.
They opened up new lands as far as the four
    seas.
Men from the four seas came in homage,
Came in homage, crowd on crowd;
Their[2] frontier was the river.
Yin received a charge that was all good;
Many blessings Yin bore.

[1] Legendary date, *c.* 1300.
[2] i.e. the Yin frontier.

254 DEEP and wise was Shang,
Always furthering its good omens.
The waters of the Flood spread wide.
Yü ranged lands and realms on earth below;
Beyond, great kingdoms were his frontier,
And when this far-flung power had been
    made lasting
The clan of Sung[1] was favoured;
God appointed its child to bear Shang.

The dark king[2] valiantly ruled;
The service of small states everywhere he
    received,
The service of great States everywhere he
    received.
He followed the precepts of ritual and did not
    overstep them;
He obeyed the showings of Heaven and carried
    them out.
Hsiang-t'u[3] was very glorious;
Beyond the seas he ruled.

God's appointment did not fail;
In the time of T'ang it was fulfilled.
T'ang came down in his due time,
Wise warnings daily multiplied,
Magnificent was the radiance that shone below.
God on high gazed down;
God appointed him to be a model to all the
    lands.
He received the big statutes, the little statutes,
He became a mark and signal to the lands
    below.

[1] From whom sprang Chien-ti, the ancestors of the Shang.
[2] Ch'i, child of the lady who swallowed the egg.
[3] Grandson of Ch'i.

He bore the blessing of Heaven,
Neither violent nor slack,
Neither hard nor soft.
He spread his ordinances in gentle harmony,
A hundred blessings he gathered upon himself.

Great laws and little laws he received,
He became great protector of the lands below.
He bore the favour of Heaven.
Far and wide he showed his valour,
Was never shaken or moved,
Never feared nor trembled;
A hundred blessings he united in himself.

The warlike king gave the signal;
Firmly he grasped his battle-axe,
His wrath blazed like a fire.
None dare do us injury.
The stem had three sprouts;[1]
None prospered nor grew.
All the regions were subdued;
Wei and Ku were smitten,
K'un-wu, and Chieh of Hsia.[2]

Of old, in the middle time,
There were tremblings and dangers.
But truly Heaven cherished us;
It gave us a minister,[3]
A true 'holder of the balance,'
Who succoured the King of Shang.

[1] The 'three sprouts' must have been three kindred enemies, but who they were we do not know.

[2] Hsia was the dynasty that T'ang the Victorious overthrew. We know very little about Wei, Ku, etc.

[3] The famous I Yin, who is connected with the Shang version of the deluge myth.

255 SWIFTLY those warriors of Yin
Rushed to the onslaught upon Ching and Ch'u,
Entered deep into their fastnesses,
Captured the hosts of Ching,
Divided and ruled their places;
Such was the work of T'ang's descendants.

O you people of Ching and Ch'u,
You must have your home in the southern
    parts.
Long ago there was T'ang the Victorious;
Of those Ti and Ch'iang[1]
None dared not to make offering to him,
None dared not to acknowledge him their
    king,
Saying, 'Shang for ever!'

Heaven bade the many princes
To make the capital where Yü wrought his
    work.[2]
The produce of the harvest they brought in
    homage:
'Do not scold or reprove us;
We have not been idle in our husbandry.'

At Heaven's bidding they[3] looked down;
The peoples below were awed,
There were no disorders, no excesses;
They dared not be idle or pause.
Heaven's charge was upon the lands below,
Firmly were their blessings planted and
    established.

[1] These are different Ti from the ones mentioned above. They and the Ch'iang were related to the Tibetans.
[2] In the lands rescued by the great Yü from the flood.
[3] The Ancestors.

Splendid was the capital of Shang,
A pattern to the peoples on every side,
Glorious was its fame,
Great indeed its magic power,
Giving long life and peace,
And safety to us that have come after.

They climbed yon Mount Ching[1]
Where the pines and cypresses grew thick.
They cut them, they carried them,
Square-hewed them upon the block.
The beams of pine-wood stuck out far,
Mighty were the ranged pillars.
The hall was finished; all was hushed and still.

[1] In northern Honan. This ballad, ending with the building of
a palace, is very similar to No. 251. It is not clear whether the palace
here referred to is one built by the men of Shang in old days or one
built by the men of Sung, their successors, about the seventh
century B.C.

Building

IN 658 B.C. the people of Wei, continually harassed by the Ti tribes, were forced to abandon their capital north of the Yellow River, in northern Honan, and transfer it to the southern enclave of Hopei that runs in a narrow strip between Shantung and Honan. In their move they were assisted and protected by Duke Huan of Ch'i, who sent a gift of three hundred horses,[1] presumably because most of the Wei people's horses had been captured by the Ti. The following song describes the building of the new capital. We do not know its exact site, nor what is meant by 'T'ang' and the 'Ching hills.'

256   THE Ting-star[2] is in the middle of the sky;
We begin to build the palace at Ch'u.
Orientating them by the rays of the sun
We set to work on the houses at Ch'u,
By the side of them planting hazels and
        chestnut-trees,
Catalpas, Pawlownias, lacquer-trees
That we may make the zitherns great and
        small.

We climb to that wilderness
To look down at Ch'u,
To look upon Ch'u and T'ang,
Upon the Ching hills and the citadel.
We go down and inspect the mulberry
        orchards,
We take the omens and they are lucky,
All of them truly good.

[1] *Kuo Yü* (Ch'i Yü). Multiplied in this song to three thousand.
[2] Part of Pegasus; also called the Building Star.

A magical rain is falling.
We order our grooms
By starlight, early, to yoke our steeds;
We drive to the mulberry-fields and there we
    rest.
Those are men indeed!
They hold hearts that are staunch and true.
They have given us mares three thousand.

257   CEASELESS flows that beck,
    Far stretch the southern hills.
    May you be sturdy as the bamboo,
    May you flourish like the pine,
    May elder brother and younger brother
    Always love one another,
    Never do evil to one another.

    To give continuance to foremothers and
        forefathers
    We build a house, many hundred cubits of
        wall;
    To south and west its doors.
    Here shall we live, here rest,
    Here laugh, here talk.

    We bind the frames, creak, creak;
    We hammer the mud, tap, tap,
    That it may be a place where wind and rain
        cannot enter,
    Nor birds and rats get in,
    But where our lord may dwell.

    As a halberd, even so plumed,
    As an arrow, even so sharp,
    As a bird, even so soaring,

As wings, even so flying
Are the halls to which our lord ascends. [1]

Well levelled is the courtyard,
Firm are the pillars,
Cheerful are the rooms by day,
Softly gloaming by night,
A place where our lord can be at peace.

Below, the rush-mats; over them the
        bamboo-mats.
Comfortably he sleeps,
He sleeps and wakes
And interprets his dreams.
'Your lucky dreams, what were they?'
'They were of black bears and brown,
Of serpents and snakes.'

The diviner thus interprets it:
'Black bears and brown
Mean men-children.
Snakes and serpents
Mean girl-children.'

So he bears a son,
And puts him to sleep upon a bed,
Clothes him in robes,
Gives him a jade sceptre to play with.
The child's howling is very lusty; [2]
In red greaves shall he flare,
Be lord and king of house and home.

[1] This verse is corrupt and not intelligible with any certainty.
[2] *Huang*, 'lusty,' suggests the *huang*, 'flare' of the red greaves.
These could only be worn by the king's command and constituted
a decoration similar to our Garter. Women (see the next verse)
received no such marks of distinction.

Then he bears a daughter,
And puts her upon the ground,
Clothes her in swaddling-clothes,
Gives her a loom-whorl to play with.
For her no decorations, no emblems;
Her only care, the wine and food,
And how to give no trouble to father and
    mother.

Hunting

We have seen in No. 31 that the word 'field' (in Chinese, *t'ien*) is used for the scene of a hunter's activity, just as it is also used for the scene of the agriculturalist's labours. I take it that the word originally means to 'lay out,' 'arrange,' and that it was used in connection with the allotment of hunting-spheres of this or that person or tribe long before agriculture began to supplement the Chinese food-supply. Chinese society, like our own in past days, comprised two strata that were at radically different cultural levels. The gentlemen, after the introduction of agriculture, continued to be in the main hunters and fighters. It was their business to see that their lands were farmed, but it was not proper for them to take any personal part in the labours of the soil. The common people are wholly absorbed in agriculture, resent the enclosure for hunting purposes of land that might otherwise have been tilled, and can only with difficulty be lured into following their lords to battle.

258 Here come the hounds, ting-a-ling,
  And their master so handsome and good;
  The hounds, with double ring,
  Their master so handsome and brave.
  The hounds, with double hoop;
  Their master so handsome and strong.

259   CHOP, chop they cut the hardwood
And lay it on the river bank
By the waters so clear and rippling.
If we did not sow, if we did not reap,
How should we get corn, three hundred stack-
      yards?
If you did not hunt, if you did not chase,
One would not see all those badgers hanging
      in your courtyard.
No, indeed, that lord
Does not feed on the bread of idleness.

Chop, chop they cut cart-spokes
And lay them beside the river,
By the waters so clear and calm.
If we did not sow, if we did not reap,
How should we get corn, three hundred barns?
If you did not hunt, if you did not chase,
One would not see the king-deer hanging in
      your courtyard.
No, indeed, that lord
Does not eat the bread of idleness.

Chop, chop they cut wheels
And lay them on the lips of the river,
By the waters so clear and whimpling.
If we did not sow, if we did not reap,
How should we get corn, three hundred bins?
If you did not hunt, if you did not chase,
One would not see all those quails hanging in
      your courtyard.
No, indeed, that lord
Does not sup the sup of idleness.

260 His team of darkies pull well;
    The six reins in his hand
    The duke's well-loved son
    Follows his father to the hunt.

    Lusty that old stag,
    That stag so tall.
    The duke says: 'On your left!'
    He lets fly, and makes his hit.

    They hold procession through the northern
        park,
    Those teams so well trained,
    The light carts, bells at bridle;
    Greyhound, bloodhound inside.

261 Our chariots are strong,
    Our horses well matched.
    Team of stallions lusty
    We yoke and go to the east.

    Our hunting chariots are splendid,
    Our teams very sturdy.
    In the east are wide grasslands;
    We yoke, and a-hunting we go.

    My lord follows the chase
    With picked footmen so noisy,
    Sets up his banners, his standards,
    Far afield he hunts in Ao.

    We yoke those four steeds,
    The four steeds so big.
    Red greaves, gilded slippers—
    The meet has great glamour.

Thimbles and armlets are fitted,
Bows and arrows all adjusted,
The bowmen assembled
Help us to lift the game.

A team of bays we drive;
The two helpers do not get crossways,
Faultlessly are they driven,
While our arrows shower like chaff.

Subdued, the horses whinny;
Gently the banners wave.
'If footmen and riders are not orderly
The great kitchen will not be filled.'

My lord on his journeys
Without clamour wins fame.
Truly, a gentleman he;
In very truth, a great achievement.

262 A LUCKY day, fifth of the week;[1]
     We have made the sacrifice of propitiation,[2]
          we have prayed.
     Our hunting chariots so lovely,
     Our four steeds so strong,
     We climb that high hill
     Chasing the herds of game.

     A lucky day, seventh of the cycle;[3]
     We have picked our steeds.
     Here the beasts congregate,
     Doe and stag abound,
     Along the Ch'i and Chü,[4]
     The Son of Heaven's domain.

     Look there, in the midst of the plain,
     Those big ones, very many!
     Scampering, sheltering,
     Some in herds, some two by two.
     We lead hither all our followers,
     Anxious to please the Son of Heaven.

     We have drawn our bows;
     Our arrows are on the bowstring.
     We shoot that little boar,
     We fell that great wild ox.
     So that we have something to offer, for
          guest, for stranger,
     To go with the heavy wine.

          [1] The ten-day week.
          [2] Compare No. 243, verse 8.
          [3] Sixty-day cycle.
          [4] North-east of the Chou capital.

As the pieces connected with hunting are very few, I
have supplemented them with a song from the so-
called 'Stone Drum' inscriptions. The date of these in-
scriptions is much disputed; but the songs themselves
must surely be contemporary with the similar pieces in
the *Book of Songs*. That is to say, they must date from
about the eighth century B.C.

> Our chariots are strong,
> Our horses well-matched,
> Our chariots are lovely,
> Our horses are sturdy;
> Our lord goes a-hunting, goes a-sporting.
> The does and deer so fleet
> Our lord seeks.
> Our horn[1] bows are springy;
> The bow-string we hold.[2]
> We drive the big beasts.
> They come with thud of hoofs; come in
>   great herds.
> Now we drive, now we stop.
> The doe and deer tread warily.
> They come big . . .[3]
> We drive the tall ones;
> They come charging headlong.
> We have shot the strongest of all, have
>   shot the tallest.

[1] See above, No. 250.
[2] Sense very doubtful.
[3] One character is indecipherable.

Friendship

263   Even the rising waters
Will not carry off thorn-faggots that are
well bound.
Brothers while life lasts
Are you and I.
Do not believe what people say;
People are certainly deceiving you.

Even the rising waters
Will not carry off firewood that is well
tied.
Brothers while life lasts
Are we two men.
Do not believe what people say;
People are certainly not to be believed.

264   In your lamb's wool and cuffs of leopard's
fur
From people like me you hold aloof.
Of course, I have other men;
But only you belong to old days.

In your lamb's wool and sleeves of leopard's
fur
To people like me you are unfriendly.
Of course, I have other men;
But it is only you that I love.

This, of course, may be a love song, just as several of
the songs at the beginning of the book may really be
songs of friendship.

265 How splendid he was!
      Yes, he met me between the hills of Nao.[1]
      Our chariots side by side we chased two
          boars.
      He bowed to me and said I was very nimble.

      How strong he was!
      Yes, he met me on the road at Nao.
      Side by side we chased two stags.
      He bowed to me and said 'well done.'

      How magnificent he was!
      Yes, he met me on the south slopes of Nao.
      Side by side we chased two wolves.
      He bowed to me and said 'that was good.'

[1] In northern Shantung.

Moral Pieces

I HAVE put in this class six songs which are wholly devoted to moral instruction; but there are naturally in other songs, too, many passages which give us information about early Chinese morality. If we put together these moral songs and scattered maxims, we see at once that there was no conception of a human morality, of abstract virtues incumbent upon all men irrespective of their social standing, but only an insistence that people of a certain class should fulfil certain rites and maintain certain attitudes. The chief duty of the gentleman is to be dignified[1] and so inspire respect in the common people. There is great emphasis on the relationship of brothers. But what is enjoined is a general harmony; there is no such insistence on the submission of the younger brother to the elder as we find in Confucianism. *Hsiao* ('filial piety') means tendence of the dead. I do not think there is any clear case in the *Songs* of its meaning devotion to living parents, as it constantly does in later times. Confucius protested against the idea that 'filial piety' meant 'feeding one's parents.' But in the *Songs* this is the one filial duty which is continually harped upon, and one of the main miseries of war was that it interfered with this sacred duty.

Jên, 'being a man,' the highest moral quality in all Confucian writings, barely figures in the *Songs*. Twice (in Nos. 30 and 258) it is coupled with *mei*, 'handsome,' and merely means 'good' in the most general sense. Once[2] it is coupled with 'reverent.' We are still far indeed from the days when *jên* was elevated to the rank of a magical, compelling power, by the use of which great kingdoms were founded and maintained. The people who wrote the *Songs* believed that empires

---

[1] And tidy; to keep his premises neat and clean.
[2] No. 271, verse 9. Here written, however, simply as 'man,' without the two extra strokes.

were won by catapults and battering-rams, at the command
of God.

266   On the wall there is star-thistle;
It must not be swept away.[1]
What is said within the fence[2]
May not be disclosed.
But what could be disclosed[3]
Was filthy as tale can be.

On the wall there is star-thistle;
It must not be cleared away.
What is said within the fence
May not be reported in full.
But what could be reported in full
Was lewd as tale can be.

On the wall there is star-thistle;
It must not be bundled for firewood.
What is said within the fence
May not be openly recited.
But what could be recited
Was shameful as tale can be.

[1] Because its prickles keep out intruders.
[2] i.e. at the secret hearing of love-disputes.
[3] The matrimonial dispute here referred to is traditionally sup-
posed to have taken place in Wei, about 699 B.C. See additional
notes.

267   THE guests are taking their seats;[1]
      To left, to right they range themselves.
      The food-baskets and dishes are in their
            rows,
      With dainties and kernels displayed.
      The wine is soft and good,
      It is drunk very peaceably.
      The bells and drums are set,
      The brimming pledge-cup is raised.
      The great target is put up,
      The bows and arrows are tested,
      The bowmen are matched.
      'Present your deeds of archery,
      Shoot at that mark
      That you may be rewarded with the cup.'

      Fluting they dance to reed-organ and drum,
      All the instruments perform in concert
      As an offering to please the glorious
            ancestors,
      That the rites may be complete.
      For when all the rites are perfect,
      Grandly, royally done,
      The ancestors bestow great blessings;
      Sons and grandsons may rejoice,
      May rejoice and make music:
      'Let each of you display his art.'
      The guests then receive the pledge-cup,
      The house-men enter anew
      And fill that empty cup,
      That you may perform your songs.

      When the guests first take their seats,
      How decorous they are, how reverent!
      While they are still sober
      Their manner is dignified and correct;

            [1] Literally, their mats.

But when they are drunk
Their manner is utterly changed.
They leave their seats and roam,
Cut capers, throw themselves about.
While they are still sober
Their manner is dignified and grave;
But when they are drunk
It becomes unseemly and rude;
For when people are drunk
They do not know what misdemeanours
  they commit.

When guests are drunk
They howl and bawl,
Upset my baskets and dishes,
Cut capers, lilt and lurch.
For when people are drunk
They do not know what blunders they
  commit.
Cap on one side, very insecure,
They cut capers lascivious.
If when they got drunk they went out,
They would receive their blessing like the
  rest.
But if they get drunk and stay,
The power of the feast is spoilt.
Drinking wine is very lucky,
Provided it is done with decency.

It is always the same when wine is drunk;
Some are tipsy, some are not.
So we appoint a master of ceremonies,
Or choose someone as recorder.
'That drunk man is not behaving nicely;
He is making the sober feel uncomfortable.
Pray do not mention at random

Things that do not belong together, that
    are quite silly.
What are not real words, do not say;
What leads nowhere, do not speak of,
Led on by drunkenness in your talk,
Bringing out "rams" and "hornless" side by
    side.
After the three cups[1] you don't know what
    you are saying;
What will become of you if you insist on
    taking more?'

268   PLIANT the horn bow;
    Swiftly its ends fly back.
    But brothers and kinsmen by marriage
    Ought not to keep their distance.

    If you are distant
    The common people will be so too;
    But if you set a good example
    The common people will follow it.

    These good brothers
    Are generous and forgiving;
    But bad brothers
    Do each other all the harm they can.

    Common people are not good;
    They turn their backs on one another, each
        his own way.
    He who has got the cup won't pass it on,
    Until there is already nothing left in it.

[1] The three ritual cups. To talk of a hornless ram is like talking
of a Manx cat's tail.

Like[1] the old horse that was changed into a
colt,
They don't look behind them.[2]
When they eat, it must be till they are
gorged,
When they pour out drink, they take huge
quantities.

Don't teach monkeys to climb trees,
Or put wet plaster on wet plaster.[3]
If gentlemen set good rules
The lesser folk will fall in with them.

Thick though the snow may have fallen,
When sunshine warms it, it melts.
But none of you offers to step down or
retire;
You remain proudly on high.

Fast though the snow may have fallen,
When sunshine warms it, it flows away.
That you should be so unseeing, so
purblind—
That is what makes me sad.

[1] 'Like' is not expressed in the original.
[2] i.e. don't consider those who come 'after them,' who have not
yet been served. The old horse, delighted by its own capers, did not
notice that the village boys were laughing at it 'behind its back.'
[3] The common people are bad enough already. Do not by your
bad example add fresh wickedness to their wickedness.

269   How the quails bicker,
       How the magpies snatch!
       Evil are the men
       Whom I must call 'brother.'

       How the magpies snatch,
       How the quails bicker!
       Evil are the men
       Whom I must call 'lord.'

270   LOOK at the rat; he has a skin.
       A man without dignity,
       A man without dignity,
       What is he doing, that he does not die?

       Look at the rat; he has teeth.
       A man without poise,
       A man without poise,
       What is he waiting for, that he does not
           die?

       Look at the rat; he has limbs.
       A man without manners,
       A man without manners[1]
       Had best quickly die.

---

[1] But *li* includes a great deal that we should call religion; for
example, sacrificing at the right time.

271 GRAVE and dignified manners
Are the helpmates of power.
Men indeed have a saying,
'There is none so wise but has his follies.'
But ordinary people's follies
Are but sicknesses of their own.
It is the wise man's follies
That are a rampant pest.

Nothing is so strong as goodness;
On all sides men will take their lesson
    from it.
Valid are the works of inward power;
In all lands men will conform to them.
He who takes counsel widely, is final in his
    commands,
Far-seeing in his plans, timely in the
    announcing of them,
Scrupulously attentive to decorum,
Will become a pattern to his people.

But those that rule to-day
Have brought confusion and disorder into
    the government;
Have upset their power
By wild orgies of drinking.
So engrossed are you in your dissipations
That you do not think of your heritage,
Do not faithfully imitate the former kings,
Or strive to carry out their holy ordinances.

Therefore mighty Heaven is displeased;
Beware lest headlong as spring waters
You should be swept to ruin.
Rise early, go to bed at night;
Sprinkle and sweep your courtyard
So that it may be a pattern to the people.

Put in good order your chariots and horses,
Bows, arrows, and weapons of offence,
That you may be ready, should war arise,
To keep at due distance barbaric tribes.

Ascertain the views of gentlemen and
          commoners,
Give due warning of your princely measures,
Take precautions against the unforeseen,
Be cautious in your utterances.
Scrupulously observe all rules of decorum,
Be always mild and good-tempered.
A scratch on a sceptre of white jade
Can be polished away;
A slip of the tongue
Cannot ever be repaired.

Do not be rash in your words,
Do not say: 'Let it pass.
Don't catch hold of my tongue!
What I am saying will go no further.'
There can be nothing said that has not its
          answer,
No deed of Power that has not its reward.
Be gracious to friends and companions
And to the common people, my child.
So shall your sons and grandsons continue
          for ever,
By the myriad peoples each accepted.

When receiving gentlemen of your
          acquaintance
Let your countenance be peaceable and mild;
Never for an instant be dissolute.
You are seen in your house;
You do not escape even in the curtained
          alcove.

Do not say: 'Of the glorious ones
None is looking at me.'
A visit from the Spirits
Can never be foreseen;
The better reason for not disgusting them.[1]

Prince, let the exercise of your inner power
Be good and blessed.
Be very careful in your conduct,
Be correct in your manners,
Never usurp or go beyond your rights,
And few will not take you as their model:
'She threw me a peach
And I requited it with a plum.'
That kid with horns[2]
Was truly a portent of disorder, my son!

Wood that is soft and pliant
We fit with strings.[3]
Reverence and goodness so mild
Are the foundations of inner power.
Mark how the wise man,
When I tell him of ancient sayings,
Follows the way of inner power.
Mark how the fool,
On the contrary, says that I am wrong,
And that everyone has a right to his ideas.

Alas, my son,
That you should still confuse right and
        wrong!
When I have not led you by the hand
I have pointed at the thing.
What I have not face to face declared to you

---

[1] Doing anything that would put them off from coming.
[2] Presumably a portent that had recently occurred.
[3] Make into zitherns.

I have hoarsely whispered in your ear.
You may say to me, 'You don't know';
But I am already a grandfather.
The people are short of supplies;
Who knew it early but deals with it late?

Oh, high Heaven so bright,
My life is most unhappy!
Seeing you so heedless
My heart is sorely grieved.
I instruct you in utmost detail;
But you listen to me very casually.
You do not treat my talks as lessons,
But on the contrary regard them as a joke.
You may say, 'You don't know';
But I am in truth a very old man.

Alas, my son,
What I tell to you are the ways of the
       ancients.
If you take my advice
You will have small cause to repent.
Heaven is sending us calamities,
Is destroying the country.
You have not far to go for an example;
High Heaven does not chop and change.
By perverting your inner power,
You will reduce your people to great
       extremities.

Lamentations

THERE are altogether about thirty-five 'lamentations,' some of them dealing with private grievances, but most of them bewailing the disorders and injustices of public life. This group is, from the general reader's point of view, by far the least interesting in the book, and I have omitted fifteen long political poems, which I have, however, discussed elsewhere.[1] They have one feature which requires explanation. The discontented poet[2] refers to the king, or more generally to those in power, under the cover-name 'god,' 'god on high.' The best example of this kind of poem is No. 288: 'God on high is very bright; don't burn yourself on him.' That in such cases 'god' is merely an ironical cover-name has been accepted by all interpreters and is certainly the case. This strikes us at first as rather strange. But there is a parallel in our own literature. Discontented public men who write memoirs use the phrase the 'powers that be' in just the same way. For example: 'I was now generally considered to be a strong candidate for the governorship of Blank; but the Powers that be willed otherwise.'

Mr. R. C. Trevelyan reminds me of Horace, *Satires*, II, 6, line 52: *Deos quoniam propius contingis*, where *deos* means 'the people in power.'

[1] In the Chinese magazine *T'ien-hsia*, October 1936.
[2] I think we may here reasonably say 'poet' and not 'singer,' for these may very well have been literary pieces from the start.

272 I GO out at the northern gate;
Deep is my grief.
I am utterly poverty-stricken and destitute;
Yet no one heeds my misfortunes.
Well, all is over now.
No doubt it was Heaven's doing,
So what's the good of talking about it?

The king's business came my way;
Government business of every sort was put
     upon me.
When I came in from outside
The people of the house all turned on me and
     scolded me.
Well, it's over now.
No doubt it was Heaven's doing,
So what's the good of talking about it?

The king's business was all piled upon me;
Government business of every sort was laid
     upon me.
When I came in from outside
The people of the house all turned upon me
     and abused me.
Well, it's over now.
No doubt it was Heaven's doing,
So what's the good of talking about it?

273   THAT wine-millet bends under its weight,
That cooking-millet is in sprout.
I go on my way, bowed down
By the cares that shake my heart.
Those who know me
Say, 'It is because his heart is so sad.'
Those who do not know me
Say, 'What is he looking for?'[1]
Oh, azure Heaven far away,
What sort of men can they be?

That wine-millet bends under its weight,
That cooking-millet is in spike.
I go on my way bowed down
By the cares that poison my heart within.
Those who know me
Say, 'It is because his heart is so sad.'
Those who do not know me
Say, 'What is he looking for?'
Oh, azure Heaven far away,
What sort of men can they be?

That wine-millet bends under its weight,
That cooking-millet is in grain.
I go on my way bowed down
By the cares that choke my heart within.
Those who know me
Say, 'It is because his heart is so sad.'
Those who do not know me
Say, 'What is he looking for?'
Oh, azure Heaven far away,
What sort of men can they be?

[1] Seeing his bowed head they think he is looking on the ground
for something he has dropped.

274 GINGERLY walked the hare,
But the pheasant was caught in the snare.
At the beginning of my life
All was still quiet;
In my latter days
I have met these hundred woes.[1]
Would that I might sleep and never stir!

Gingerly walked the hare;
But the pheasant got caught in the trap.
At the beginning of my life
The times were not yet troublous.
In my latter days
I have met these hundred griefs.
Would that I might sleep and wake no
        more!

Gingerly walked the hare;
But the pheasant got caught in the net.
At the beginning of my life
The times were still good.
In my latter days
I have met these hundred calamities.
Would that I might sleep and hear no
        more!

[1] The fall of the western Chou dynasty?

275   In the garden is a peach-tree;[1]
But its fruits are food.
It is my heart's sadness
That makes me chant and sing.
Those who do not know me
Say, 'My good sir, you are impudent.
That man is perfectly right.
What is this that you are saying about him?'
My heart's sorrow,
Which of them knows it?
Which of them knows it?
The truth is, they do not care.

In the garden is a prickly jujube;
But its fruits are good to eat.
It is my heart's sadness
That makes me travel from land to land.
Those who do not know me
Say, 'My good sir, you are a scamp.
That man is perfectly right.
What is this that you are saying about him?'
My heart's sorrow,
Which of them knows it?
Which of them knows it?
The truth is, they do not care.

---

[1] As it balances the prickly jujube, it cannot be the ordinary peach that is meant, but the *yang-t'ao*, 'sheep's peach,' which was thorny. See No. 2.

276   BIG rat, big rat,
     Do not gobble our millet!
     Three years we have slaved for you,
     Yet you take no notice of us.
     At last we are going to leave you
     And go to that happy land;
     Happy land, happy land,
     Where we shall have our place.

     Big rat, big rat,
     Do not gobble our corn!
     Three years we have slaved for you,
     Yet you give us no credit.
     At last we are going to leave you
     And go to that happy kingdom;
     Happy kingdom, happy kingdom,
     Where we shall get our due.

     Big rat, big rat,
     Do not eat our rice-shoots!
     Three years we have slaved for you.
     Yet you did nothing to reward us.
     At last we are going to leave you
     And go to those happy borders;
     Happy borders, happy borders
     Where no sad songs are sung.

277 TALL stands that pear-tree;[1]
Its leaves are fresh and fair.
But alone I walk, in utter solitude.
True indeed, there are other men;
But they are not like children of one's own
    father.
Heigh, you that walk upon the road,
Why do you not join me?
A man that has no brothers,
Why do you not help him?

Tall stands that pear-tree;
Its leaves grow very thick.
Alone I walk and unbefriended.
True indeed, there are other men;
But they are not like people of one's own
    clan.
Heigh, you that walk upon the road,
Why do you not join me?
A man that has no brothers,
Why do you not help him?

[1] The image of the pear-tree works by contrast, exactly as in
No. 145.

278 'Kıo' sings the oriole
As it lights on the thorn-bush.
Who went with Duke Mu to the grave?
Yen-hsi of the clan Tzŭ-chü.
Now this Yen-hsi
Was the pick of all our men;
But as he drew near the tomb-hole
His limbs shook with dread.
That blue one, Heaven,
Takes all our good men.
Could we but ransom him
There are a hundred would give their
            lives.

'Kio' sings the oriole
As it lights on the mulberry-tree.
Who went with Duke Mu to the grave?
Chung-hang of the clan Tzŭ-chü.
Now this Chung-hang
Was the sturdiest of all our men;
But as he drew near the tomb-hole
His limbs shook with dread.
That blue one, Heaven,
Takes all our good men.
Could we but ransom him
There are a hundred would give their
            lives.

'Kio' sings the oriole
As it lights on the brambles.
Who went with Duke Mu to the grave?
Ch'ien-hu of the clan Tzŭ-chü.
Now this Ch'ien-hu
Was the strongest of all our men.
But as he drew near the tomb-hole
His limbs shook with dread.
That blue one, Heaven,

Takes all our good men.
Could we but ransom him
There are a hundred would give their
         lives.

Duke Mu of Ch'in died in 621 B.C., so that the exact
date of No. 278 is known. The extent to which kings
were followed into the grave by their servitors differed
very much at various times and in various localities.
The practice existed on a grand scale during the dynasty
which preceded Chou. It was disapproved of by the
Confucians, but revived by the Ch'in when they con-
quered all China (middle of the third century B.C.). So
far as I know it was never revived after the rise of the
Han in 206 B.C.

279   OH, what has become of us?
      Those big dish-stands that towered so high!
      To-day, even when we get food, there is
            none to spare.
      Alas and alack!
      We have not grown as we sprouted.

      Oh, what has become of us?
      Four dishes at every meal!
      To-day, even when we get food, there is
            never enough.
      Alas and alack!
      We have not grown as we sprouted.

280 In flood those running waters
Carry their tides to join the sea.
Swift that flying kite
Now flies, now lights.
Alas that of my brothers,
My countrymen and all my friends,
Though each has father, has mother,
None heeds the disorders of this land!

In flood those running waters
Spread out so wide, so wide.
Swift that flying kite;
Now flying, now soaring.
Thinking of those rebellious ones
I arise, I go.
The sorrows of my heart
I cannot banish or forget.

Swift that flying kite
Makes for that middle mound.
The false words of the people,
Why does no one stop them?
My friends, be on your guard;
Slanderous words are on the rise.

The meaning is: we are heading for rebellion swift as a
kite or as a stream in flood.

281   WHEN a crane cries at the Nine Swamps
Its voice is heard in the wild.
A fish can plunge deep into the pool
Or rest upon the shoals.
Pleasant is that man's garden
Where the hardwood trees are planted;
But beneath[1] them, only litter.
There are other hills whose stones
Are good for grinding tools.

When a crane cries at the Nine Swamps
Its voice is heard in Heaven.
A fish can rest upon the shoal
Or plunge deep into the pool.
Pleasant is that man's garden
Where the hardwood trees are planted.
But beneath them are only husks.
There are other hills whose stones
Are good for working jade.

[1] The 'beneath' certainly has a double sense and hints that the lower classes are treated as of no account. The refrain is a cryptic threat to emigrate. Compare No. 276

282 AN ornament here, a decoration there
     Make up this shell-embroidery.
     Those slanderers of men
     Indeed have gone too far!

     A spread here, a gape there
     Make up the Southern Fan.[1]
     Such slanderers of man,
     Who would consent to join their counsels?

     Jibber-jabber, blither-blather!
     Their idea of 'counsel' is to slander men.
     And if you speak with any caution
     They say that you are not loyal.

     Gabble-gabble, tittle-tattle!
     Their idea of 'counsel' is to slander men.
     You think they won't get *you*?
     Already they are moving your way.

     The proud man enjoys himself,
     The toiler lives in woe.
     Oh, Heaven, azure Heaven,
     Take note of that proud man,
     Take pity upon that toiler!

     Those slanderers of men,
     Who would consent to join their counsels?
     I take those slanderers of men
     And throw them as an offering to the
          jackals and tigers.

     If jackals and tigers will not eat them
     I throw them as an offering to Him of the
          North.[2]

[1] The constellation of the Winnowing Fan; part of Sagittarius.
[2] The spirit of the Pole-star?

If He of the North will not accept them
I throw them as an offering to Him on high.

The way through the willow garden
Leads to the acred hill.
The palace-attendant[1] Mêng Tzǔ
Made up the words of this song.
May all gentlemen, whosoever they be,
Listen to it with attention!

283 THICK grows that tarragon.
It is not tarragon; it is only wormwood.
Alas for my father and mother,
Alas for all their trouble in bringing me up!

Thick grows that tarragon.
It is not tarragon; it is mugwort.
Alas for my father and mother,
Alas for all their toil in bringing me up!
'That the cup should be empty
Is a humiliation to the jar.'[2]
Than to live the life of the common people
Better to have died long ago!

Without a father, on whom can we rely?
Without a mother, whom can we trust?
At every turn we should encounter trouble,
At every turn meet failure.

My father begot me,
My mother fed me,
Led me, bred me,

[1] The word came to mean 'eunuch'; but we do not know at what
date eunuchs were first used in Chinese palaces.
[2] Proverb?

Brought me up, reared me,
Kept her eye on me, tended me,
At every turn aided me.
Their good deeds I would requite.
It is Heaven, not I, that is bad.

The southern hills, they rise so sharp,
The storm-wind blows so wild.
Other people all prosper;
Why am I alone destroyed?

The southern hills, they rise so jagged,
The storm-wind blows so fierce.
Other people all prosper;
I alone can find no rest.

The situation in the next song is very clear. A man of
the east (Shantung) complains that all the best jobs go
to the men of the west, to the people from the Chou
capital, while all the real work is done by local people.
The Chou aristocracy, who are supposed to administer
the country, are given positions with high-sounding titles,
but do none of the work that these titles imply. Hence
they are compared to the stars, which bear the names of
all sorts of useful things but perform no useful function: 'In
the south there is a Winnowing Fan; but it cannot sift or
raise the chaff,' etc. Tradition says that the song was
made by a minister of the Lord of T'an, a small State
that was thirty miles east of the modern treaty-port
Tsinan. The date of the song has generally been supposed
to be the reign of King Yu of Chou (781–771 B.C.). It is
certainly more likely that it dates from western Chou
times, when the dynasty was still powerful, than after its
virtual eclipse in 771. But the ascription to King Yu's
time is no doubt merely due to the fact that he ranks in

history as a 'bad king.' It may in point of fact just as well belong to the reign of one of the 'good kings.' In order not to disfigure the page with too great a mass of footnotes, I will explain the star-names here. The Han River in Heaven is the Milky Way. The Weaving Lady and the Draught Ox are constellations on opposite sides of the Milky Way. Later legend turned the Ox into a Herdboy, and made him the lover of the Weaving Lady. The Opener of Brightness is the Morning Star; the Long Path, the Evening Star. The Net is the Hyades; the Winnowing Fan part of Sagittarius.

284   MESSY is the stew in the pot;
       Bent is the thornwood spoon.
       But the ways of Chou are smooth as a
            grindstone,
       Their straightness is like an arrow;
       Ways that are for gentlemen to walk
       And for commoners to behold.
       Full of longing I look for them;
       In a flood my tears flow.

       In the Lesser East and the Greater East[1]
       Shuttle and spool are idle.
       'Fibre-shoes tightly woven
       Are good for walking upon the dew.'[2]
       Foppishly mincing the young lords
       Walk there upon the road.
       They go away, they come back again;
       It makes me ill to look at them!

[1] Fu Ssŭ-nien discusses the meaning of these terms in *Academia Sinica*, Vol. II, Pt. I. Roughly speaking, the Lesser East means the extreme west of Shantung; the Greater East means central Shantung, between Tsi-nan and Tai-an. Cf. No. 251, verse 5.

[2] Allusion to No. 73, or at any rate a utilization of the same theme.

That spraying fountain so cold
Does not soak firewood that is gathered
   and bundled.
Heigh-ho! I lie awake and sigh.
Woe is me that am all alone!
Firewood that is gathered firewood
May still be put away.
Woe is me that am all alone!
I too could do with rest.

The men of the East, their sons
Get all the work and none of the pay.
The men of the West, their sons,
Oh, so smart are their clothes!
The men of Chou, their sons
Wear furs of bearskin, black and brown.
The sons of their vassals
For every appointment are chosen.

Fancy taking the wine
And leaving the sauce,
Having a belt-pendant so fine
And not using its full length!

In Heaven there is a River Han
Looking down upon us so bright.
By it sits the Weaving Lady astride her
   stool,
Seven times a day she rolls up her sleeves.
But though seven times she rolls her sleeves
She never makes wrap or skirt.
Bright shines that Draught Ox,
But can't be used for yoking to a cart.
In the east is the Opener of Brightness,
In the west, the Long Path.
All-curving are the Nets of Heaven,
Spread there in a row.

In the south there is a Winnowing Fan;
But it cannot sift, or raise the chaff.
In the north there is a Ladle,
But it cannot scoop wine or sauce.
Yes, in the south is a Winnowing Fan;
There it sucks its tongue.
In the north there is a Ladle,
Sticking out its handle towards the west.

285   I CLIMB those northern hills
And pluck the boxthorn.
Very strenuous are the knights,
Early and late upon their tasks;
The king's business never ends.
But for my father and mother I grieve.

'Everywhere under Heaven
Is no land that is not the king's.
To the borders of all those lands
None but is the king's slave.'[1]
But the ministers are not just;
Whatever is done, I bear the brunt alone.

[Like] a team of steeds so strong
The king's business bears down upon me.
Everyone congratulates me on my
        youthfulness,
Is surprised I am still so strong,
That with muscles still so tough
I build the frontiers on every hand.

Some people sit quietly at home;
Others wear themselves out in serving
        their country.

        [1] Proverbial saying?

Some lie peacefully in bed;
Others are always on the move.

Some senselessly yell and bawl;[1]
Others fret and toil.
Some loll about at their ease;
Others in the king's business are engrossed.

Some sunk in pleasure swill their wine;
Others are tortured by the fear of blame.
Some do nothing but scold or advise;
Others in every trouble must act.

286 DON'T escort the big chariot;
You will only make yourself dusty.
Don't think about the sorrows of the world;
You will only make yourself wretched.[2]

Don't escort the big chariot;
You won't be able to see for dust.
Don't think about the sorrows of the world;
Or you will never escape from your despair.

Don't escort the big chariot;
You'll be stifled with dust.
Don't think about the sorrows of the world;
You will only load yourself with care.

[1] See the *Tz'ŭ T'ung* of Chu Ch'i-fêng, p. 722.
[2] This song uses the same formula as No. 47.

287 Buzz, buzz the bluebottles
That have settled on the hedge.
Oh, my blessed lord,
Do not believe the slanders that are said.

Buzz, buzz the bluebottles
That have settled on the thorns.
Slanderers are very wicked;
They disturb the whole land.

Buzz, buzz the bluebottles
That have settled on the hazel-bush.
Slanderers are very wicked;
They have joined[1] us two men.

---

[1] Joined our names in scandal? This may, of course, be a love poem; 'men' means 'human beings,' not 'males.' But the meaning of the last line is uncertain.

288 VERY leafy is that willow-tree,
But I would not care to rest under it.[1]
God[2] on high is very bright;
Don't go too close to him!
Were I to reprove him,
Afterwards I should be slaughtered by
 him.

Very leafy is that willow-tree,
But I would not care to repose under it.
God on high is very bright;
Don't hurt yourself on him!
Were I to reprove him,
Afterwards I should be torn to pieces
 by him.

There is a bird, flies high,
Yes, soars to Heaven.
But that man's heart
Never could it reach.
Why should I rebuke him,
Only to be cruelly slain?

[1] Because *liu* (willow) also means 'slaughter.'
[2] i.e. the ruler.

289   Oh, the flowers of the bignonia,
      Gorgeous is their yellow!
      The sorrows of my heart,
      How they stab!

      Oh, the flowers of the bignonia,
      And its leaves so thick!
      Had I known it would be like this,
      Better that I should never have been born!

      As often as a ewe has a ram's head,
      As often as Orion is in the Pleiads,
      Do people to-day, if they find food at all,
      Get a chance to eat their fill.

290 BRIGHT are the flowers
     On those plains and lowlands.
     In a great host go the travellers,
     Each bent on keeping his place.

     'My horses are colts,
     My six reins are glossy;
     I will speed, I will gallop,
     Everywhere asking for counsel.'

     'My horses are dappled,
     My six reins are like the threads of a
          loom.
     I will speed, I will gallop,
     Everywhere asking for instructions.'

     'My horses are white with black manes,
     My six reins are all greased.
     I will speed, I will gallop,
     Everywhere asking for good plans.'

     'My horses are brindled,
     The six reins very level.
     I will speed, I will gallop,
     Everywhere asking for advice.'

I have included this song here because it would be
difficult to put it into any other class, and it at any rate
concerns public life; for it is nominally a song of envoys,
about to embark on a diplomatic mission. I have a
feeling, however, that the words may be those of the
'visiting' movement in a dance or dance-game.

In this book a good deal of space is devoted to discussing questions of literary mechanism, ritual, folk-lore, and sociology; I have said nothing about the intrinsic quality of the *Songs*. But when in 1913 I first began to read them, using Couvreur's text and translation, it was not as documents of the past that they interested me. I knew then no more about the varieties of human culture than an ordinary classical education can teach. It was simply as poetry that I read the *Songs*, and strangely enough, perhaps, even more as music than as poetry. For though I soon distrusted the Confucian interpretation, I had nothing to put in its place, and was often forced to accept the *Songs* as meaningless incantations. The sounds that I gave to them were those of an untutored attempt at Pekingese, coloured here and there by Couvreur's fictitious 'ancient pronunciations,' fanciful products of a pseudo-archaeology. And yet as I read there sprang up from under the tangle of misconceptions and distortions that hid them from me a succession of fresh and lovely tunes. The text sang, just as the lines of Homer somehow manage to sing despite the barbarous ignorance with which we recite them.

The *Songs* are no longer unintelligible to me; save for a line here and there I believe that I understand them fairly well, and they have become, through their unique importance as documents of early metric, ritual mythology, an incentive to studies that extend far beyond ancient China. But they have never lost for me their early attraction. The music, perhaps utterly unauthentic, that accompanied my first discovery of them, has followed me through repeated reading and re-reading. Above all, in the last three years, when the text has been continually before me, the jumble of problems linguistic, botanic, zoological, historical, geographical which the translator of such a work must face, has never robbed the *Songs* of their freshness; and I trust that some part of my delight in them, despite the deadening lack of rhyme and formal metric, has found its way to the reader of the foregoing translations.

Additional Notes

The first figure is the number of the poem, the second that of the verse, unless marked as referring to the line.

3. 2. Dr. K. Kaku (in *Tōyō Gakuhō*, Vol. XX, No. 3) holds that *shêng* originally meant 'my sister's sons or daughters,' the speaker being a woman. According to the *Êrh Ya*, it means 'my mother-in-law's children,' 'my father-in-law's children,' 'my wife's brother,' 'my sister's husband.'

9. 2. I very much doubt whether *shih yeh* can mean 'in the market.' I suspect that *shih* is corrupt.

9. 2. Yüan is a woman's family name, like Chiang and Tzŭ in No. 13, Chi in No. 16, Chiang, I and Yung in No. 23, Chi in No. 52, etc. Such names are often preceded by age-terms, such as Mêng (eldest), Shu (third daughter), or by local names, e.g. Pao Ssŭ, 'The Ssŭ-woman from the land of Pao'; or by the father's title, e.g. (No. 52) Yin Chi, 'The Chi whose father is a *yin* (i.e. an official or scribe).'

Tzŭ-chung is a man's family name; compare the Tzŭ-chü of No. 278. In the courtship and marriage poems men are usually referred to by typical names, which function like the Sepp or Hänsel of German traditional songs.[1] These names, however, are not personal names but relationship or age terms; for example, Shu (uncle), Nos. 30 and 31, Pai or Po (elder), No. 49.

14. *Kan.* This is only another way of writing the word *lan* (Archaic, *klan*), which in later Chinese means the cultivated orchid. In early Chinese it is a general name for sweet-smelling herbs. The variants here and in No. 37 are due to the fact that Han interpreters were not used to seeing *lan* written as it is written here.

Legge's 'valerian' is based on a misunderstanding of a plate in an eighteenth-century Japanese book.[2] The plate is

[1] Or Iwantscho in Bulgarian, Jovan in Serbian traditional songs.

[2] *Mōshi Himbutsu Zukō*, by Oka Gempō, pictures by Tachibana Kunio, 1785.

labelled *fujibakama*, which means 'Chinese agrimony.' The strongly serrated leaves are quite unlike valerian.

24. The *t'an* that means 'sandal-wood' is derived from a Sanskrit word. The *t'an* of the *Songs* may have been a kind of ash.

40. 'Horn-cup.' Literally 'drinking-horn,' made of the horn of the *ssŭ*.' This word may have originally meant rhinoceros. In Chou times it meant wild cattle. To-day it again means rhinoceros. The link is that the hide of both animals was used for defensive armour.

47. 3. 'Side-locks looped' is the typical coiffure of a boy before he comes of age. The famous Japanese picture of Prince Shōtoku, the early patron of Buddhism, as a boy, shows him with his hair done like this. In China the 'coming of age' rite for boys centred round the first wearing of a grown-up person's cap (*kuan*).

54. She uses the unusual *ang* for 'I' (first person singular) because she is addressing the boatman, a social inferior. Cf. the use of *ang* by the Emperor when addressing subjects.

60. 4. Literally 'open-meshed fibre-cloth and wide-meshed fibre-cloth.' The second word is etymologically the same as *ch'i*, 'a fissure,' 'a crack' (Karlgren, 341).

64. The character with which 'rainbow' is here written means 'spider' and is simply a phonetic borrowing for the 'girdle' character. See textual notes. Characters for rainbow presumably have the 'serpent' radical because at an earlier stage of their mythology the Chinese regarded the rainbow as a snake, a belief very common in Africa and elsewhere. For the rainbow as a woman's belt, see Phyllis Kemp, *Healing Ritual in the Balkans* (p. 199); Françoise Legey, *Folk-lore of Morocco*, p. 47 (rainbow as girdle of Mohammed's daughter). The fact that elsewhere than in China the rainbow is regarded as a girdle makes it unlikely that the 'girdle' element in the Chinese character is simply phonetic.

MARRIAGE

There were also various forms of runaway match, but these cannot properly be called 'marriage,' for the woman did not become a wife (a mother of legitimate heirs), but merely a handmaid. There is no evidence for the existence in Chou times (i.e. till the second half of the third century B.C.) of any form of marriage in which the wife remained with her people and the husband came to live with her, instead of taking her to live with him—the sort of marriage which ethnologists call matrilocal. We first hear of this practice in 214 B.C., when the First Emperor ordered that all fugitives, matrilocal husbands and 'pedlars' were to be enrolled for service on the southern front. M. Granet[1] represents this as a 'Draconian measure' against an ancient form of marriage obstinately clung to by a conservative peasantry. In reality it was an attempt to press into military service various classes of people who, living at a distance from the place where their names were registered, had tended to escape the notice of recruiting officials. Another ethnologist, Robert Briffault (*The Mothers*, Vol. I, p. 365), uses the closing passage of the Fang Chi chapter in the *Li Chi* as proof of the existence of matrilocal marriage in early times. What the text says, however, is that despite all the safeguards of marriage-custom, wives sometimes fail to arrive at the husband's home.

From the Han dynasty onwards it was a regular practice for a young husband, whose parents could not fulfil their part in the exchange of property which accompanied marriage, to pay off the obligation by living as a *chui-hsü* (matrilocal husband) with the wife's family and working as a servant in the household. This form of marriage may have existed in Chou times, may indeed have been of immemorial antiquity in China; but, as I have said above, we have not the slightest evidence that this was so. The only proof that the Chou once reckoned descent through the females (i.e. had a matrilinear society, which often goes with matrilocal marriage) is afforded by their kinship terms and various small points of ritual.[2]

73. The *ti* of the *Songs* is a belt-pendant and not a hair-pin, as in later times.

81. This poem has generally been supposed to deal with the

---

[1] *Danses et Légendes*, I, 17.
[2] See additional notes on No. 3 and 225.

visit of a wife to her parents' house; but this does not fit the wording. I take it that the lady had fallen in love with her future husband at the Wei capital, in northern Honan, and had afterwards gone to live farther north. The only identifiable place-name is Mei, which was close to the capital. Ts'ao must also have been near by. It cannot be the Ts'ao on the far side of the Yellow River, which became the Wei capital after *c.* 600 B.C.

108, 109. That these two poems, which stand far apart in the original text, are closely connected, was first pointed out in the *Yen-Ching Hsüeh Pao* (No. 1, 1927) by Yü P'ing-po.

118. 3. 'To signal with a circular movement of the flag' is the proper meaning of *hsüan*. See *Shuo Wên*.

119.   'Give his life.' See T.T. 2126. *Shê ming* also means 'to disseminate royal edicts,' as, for example, in the inscription on the tripod of Duke Mao (Karlgren, B. 143), but that has no relevance here. The tripod may well be two hundred years earlier than this poem and the context is quite different.

120.   The results of recent excavation are likely, when fully published, to give us a much clearer notion of the Chou war-chariot. I think the 'flank-checks' in verse 1, line · 4, were spiked balls, hung on the girth of the inner horse to prevent the outer horse getting too close to it. Something similar was used by the Assyrians. I do not doubt that the word usually translated 'traces' means ropes or reins used to drag a chariot by hand, when the horses could not get it through muddy or difficult places. 'Traces,' in our sense of the word, seldom occur in antiquity.

Line 3. There is not the slightest evidence that *hsü* can mean a ring. My translation of the poem is, however, merely provisional. It is very doubtful whether *wo* means silver-inlay (cf. J. G. Andersson in *Yin and Chou Researches*: the Goldsmith in Ancient China, p. 2); or indeed has anything to do with silver at all. It was about their own techniques that the Han commentators knew, and not about those of a previous period.

125. 4. The idea that *li* means 'scent-bag' is due, I think, to a series of misconceptions.

131.   Hsien-yün. They are also mentioned in several bronze inscriptions (e.g. Karlgren, B. 107, B. 133, B. 205). The

only place-name in these inscriptions which can be identi-
fied with certainty is 'north side of the Lo' (B. 107), which
can only mean north of the Northern Lo River in Eastern
Shensi. Similarly, the only place-name in our songs with a
certain identification is the 'north side of the Ching' in
No. 133. The Ching (cf. No. 105) is the next great Shensi
river west of the Lo.

132.   For an example of 'trying' a defeated chieftain, see the
inscription Karlgren, B. 19. The defendant's plea is that
he had been maltreated by a certain Chou lord and had
therefore thrown in his lot with the Shang. The farce of
interrogation having been accomplished, the rebel chieftain
was, of course, beheaded.

136.   'All the way to the southern seas.' This is probably merely
a hyperbole.

136.   Wên-jên. Cf. the *Wên-hou chih Ming* in the *Shu Ching* and
the well-known Shan tripod (Kuo Mo-jo, *K'ao Shih*,
p. 65). We could translate 'I have announced it to my
Mighty ones.'

139.   I translate T'ai-shih 'Leader,' i.e. war-leader and not
'Master,' because there is no evidence that the theory of
three superfunctionaries without definite duties (the Grand
Master, Grand Helper, Grand Protector) existed before Han
times.

143.   'The meshes of crime.' The idea that sin is a net in which
Heaven catches those whom it would destroy was very
widely spread in antiquity. Scheftelowitz[1] has shown that
it existed among the Sumerians, Babylonians, Indians (in
the Vedas), and ancient Persians (in the Zend Avesta). It
also occurs in the Bible.[2] It is therefore likely to be no
accident that so many of the words connected with sin
in Chinese are written with the 'net' radical. Compare
No. 304 , 'Sin's net is not taken in,' and No. 305, 'Heaven
sent down the net of sin.' The ordinary character for sin
(*tsui*), which has the 'net' radical, is said indeed to have
been invented by the Emperor Shih-huang in the third
century B.C. But it is much more likely that it was an old
form, preserved in the State of Ch'in and made current

[1] *Das Schlingen und Netzmotiv* . . ., 1912.
[2] Hosea vii. 12; Ezekiel xii. 13; xvii. 19-20.

in the rest of China when Ch'in established itself as supreme.

152.   In the 'Chin Sayings' of the *Kuo Yü*, Duke Wên of Chin is made to quote this poem while still in exile. That is to say, tradition associated him with the poem, though in a way·different from that which I have assumed. The whole story of this ruler, both in the *Kuo-yü* and the *Tso Chuan*, is interspersed with folk-lore elements. For example, his 'ribs all in one piece,' an obvious 'invulnerability-motif.' Certain facts about him (I think we may take them as such) facilitated the linking of his story with traditional folk-lore. His birth involved the breaking of a taboo, for his parents were of the same clan (*hsing*), and this could be taken as putting him on a par with heroes whose parents were brother and sister, human and animal, or the like.

157.   'Headman and overseer.' *Ya* is literally 'seconder.' I take *lü* in the sense of government inspector, who sees that a due proportion of land is tilled for tithe purposes. See *Chou Li*, chap. 30, folio 1. But this is pure speculation.

157.   *K'ao* means 'deceased fathers,' the term 'father' including paternal uncles.

159.   *Mei-shou.* This phrase means 'great old age'; we cannot etymologize it any further. It is written in many different ways (on inscriptions never with 'eyebrow' till Han times), suggesting pronunciations *mên, wei, mei, mou.*

161.   *Ho*, 'crops,' is very likely a corruption of *kua*, 'melons.' Cf. 160, 4.

168.   The interpretation of the last stanza is mere guess-work.

171.   *Pu*, here as in No. 238 and elsewhere, represents a labial prefix, and is not a negative.

176. 2. Literally, 'It is in teams . . . that (*so*) the princes arrive.'

187.   I am not confident that I have understood this poem rightly.

197.   'Shuffling steps.' See Ch'ên Huan's commentary, Chap. VI, folio 10.

198.   The fact that the *Tso Chuan* chronicle (Chao kung, twenty-third year) interprets the song in the same way as Mao (the earliest commentator) proves nothing. For the *Tso Chuan*, in its existing state, is full of Confucian lore drawn from just the same sources as the traditional Confucian

commentaries. What matters is not whether the chronicle supports an interpretation, but whether that interpretation is compatible with the wording of the text in question.

199. 4. 'Hopes and rules.' This is very likely corrupt; but to interpret it as 'spring and sight' of a cross-bow, as does Hsü Chung-shu (*Academia Sinica*, IV, 4, p. 422), is hazardous.

218. This poem has recently been discussed by Yü Hsing-wu, in *Yü Kung* for March 1936.

225, line 7. Ancestors were called *chao* 'bright' and *mu* 'quiet' 'solemn' in alternate generations. The *chao* ancestral tablets were on the left, the *mu* ancestral tablets were on the right side of the ancestral temple. Thus father, grandson, great-great-grandson[1] came together on one side. Son, great-grandson, great-great-great-grandson on the other. This no doubt merely reflects the original habits of the living; hence the double nomenclature of Chinese officials, scribe of the left, scribe of the right, etc. Compare the prohibition against a father carrying his son in his arms (separation of immediate male generations), or teaching him. All this implies an original system of exchange marriage between two matrilineal units. The odd generations would then all belong to one unit, the even generations to the other.

238. I take the particle *tan*, so frequent in this poem, to mean 'truly,' 'verily,' or something of that sort. I do not think Wu Shih-ch'ang's recent study of the word[2] gets us much further.

246. 2. 'There came a command from Heaven . . .' Here the song retraces its steps. This verse does not go on to a fresh narration, but echoes the last. The narrative songs developed out of lyric poems in which each verse deliberately echoes the last, and there are considerable survivals of this structure in the long ballads. There is not the slightest reason to suppose that two successive marriages are being spoken of. We may regard Hsin (a domain of whose history we know nothing) as scarcely deserving the name of 'great country.' But compare No. 102, where another small State is conventionally spoken of as a 'great country.'

[1] i.e. son's son; son's son's son's son, etc.
[2] In the Yenching *Journal of Chinese Studies*, No. 8, 1930.

251. 'You shall be (the star) Orion's peer.' See Kuo Mo-jo, on the Tsung Chou bell inscription, *Ta Hsi K'ao Shih*, I, 53 verso. Some inscriptions have the character '3' instead of the proper character for 'Orion's belt,' just as here. I only accept this explanation provisionally; the relevant inscriptions have not been satisfactorily deciphered.

266. When Hui, still in his minority, succeeded Hsüan as Duke of Wei in 699, the men of Ch'i, who at this period dominated the affairs of the central Chinese States, forced Hui's half-brother Wan to marry Hui's widowed mother, who was a Ch'i princess, in order to ensure a succession favourable to Ch'i interests. The princess was Hui's stepmother, and it is supposed that a dispute arose concerning the legitimacy of the union. Something very shocking evidently transpired during the hearing of the case (if we accept that this explanation of the poem is correct). Presumably what transpired was that Wan had already had intercourse with his step-mother during his father's lifetime.

Chêng Hsüan, in his commentary on the last words of *Chou Li*, Chap. 26, says that the place where love-disputes were heard was 'covered over on top and fenced in below.' I take the *kou* of the present song as equivalent to the *chan* (fencing) of Chêng's note. Both words mean trellis-work made of thin strips of wood. *Kou* is usually taken to mean the partition which divided the woman's rooms from the man's. But it was deeds not words which disgraced the harem. The 'words' that were shocking were the stories told at the trial. My interpretation certainly makes better sense; but we know so little of these *yin sung* (trials in camera) that I only put it forward as an hypothesis.

267. 'Grandly, royally done.' As we do not know what *jên* and *lin* mean, I have followed the traditional interpretation as preserved by Mao, simply in order to avoid leaving a blank. 'Receive the pledge-cup.' *Shou ch'iu* is corrupt, and impossible to emend with any certainty.

Appendices

Appendix I

The Allegorical Interpretation

THE preservation of the *Songs* is due to the fact that they were used for a variety of social and educational purposes which had nothing to do with their original intention. Confucius,[1] for example, tells us that a knowledge of the *Songs* enables us to incite other men to desirable courses, helps us to observe accurately their inmost feelings and to express our own discontents, to do our duty both to parent and prince, and finally 'to widen our acquaintance with the names of birds, beasts, plants and trees.' In anecdote after anecdote of the *Tso Chuan* chronicle and the 'Sayings of the Kingdoms' (*Kuo Yü*) we can see the *Songs* in actual use as 'incitements,' as diplomatic 'feelers,' as a veiled means of displaying one's own intentions or sounding those of a fellow-diplomatist. For example, when the Duke of Lu in 544 B.C. has taken refuge in a foreign land, owing to the menaces of the Chi family, and hesitates to return, his Minister 'incites' him by intoning No. 122, with its refrain 'let us go back.' The emotional effect of the familiar poem is greater than that of any direct appeal. A guest at a banquet given by the Prince of Chêng 'observes' the dispositions of the seven Ministers of Chêng by noting the *Songs* that they recite at the banquet. An ambassador from Chin prepares the way for an alliance between his native State and Lu by reciting No. 268, 'Brothers should draw together'; for the ducal houses of Chin and Lu were related. In public life a man who does not know the *Songs* is 'as one whose face is turned towards the wall.' An envoy sent from Sung to Lu in 530 B.C. fails to recognize the allusion in a song recited on his arrival, and is at a loss how to reply. His mission is completely discredited, and it is predicted that he will come to speedy ruin. This may seem to us bizarre; but much the same fate would have befallen an eighteenth-century Member of

[1] *Analects*, XVII, 9.

Parliament who failed to understand an allusive quotation from Vergil.[1]

In 614 B.C., when the Prince of Chêng visits Lu, a long diplomatic 'exchange of views' takes place entirely in the discreet medium of quotations from the *Book of Songs*.

We have seen that besides regarding the *Songs* as an aid to social and political intercourse Confucius saw in them a text-book of personal morality. A small minority of the songs are indeed didactic and could therefore be taken at their face value. From the political and historical pieces it was very easy to draw a moral, even where none was intended. But there remained a class of song (the largest in the book) which was refractory. The courtship and marriage songs, numbering about one hundred and twenty, could only be used for moral instruction if interpreted allegorically. Take, for example, a verse like

> In the lowlands is the goats-peach;
> Very delicate are its boughs.
> Oh, soft and tender,
> Glad I am that you have no friend!

followed by other verses, with 'glad I am that you have no home,' 'glad I am that you have no house.' This song is interpreted as the outburst of someone 'groaning under the oppression of the Government, and wishing he were an unconscious tree.' This feat of interpretation was very simply accomplished. *Chih*, 'someone whom one knows,' 'a friend,' 'a mate,' is taken in the sense 'consciousness,' both words being meaning-extensions of *chih*, 'to know,' and both being written with the same character. So for the last line we get Legge's translation,[2] 'I should rejoice to be like you (O tree), without consciousness.'

This type of reinterpretation is not confined to China. Parts of our own Bible have been explained on similar lines, particularly the Song of Solomon and certain of the Psalms. Thus in, 'I raised thee up under the apple-tree' (Song of Solomon viii. 5), the tree in question was taken to be the Cross of Christ, prophetically described by King Solomon.

[1] Burke constantly quoted Vergil in his speeches, using these tags of Classical poetry exactly as the *Songs* were used by Chinese politicians. For example, by an allusion to the Trojan horse he warns Parliament against the commercial machinations of the French.

[2] *Chinese Classics*, IV, p. 217.

Just as words can have more than one meaning, as in the case of *chih* above, so too social practices can have more than one meaning. People wear plain, inconspicuous clothing either because they are poor or because they are in mourning. It was very easy (see No. 10) to turn a song about a humble, plainly dressed lover into a sermon about mourning observances.

The true nature of the poems was realized by M. Granet, whose *Fêtes et Chansons de la Chine Ancienne*, published in 1911, deals with about half the courtship and marriage songs. Since that time sinology has made enormous advances. I differ from M. Granet as regards some general questions and many details. But his book was epoch-making, and I can only hope that the next translator of the *Songs* will feel as much respect for my present versions as I do for those of M. Granet.

The best translation of the *Songs* in their traditional interpretation is that of Couvreur, which faithfully follows the commentary of Chu Hsi.[1] Legge mixes up the Chu Hsi interpretation with that of the Han commentators and dilutes both with suggestions of his own, so that to-day his translation serves no useful purpose. A translation like that of Couvreur is, however, still indispensable; for unless one knows how the *Songs* have been allegorized in the past, one will fail to understand not only innumerable allusions in later literature, but even expressions (drawn from the moral interpretation of the *Songs*) that are still current in everyday speech.

[1] Died A.D. 1200.

The Wan Dance

A LL that we can know of this dance is contained in half a dozen passages of Chou literature. The Han commentators, writing hundreds of years afterwards, have much to say on the subject; but it does not appear that they really know anything more about it than we do.

We learn from No. 208 that in the land of Wei (northern Honan) the *wan* was danced at midday in the courtyard in front of the duke's palace, the dancer[1] holding in his left hand the flute and in his right hand the pheasant plumes. The song accompanying the dance (it is impossible to regard the last verse in any other light) was a love-song.

In No. 213 we find the *wan* dance being performed in Sung, to the south-east of Wei, at a musical ceremony designed to 'please the glorious ancestors.' In No. 251 we find it being danced at a sacrificial feast held in the country of Lu, east of Wei and Sung.

Now let us turn to the *Springs and Autumns*. In the fifth year of Duke Yin of Lu (718 B.C.) the shrine of the consort Chung Tzŭ was finished, 'and for the first time six sets[2] of plume-dancers were used in her honour.' The *Tso Chuan* chronicle says that when the shrine was finished and the *wan* dance was about to be held, Duke Yin asked his Minister Ch'ung-chung how many sets of plume-dancers there should be. He replied, 'The Son of Heaven uses eight, barons use six, ministers use four and knights only two.' As a baron, the Duke of Lu therefore used six sets of dancers.

In the eighth year of Duke Hsüan of Lu (601 B.C.) a member of the ducal family died during the course of a big sacrificial ceremony held at the duke's ancestral hall. It was decided to continue the ceremony, but 'when the *wan* dancers entered, they discarded their flutes,' as a sign of respect to the dead.

In the account of the twenty-eighth year of Duke Chuang of Lu,[3] the *Tso Chuan* tells us that in the country of Ch'u a brother of the late King Wên of Ch'u fell in love with the widowed queen

---

[1] Or dancers. But I think it is better to regard the song as being in praise of a particular dancer.

[2] Eight dancers went to a set.

[3] 666 B.C.

and in order to 'bewitch' her, set up a pavilion alongside of her palace and had a *wan* dance performed in it. 'Hearing of this the queen wept, saying, "When my late lord had this dance performed, it was to keep his warriors in training for battle. His Excellency, instead of directing it against the enemy, aims it at one who is not yet dead.[1] What a difference!" '

In the twenty-fifth year of Chao of Lu,[2] at a time when a cadet branch of the ducal family, Chi Shih, was rapidly usurping the powers of the duke, there was an ancestral sacrifice (*ti*) to the late Duke Hsiang. Only two sets of *wan*-dancers performed at the ancestral hall; all the rest danced the *wan* in the mansion of the Chi Shih.

It is my impression that the King of Ch'u, in using the dance as a part of military training, was diverting it from its original purpose.[3] War-dances were danced with spear and shield; peace-dances with flute and plumes. We have seen that the *wan* was performed with flute and plumes. There is no passage that contradicts this. There is also considerable reason to suppose that it was amorous in character. In No. 208 it is danced to the accompaniment of a love-song; in the first *Tso Chuan* passage it is used as a love-enchantment. Its licentious character is further illustrated in the legend of the five grandsons of the Great Yü, shaper of hills and streams. It is said[4] of them that they gave themselves over to feasting, drinking, and every form of licence: 'the gorgeousness of their *wan* dances was duly marked in Heaven, and Heaven was not at all pleased.'

The Han theories about the dances are as follows: (1) It was a peace dance, (2) it was a war-dance, (3) it was both, (4) *wan* merely means 'great,' (5) *wan* is merely an old word for 'dance.'

(5) is clearly untrue. *Wan* is used as an adjective qualifying *wu*, 'dance.' There is no evidence in favour of (4). The other three opinions are all derived from the passages in Chou literature which we have been considering. There is at present no evidence for the use of the dance in the Chou home country (north-west China); but I think it would be premature to conclude, as some writers

---

[1] But might as well be, i.e. a widow.   [2] 517 B.C.
[3] This king was very bellicose. He conquered thirty-nine States (*Lü Shih Ch'un Ch'iu*, 138).
[4] In a lost book of the *Shu Ching* quoted in Mo Tzŭ's chapter, 'Down with Music!'

have done, that it was particularly connected with the Shang people, predecessors of the Chou.

With regard to the meaning of the word *wan* itself, only tentative speculation is possible. All over the world to-day, alike in the most primitive and the most sophisticated societies, people are dancing dances the names of which they would be hard put to it to explain. What, for example, does 'tango' mean? I have heard it connected with the Basque *zango*, 'foot'; but there are many other theories. Normally *wan* means 'a great many,' and more specifically ten thousand.[1] In order to write it the Chinese borrowed the pictogram for scorpion, which had approximately the same sound, perhaps originally something like 'tmuand.' There is, therefore, a possibility that the dance was a 'scorpion' dance; the pattern the dancers traced may have resembled a conventionalized picture of a scorpion. The same character with the radical 'walk' appended to it, besides being used for ten thousand (as it often is on inscriptions), is used of going in processions, and the dance may have been a processional dance. But this does not accord with its seductive character. Once we assume that the ideogram with which *wan* is written is a phonetic transcription of some other word, innumerable possibilities open up, none of which it is possible either to disprove or to confirm.

Concerning the dance itself, as opposed to its name, we can say at any rate that it was usually connected with the tendance of ancestors, that the performers always carried plumes and generally carried flutes; that the minimum number of dancers was two rows of eight, and that in theory at any rate a very grand *wan* needed sixty-four performers.

[1] And Ho Hsiu, in the second century A.D., maintained the *wan* was the war-dance of the ten thousand soldiers who fought with King Wu, the conqueror of the Shang. But I feel convinced that it was originally a sacrificial dance and not a war-dance.

Comparison between Early Chinese and European Culture

I T is no accident that early Chinese songs and ballads are on the whole very like those of Europe, and that even when their content is different it still remains of a kind fairly easy for us to understand. The two civilizations are fundamentally very similar. I shall here do no more than indicate in a broad way where the resemblances lie. To begin with, the early Chinese conception of God comes very near to our own, and just as we use the word Heaven as a substitute for God, they used the word *t'ien*, which also means 'sky.' This use of the current word for 'sky' as an alternative to God is certainly very uncommon, if it indeed exists at all, outside historic Europe and ancient China. Indra may be a sky-god and chief of the gods; but Indra did not mean God, nor did it currently mean 'sky.' The same is true of Zeus.

The difference between us and the Chinese is that whereas our word God has no connotation 'Ancestor,' the Chinese word *ti* was applied also to dead rulers. To sacrifice to a dead ruler is to *ti*, however recent and historical he may be. *Ti* does not mean a remote, mythological royal ancestor, floating in an undetermined past. Whether our conception 'God' also grew out of a conception 'royal ancestor' is a matter for future research. The whole of Chinese religion centred round the feeding of ancestors with offerings whether animal or vegetable. In our own religious life this preoccupation is reduced to very small survivals, such as harvest offerings. But our religious terminology still teems with sacrificial metaphors. Our liturgies and hymns are full of words like sacrifice, blood, offering, lamb, and though few of us have ever performed a sacrifice, the conceptions which centre round sacrifice and offering are extremely familiar to us.

Early Chinese dancing has two aspects, one of which is familiar to us, while the other seems strange. With us, in all ranks of society, dancing is intimately connected with courtship. Dukes give balls in order to marry off their daughters; dances are held in village halls in order that young people may meet. Many middle-class men learn dancing (often reluctantly) solely in order to find a wife. This was one aspect of dancing in early China; whereas in later China, though courtship-dancing continued as a rural survival, to the mass of culture-bearing society dancing ceased to mean something that one did oneself; it meant a performance by professionals, generally women, whose lives were spent doing nothing else. We too have our professional dancers, but the part that their dancing plays in our society is insignificant compared with that played by the social dancing in which everyone takes part. Here, as in so many instances, Europe and early China have started at the same point, but whereas China has lost contact with the past, Europe has retained it. This applies, for example, to the conception 'God.' By the first century A.D. the term *ti* and all the ideas that centred round it were already obsolete. The Han commentators either explain that *ti* means Heaven (which would certainly not have been necessary a few hundred years before) or identify the word with some particular legendary monarch.

But to return to dancing. It had in ancient China another aspect which is less familiar to us. One danced 'to please the ancestors,' and it is this kind of dancing which is chiefly mentioned in early literature. Here as regards conservatism, Europe and China are on an equal footing. We have a few survivals of religious dancing (such as the dance of the Seises in Seville Cathedral, which still went on a few years ago and is likely now to be revived), and the Chinese still retain an echo of the old religious dances in their cult of the god Confucius.

The Chinese were settled agriculturalists. With some of the points in which their agricultural rites and technique resembled ours I have dealt in my foreword to the agricultural poems. The matter urgently requires more expert treatment. I will here pass on to marriage, the form of which is largely determined by the method of food-production. A society of nomad pastors (to give a very obvious instance) will be unlikely to have the same marriage institutions as a community of settled corn-growers. The main features of marriage, as we meet with it in the *Songs*, are also found in our own system. In many parts of the world the husband goes to live with his wife's people. In the *Songs*, as with us, he brings the wife to live with his people. In many parts of the world (for example, often in Melanesia and India) the legal and residential side of marriage takes place long before puberty. In China, as here, the boy and girl must both be adult. In China of the Chou dynasty,[1] succession went to the eldest son,[2] as it does with us. Courtship, as I have pointed out in connection with poems like No. 26, included a quasi-illicit element, like the French institution of the *maîtresse*, tolerated by society and even expected, on the condition that it was carried on secretly. This led to songs surprisingly like certain types of European love-song. But part of the likeness is due to accidental and quite late convergence. If it were not for the fact that the metrical shape of our songs and theirs is strikingly similar the resemblance would cease to be so sensational. The metrical shape of the European songs is, however, largely determined by the fact that they are in rhyme. But rhyme began in Europe at a comparatively late period, and if such songs have any antiquity at all in Europe, they must first have existed in an unrhymed form. For example, the Germanic songs of this type (if they existed) must have been alliterative, which would at once go far towards obliterating the superficial resemblance.

I cannot go into all the miscellaneous points of technique which link our societies to that of ancient China. But it may be worth pointing out that they shared with us the cartwheel and its cognate the potter's wheel, elements unknown to certain great civilizations of the past. The mention of carts brings us to the question of war. Chinese warriors, like our own in the Middle Ages, were divided into two social categories, those that rode and those that followed on foot. Until about 400 B.C., however, they rode in war-chariots and not on horseback. Those that rode were gentlemen and those that walked were 'people.' In vast parts of the world this social dichotomy in warfare has never existed.

The wars of which we read in the *Songs* were of two kinds. Those in the north and north-west were wars of conservation. Their aim was to protect the existing agricultural area against the raids of nomads from the steppe. The wars in the south and south-east were wars of annexation. Their aim was to secure fresh territory suitable for agriculture. Among many peoples war of annexation is quite unknown. War often exists, for example, only in order to procure products that are regarded as essential to the maintenance of society; but these are human products, such as scalps, heads,

[1] Among their predecessors, the Shang, it went to the next brother.
[2] This was certainly the usual practice. Wang Chi ('king the younger'), the father of King Wên, was the third son. But there is no evidence that this represents an earlier institution.

ears, and do not involve wholesale slaughter or annexation. We also fight in order to obtain control of products (iron, coal, oil, and so on); but this involves annexation. We are not, however, altogether comfortable about annexation and find it necessary to assure ourselves that the previous possessors were criminals, utterly unworthy to enjoy such advantages. The Chinese had just the same attitude towards their wars of annexation. Not only did they find it necessary to take a high moral tone about the wickedness of those whom they despoiled,[1] but they were willing to invent the most far-fetched reasons (King Wu accuses the Shang of going to bed late)[2] rather than admit that they were themselves bent on expansion. This is indeed not the tone of our medieval ballads, which show less moral sensitivity. But it is very reminiscent of the style in which Cromwell addressed the Irish.

As regards mythology, the main Chou legend, that of Hou Chi, is of an international type. The attempt on his life and the friendly intervention of birds are features that his story shares with that of Gilgamesh, the earliest epic hero. If we take into account other sources apart from No. 238 in the *Songs*, we find that he scores seven out of ten points in Lord Raglan's scheme of the early career of a hero,[3] and is thus in the company of Asclepius, Dionysus, Zeus, Moses, to name only a few of the band.

Probably the fact that most contributes to the ease with which it is possible to turn the songs into a comprehensible English form, is the close relationship between the two languages. I do not mean by this that English is 'derived' from Chinese, or that they belong to the same 'family.' It is perhaps time that we stopped promiscuously using kinship metaphors in relation to languages. I merely mean that in many of its essentials early Chinese stands very close to English and to Germanic in general.[4] The word order is practically the same; whereas the word order of, for example, Japanese, is almost the opposite of ours. English preserves a large onomatopoeic element, and is rich in binomes of the 'zigzag,' 'shilly-shally' type. These are the backbone of early Chinese.

[1] See No. 242.

[2] I cannot think that to the Shang these pleas would have been any more convincing than they are to us to-day.

[3] Points 1–10, *The Hero*, p. 179.

[4] Certain differences exist between German and English word order, but these are not really fundamental.

Finally, both have in common a number of roots, not purely imitative but no doubt immediately derived from sound-imitation; among these I should put *sied* (almost certainly for earlier *sled*), which means 'to drag.' Compare our 'sledge,' 'sled,' 'sleigh.' But this is, of course, very risky and speculative ground.

Another point of contact between Chou civilization and ours is the lack of cruel or violent manhood-initiation rites, such as prevail in many parts of Africa. These were, so far as I know, also lacking among the nomadic Turks and Mongols.

Appendix IV

Wên and Tê

1. Wên.—This word occurs hundreds of times in inscriptions as a stock epithet of ancestors. We do not know what it means, any more than the Romans knew what 'augustus'[1] meant. Possibly quite distinct from this is another word, written with the same character. This means a pattern, and hence 'a written symbol,' book-learning as opposed to battle-prowess, the 'pen' as opposed to the 'sword,' the arts of peace as opposed to those of war. But sacrifices are also called 'deeds of wên,' and it is not clear whether the contrast between wên and wu (war) does not far antedate the idea of a contrast between clerks and soldiers. When the songs say 'great in wên and wu,' I doubt whether wên includes any idea of literary accomplishment.

It would be dangerous to connect wên with the other words which are written with the same phonetic. Wên on top of 'heart' means 'strong,' and 'day' on top of wên is a stock epithet of Heaven. Is it connected with wên, the stock epithet of ancestors? I see no means of deciding. If I translate wên, 'mighty,' it is because one is bound to use an equivalent of some kind, and not because I have any confidence that this was the meaning.

2. Tê.—This does not mean 'virtue' in our sense of the word; for there is bad tê as well as good tê. It means 'virtue' in the sense in which we speak of the 'virtue' of a drug. The Latin word 'virtus' frequently has this sense. Tê means what mana means, as defined by Tregear in his Maori-Polynesian Comparative Dictionary; 'magic power, prestige, influence.' In the first draft of my translation I left the word untranslated. But tê is not easy to acclimatize in English, and in the end I translated it power (compare my book The Way and its Power), inner power (for it excludes physical strength); but sometimes virtue, in contexts where this is not misleading.

Often tê comes very near to being a noun-ending, forming an abstract word. In such sentences as 'his luan tê (turbulent virtue) was his undoing,' luan tê could very well be translated 'turbulence.' Possibly the abstract endings in, for example, Latin (-entia, -tas, -tus, and so on) had a similar origin.

[1] Etymologies put forward by classical writers are (1) from augere, 'to increase'; (2) from avis, 'bird'; (3) from a root, 'to shine.'

Appendix V

Questions Awaiting Research

1. ORIGIN of the names of the books into which the work is divided—Chou Nan, Shao Nan, Pin. Meaning of the headings under which individual songs appear in cases where these are not words taken from the first line. The distinction between Big *Ya* and Little *Ya*.
2. Do the various local sections show dialectical differences?
3. History of the Mao text and the difference (order and contents) between it and the three other versions. That the order of the Lu text was different is shown by the fragments of the Lu text carved on stone in Han times.
4. On what principle was the anthology made? Why do the local sections lack songs from such important centres as Lu and Sung?
5. Which (if any) of the songs are literary compositions, written down when they were first made?
6. Who were the enemies against whom the Chinese fought? To what extent were they culturally different from the Chinese? Compare *Tso Chuan*, Duke Yin, ninth year (714 B.C.), where the Northern Jung who attacked Chêng are said to fight on foot, as opposed to the Chinese, who used war-chariots.

Notes on Books Used

(1) *Shang Shu Chin Ku Wên Chu Su.* Basic Sinological Series. By Sun Hsing-yen (1753–1818). The most convenient text of the authentic (i.e. pre-Han) books of the *Shu Ching.* Gives the more important variants. The editor's own interpretations are not, from our point of view, of much value.

(2) *Ching I Shu Wên.* Basic Sinological Series. Critical observations of Wang Nien-sun (1744–1832) recorded by his son Wang Yin-chih (1766–1834). The section on the *Songs* contains some of the best linguistic work that has been done.

(3) *Shuo Wên T'ung Hsün Ting Shêng.* By Chu Chün-shêng (1788–1858). A dictionary of the phonetic series, based on the *Shuo Wên.* The best existing key to phonetic borrowing. Contains much original speculation.

(4) *Shih Mao Shih Chuan Su.* Basic Sinological Series. By Ch'ên Huan (1786–1863). Absolutely tied down to Mao's glosses, but gives some of the more important variants. Mao's glosses are indeed almost always right, in the sense that when he says A = B, B really is one of the senses of A. But in cases where A has several meanings, Mao sometimes gives the wrong one, regardless of the fact that it makes nonsense.

(5) *Mao Shih I Wên Chien,* in Nan Ch'ing Shu Yüan Ts'ung Shu. By Ch'ên Yü-shu (1853–1906). A study of different ways in which the same word is written in different parts of Mao's text. A little-known work which is very useful.

(6) *Shih San Chia I Chi Su.* By Wang Hsien-ch'ien (1842–1917), author of a well-known commentary on *Chuang Tzǔ.* The most complete collection of variants.

(7) *Chung Hua Ta Tzǔ Tien.* By Hsü Yüan-k'ao and others. Four volumes, Shanghai, 1935. The fullest and best dictionary of early Chinese. Referred to as *Ta Tzǔ Tien.*

(8) *Liang Chou Chin Wên Tz'ǔ Ta Hsi K'ao Shih.* By Kuo Mo-jo. 1935. A study of all the more important Chou inscriptions. Referred to as *K'ao Shih.*

(9) References such as 'Karlgren, B. 119' refer to *Yin and Chou Researches,* 1935. The word Karlgren alone refers to the *Analytic Dictionary,* 1923.

Chinese characters for the titles and names above will be found at the end of Vol. II (Textual Notes).

(10) *Shuang Chien Ch'ih Shih Ching Hsin Chêng.* By Yü Hsing-wu (1936). Notes on the *Songs*, with special reference to parallels in Chou inscriptions. Contains many emendations, all scrupulously supported by quotation. The same author's similar work on the *Shu Ching* is also of importance; but both works are marred by disregard of Chou phonology.

Finding List

My number	Mao	My number	Mao	My number	Mao
1	94	36	93	71	101
2	148	37	145	72	158
3	106	38	146	73	107
4	99	39	87	74	116
5	122	40	3	75	26
6	18	41	63	76	15
7	108	42	55	77	43
8	117	43	59	78	32
9	137	44	61	79	22
10	147	45	72	80	132
11	75	46	91	81	39
12	111	47	102	82	83
13	138	48	89	83	47
14	95	49	62	84	24
15	56	50	125	85	104
16	139	51	142	86	57
17	20	52	225	87	1
18	64	53	45	88	9
19	74	54	34	89	12
20	88	55	60	90	173
21	98	56	81	91	90
22	42	57	140	92	228
23	48	58	73	93	14
24	76	59	226	94	118
25	82	60	27	95	218
26	96	61	69	96	67
27	100	62	150	97	126
28	41	63	23	98	13
29	159	64	51	99	8
30	77	65	151	100	66
31	78	66	29	101	30
32	143	67	33	102	54
33	44	68	17	103	187
34	129	69	141	104	58
35	86	70	105	105	188

My number	Mao	My number	Mao	My number	Mao
106	19	145	169	184	175
107	71	146	162	185	186
108	35	147	10	186	213
109	201	148	133	187	214
110	229	149	149	188	134
111	176	150	68	189	231
112	2	151	121	190	114
113	6	152	153	191	115
114	28	153	275	192	174
115	21	154	276	193	221
116	124	155	277	194	164
117	7	156	279	195	165
118	79	157	290	196	217
119	80	158	291	197	246
120	128	159	154	198	144
121	31	160	190	199	209
122	36	161	211	200	210
123	37	162	212	201	239
124	110	163	4	202	247
125	156	164	5	203	248
126	181	165	152	204	302
127	185	166	160	205	280
128	230	167	166	206	11
129	232	168	170	207	25
130	234	169	171	208	38
131	167	170	172	209	84
132	168	171	215	210	85
133	177	172	249	211	136
134	178	173	251	212	298
135	227	174	252	213	301
136	262	175	216	214	266
137	259	176	222	215	267
138	16	177	278	216	268
139	263	178	284	217	269
140	204	179	53	218	270
141	208	180	123	219	271
142	260	181	130	220	272
143	207	182	182	221	273
144	261	183	161	222	274

My number	Mao	My number	Mao	My number	Mao
223	281	251	300	279	135
224	282	252	297	280	183
225	283	253	303	281	184
226	285	254	304	282	200
227	286	255	305	283	202
228	287	256	50	284	203
229	258	257	189	285	205
230	289	258	103	286	206
231	155	259	112	287	219
232	157	260	127	288	224
233	292	261	179	289	233
234	293	262	180	290	163
235	294	263	92	291	191
236	295	264	120	292	192
237	296	265	97	293	193
238	245	266	46	294	194
239	250	267	220	295	195
240	237	268	223	296	196
241	235	269	49	297	197
242	255	270	52	298	198
243	241	271	256	299	199
244	242	272	40	300	253
245	240	273	65	301	254
246	236	274	70	302	257
247	244	275	109	303	258
248	243	276	113	304	264
249	238	277	119	305	265
250	299	278	131		

Mao	My number	Mao	My number	Mao	My number
1	87	8	99	15	76
2	112	9	88	16	138
3	40	10	147	17	68
4	163	11	206	18	6
5	164	12	89	19	106
6	113	13	98	20	17
7	117	14	93	21	115

Mao	My number	Mao	My number	Mao	My number
22	79	61	44	100	27
23	63	62	49	101	71
24	84	63	41	102	47
25	207	64	18	103	258
26	75	65	273	104	85
27	60	66	100	105	70
28	114	67	96	106	3
29	66	68	150	107	73
30	101	69	61	108	7
31	21	70	274	109	275
32	78	71	107	110	124
33	67	72	45	111	12
34	54	73	58	112	259
35	108	74	19	113	276
36	122	75	11	114	190
37	123	76	24	115	191
38	208	77	30	116	74
39	81	78	31	117	8
40	272	79	118	118	94
41	28	80	119	119	277
42	22	81	56	120	264
43	77	82	25	121	151
44	33	83	82	122	5
45	53	84	209	123	180
46	266	85	210	124	116
47	83	86	35	125	50
48	23	87	39	126	97
49	269	88	20	127	260
50	256	89	48	128	120
51	64	90	91	129	34
52	270	91	46	130	181
53	179	92	263	131	278
54	102	93	36	132	80
55	42	94	1	133	148
56	15	95	14	134	188
57	86	96	26	135	279
58	104	97	265	136	211
59	43	98	21	137	9
60	55	99	4	138	13

Mao	My number	Mao	My number	Mao	My number
139	16	178	134	217	196
140	57	179	261	218	95
141	69	180	262	219	287
142	51	181	126	220	267
143	32	182	182	221	193
144	198	183	280	222	176
145	37	184	281	223	270
146	38	185	127	224	288
147	10	186	185	225	52
148	2	187	103	226	59
149	149	188	105	227	135
150	62	189	257	228	92
151	65	190	160	229	110
152	165	191	291	230	128
153	152	192	292	231	189
154	159	193	293	232	129
155	231	194	294	233	289
156	125	195	295	234	130
157	232	196	296	235	241
158	72	197	297	236	246
159	29	198	298	237	240
160	166	199	299	238	249
161	183	200	282	239	201
162	146	201	109	240	245
163	290	202	283	241	243
164	194	203	284	242	244
165	195	204	140	243	248
166	167	205	285	244	247
167	131	206	286	245	238
168	132	207	143	246	197
169	145	208	141	247	202
170	168	209	199	248	203
171	169	210	200	249	172
172	170	211	161	250	239
173	90	212	162	251	173
174	192	213	186	252	174
175	184	214	187	253	300
176	111	215	171	254	301
177	133	216	175	255	242

Mao	My number	Mao	My number	Mao	My number
256	271	273	221	290	157
257	302	274	222	291	158
258	303	275	153	292	233
259	137	276	154	293	234
260	142	277	155	294	235
261	144	278	177	295	236
262	136	279	156	296	237
263	139	280	205	297	252
264	304	281	223	298	212
265	305	282	224	299	250
266	214	283	225	300	251
267	215	284	178	301	213
268	216	285	226	302	204
269	217	286	227	303	253
270	218	287	228	304	254
271	219	288	229	305	255
272	220	289	230		

Index

THE Harvard-Yenching *Concordance* furnishes the specialist with a full index to the *Songs*. What follows here refers chiefly to my own notes and explanations. The references are to pages.

Religion & Philosophy Titles
From Grove Weidenfeld

___ BIALI	0-8021-3146-8	Aberbach, David BIALIK	$6.95
___ BIALIC	0-8021-1062-2	Aberbach, David BIALIK	$15.00 (cl)
___ ALONE	0-8021-5127-2	Batchelor, Stephen ALONE WITH OTHERS: An Existential Approach to Buddhism	$8.95
___ ANTHO	0-8021-5038-1	Birch, Cyril (ed.) ANTHOLOGY OF CHINESE LITERATURE, Vol. 1	$17.50
___ ANTH2	0-8021-5090-X	Birch, Cyril (ed.) ANTHOLOGY OF CHINESE LITERATURE, Vol. 2	$14.95
___ MING	0-8021-5031-4	Birch, Cyril (trans.) STORIES FROM MING COLLECTION: Art of The Chinese Story-Teller	$9.95
___ ZENTEA	0-8021-5092-6	Blofeld, John THE ZEN TEACHING OF HUANG PO	$10.95
___ KISSI	1-55584-194-5	Calisher, Hortense KISSING COUSINS	$14.95 (cl)
___ CRUCI	0-8021-1094-0	Fricke, Weddig THE COURT-MARTIAL OF JESUS	$18.95 (cl)
___ BANKR	0-8021-3184-0	Haskel, Peter BANKEI ZEN: Translation from the Record of Bankei	$9.95
___ BANKC	0-8021-1211-0	Haskel, Peter BANKEI ZEN	$27.50 (cl)
___ ANTHJ	0-8021-5058-6	Keene, Donald (ed.) ANTHOLOGY OF JAPANESE LITERATURE	$14.95
___ MODJAP	0-8021-5095-0	Keene, Donald (ed.) MODERN JAPANESE LITERATURE	$14.95
___ ZENTR	0-8021-3162-X	Kraft, Kenneth ZEN: Tradition and Transition	$8.95
___ FRONPA	1-55584-197-X	Levi Peter THE FRONTIERS OF PARADISE	$16.95 (cl)
___ LIVIN	0-8021-3136-0	Linssen, Robert LIVING ZEN	$9.95
___ SIMON	1-55584-021-3	Miles, Sian SIMONE WEIL: An Anthology	$8.95
___ DROPP	0-8021-3052-6	Mitchell, Stephen DROPPING ASHES ON BUDDHA: The Teaching of Zen Master Seung Sahn	$11.95
___ CRAZY	0-8021-5184-1	Oe, Kenzaburo THE CRAZY IRIS AND OTHER STORIES OF THE ATOMIC AFTERMATH	$6.95
___ CRAZYC	0-8021-1212-9	Oe, Kenzaburo THE CRAZY IRIS AND OTHER STORIES OF THE ATOMIC AFTERMATH	$22.50 (cl)
___ PERMAT	0-8021-5061-6	Oe, Kenzaburo A PERSONAL MATTER	$7.95
___ TEACH	0-8021-5185-X	Oe, Kenzaburo TEACH US TO OUTGROW OUR MADNESS (The Day He Himself Shall Wipe My Tears Away; Prize Stock; Teach Us To Outgrow Our Madness; Aghwee The Sky Monster)	$9.95
___ RASHI	0-8021-3147-6	Pearl, Chaim RASHI	$6.95
___ RASHIC	0-8021-1063-0	Pearl, Chaim RASHI	$15.95 (cl)
___ WHATBU	0-8021-3031-3	Rahula,Walpola WHAT THE BUDDHA TAUGHT	$8.95
___ HEINE	0-8021-3148-4	Robertson, Ritchie HEINE	$6.95
___ HEINEC	0-8021-1064-9	Robertson, Ritchie HEINE	$15.95 (cl)
___ PALAC	1-55584-068-X	Shahar, David THE PALACE OF SHATTERED VESSELS	$22.50 (cl)
___ TRAIN	0-8021-5023-3	Singh, Khushwant TRAIN TO PAKISTAN	$5.95
___ WORBUD	0-8021-3095-X	Stryk, Lucien (ed.) WORLD OF THE BUDDHA: An Introduction to Buddhist Literature	$12.95
___ ZENPOE	0-8021-3019-4	Stryk, Lucien (ed.) ZEN POEMS OF CHINA AND JAPAN	$7.95
___ ESSAY	0-8021-5118-3	Suzuki, D.T. ESSAYS IN ZEN BUDDHISM	$13.95
___ INTRO	0-8021-3055-0	Suzuki, D.T. INTRODUCTION TO ZEN BUDDHISM	$4.95
___ MANUA	0-8021-3065-8	Suzuki, D.T. MANUAL OF ZEN BUDDHISM	$10.95
___ BUBER	0-8021-3149-2	Vermes, Pamela BUBER	$6.95
___ BUBERC	0-8021-1061-4	Vermes, Pamela BUBER	$15.95 (cl)
___ BOOKSO	0-8021-3021-6	Waley, Arthur (trans.) THE BOOK OF SONGS	$9.95

Religion & Philosophy Titles *(continued)*

___ MONKE	0-8021-3086-0	Waley, Arthur (trans.) MONKEY	$11.95
___ NOPLAY	0-8021-5206-6	Waley, Arthur (trans.) NO PLAYS OF JAPAN	$9.95
___ WAYPOW	0-8021-5085-3	Waley, Arthur THE WAY AND ITS POWER	$10.95
___ ENDUR	0-8021-3132-8	Warner, Langdon THE ENDURING ART OF JAPAN	$9.95
___ SPIRI	0-8021-3056-9	Watts, Alan THE SPIRIT OF ZEN	$8.95

TO ORDER DIRECTLY FROM GROVE WEIDENFELD:

YES! **Please send me the books selected above.**

Telephone orders—credit card only: 1-800-937-5557.
Mail orders: Please include $1.50 postage and handling, plus $.50 for each additional book, or credit card information requested below.
Send to: Grove Weidenfeld
    IPS
    1113 Heil Quaker Boulevard
    P.O. Box 7001
    La Vergne, TN 37086-7001

☐ I have enclosed $_____ (check or money order only)

☐ Please charge my Visa/MasterCard card account (circle one).

  Card Number _____

  Expiration Date _____

  Signature _____

Name _____

Address _____ Apt. _____

City _____ State _____ Zip _____

Please allow 4–6 weeks for delivery.
Please note that prices are subject to change without notice.
For additional information, catalogues or bulk sales inquiries, please call 1-800-937-5557.   ADCD